The Metamorphoses of
Shakespearean
Comedy

The Metamorphoses of Shakespearean Comedy

William C. Carroll

Princeton
University
Press

Published by Princeton University Press, 41 William Street, Princeton,
New Jersey 08540
In the United Kingdom: Princeton University Press, Guildford, Surrey

All Rights Reserved

Library of Congress Cataloging in Publication Data will be found on the
last printed page of this book

ISBN 0-691-06633-7

This book has been composed in Linotron Sabon and Weiss

Clothbound editions of Princeton University Press books are printed on
acid-free paper, and binding materials are chosen for strength
and durability.
Printed in the United States of America by Princeton University Press
Princeton, New Jersey

*For my Mother
and Father*

Contents

Acknowledgments

This book has passed through a number of metamorphic stages of its own. It began with the very great assistance of a NEH Fellowship for Independent Study in 1978-79, and took final shape during a sabbatical research leave from Boston University; I am very grateful to both institutions for providing me the time to think and to write. Along the way, several friends and colleagues generously offered advice, encouragement, and their own inspirational example: my special thanks to Patricia Craddock, Albert Gilman, David Young, Garrett Stewart, James Siemon, and Rosemary Oxenford. My wife Carol provided encouragement and support throughout this project, which was concluded just as our son David was born.

I owe an enormous debt of gratitude to three friends who carefully read my manuscript at different stages of its development. George Park saw the earliest stages of writing, and wielded a sharp editorial pen with wit, judgment, and an unerring sense of what worked and what did not; his suggestions proved invaluable. Stuart Johnson read the manuscript roughly at midpoint in its history, and precisely focused his and my attention on many of the most crucial theoretical and interpretive problems; his provocative imagination helped shape this study decidedly for the better. John Matthews read the manuscript in its final stages, and brought the great clarity of his insight to bear on troubling questions of structure and argument; his generosity is deeply appreciated. The book has been brought to a far greater coherence as a result of their efforts, while its faults remain my own. All I can offer them is my heartfelt thanks and the continuity of our lasting friendship.

Part of Chapter Three was first published in "The Ending of *Twelfth Night* and the Tradition of Metamorphosis," in *Shakespearean Comedy*, ed. Maurice Charney (Special Issue of *New York Literary Forum*, 1980). Several pages in Chapter Four first appeared in "Metalanguage in Shakespearean Comedy," in *Shakespearean Metadrama*, ed. John W. Blanpied (Rochester: Univ. of Rochester Dept. of English, 1977). Part of Chapter Six first appeared in " 'A Received Belief': Imagination in *The Merry Wives of Windsor*," in *Studies in Philology*, LXXIV (1977). I am grateful to these journals for permission to republish parts of these works.

Part One ❧ Introduction

. . . all these things, which thou seest, change immediately and will no longer be; and constantly bear in mind how many of these changes thou hast already witnessed. The universe is transformation: life is opinion.

MARCUS AURELIUS
Meditations, IV. 3

Full sail, I voyage
Over the boundless ocean, and I tell you
Nothing is permanent in all the world.
All things are fluent; every image forms,
Wandering through change. Time is itself a river
In constant movement, and the hours flow by
Like water, wave on wave, pursued, pursuing,
Forever fugitive, forever new.
That which has been, is not; that which was not,
Begins to be; motion and moment always
In process of renewal.

OVID
Metamorphoses, XV. 176-86

Preface

"O Bottom, thou art changed!" (MND, III. i. 113)
"We shall all be changed." (I. Cor. 15:51)

"Metamorphosis" seldom remains in the cocoon of its narrowest definition. The word constantly breaks free, sheds its old skin, and emerges in contexts having little to do with butterflies. It can refer to a physical shifting of shape, an internal transformation, or simply to change itself. In the Renaissance the word might apply to something as specific as the myth of Proteus or to something so commonplace as poetic encounters with that most inconstant of mistresses, Mutability. The word might range from the height of I Corinthians to the bottom of Bottom. In Shakespearean comedy, the terms "transformation" and "metamorphosis" have been used to refer to an actual physical change, such as Bottom's fitting appearance as an ass, or the assumption of mask or disguise, as well as emotional and psychological shifts such as Claudio's apparent change of heart at the end of *Much Ado About Nothing* or Oliver's abrupt reformation in *As You Like It*. Although the concept of metamorphosis seems as slippery as these definitions, throughout this study I will nevertheless distinguish, as I think Shakespeare did, between metamorphosis proper and more mundane though related forms of change, such as natural mutability or normal human maturation.

3

The proof of transformation is essentially perceptual. A transformation has occurred when something (whether animate or inanimate) recognizably changes its nature. It requires our ability to mark difference and similarity at once, to remember what was while we realize what is. How can we recognize and speak of something as being the same thing and yet no longer itself? We may say that a boundary exists, which marks the limits of object X, so that transformation occurs when the boundary is crossed, and X becomes Y. Here we encounter, not for the last time, the elusiveness of metamor phosis as a concept, for "crossing a boundary" implies that something has left one space and gone into another; the spatialization can only be misleading. In fact, the identity of an object is known *by* its boundaries, so *it* cannot cross its *own* boundaries—at least linguistically. It might be more useful to think of a boundary simply dissolving and reforming elsewhere; but all such formulations are spatial, and passive constructions as well, the implied agent unknown. An accident versus essence distinction might be useful, suggesting that in most metamorphoses the essence of central identity is unchanged but the accidental properties of the boundary have been altered—thus the outer shape of Bottom's head is transformed but the inner substance is not. Yet even this qualification, a favorite from St. Augustine to Reginald Scot and King James, raises as many questions as it answers, as we will see. Some such terminology of the boundary nevertheless seems necessary, and will be employed in this study.[1]

Tzvetan Todorov has briefly employed a similar vocabulary of transgression in *The Fantastic:*

> We say readily enough that someone monkeys around, or that he fights like a lion, like an eagle, etc. The supernatural begins the moment we shift from words to the things these words are supposed to designate. The metamorphoses too, therefore, constitute a transgression of the separation between matter and mind as it is generally conceived.

4

Todorov's formulation, however, seems to account for only half the phenomenon. To reverse his phrase, the transgression constitutes the metamorphosis; in Shakespeare, moreover, the boundary between matter and mind is rarely the crucial one.[2]

Boundaries are not effectively known until they have been violated. Metamorphosis is simultaneously both the transgression and the establishment of boundary. It can be conceptualized only after it has ceased, when we can compare the memory of past and present. A human being can therefore experience metamorphosis only by not being completely transformed. Turn a man into an ass or a prince into a frog and your lesson will be lost unless you leave him a human mind in his animal shape. Otherwise he won't *know* that he has been transformed. Anything can be transformed, then, but only human beings can *experience* metamorphosis; the recognition of transformation signals the human presence. It follows that every human transformation, if perceived by the metamorph, must be incomplete.

These are the puzzles which Shakespeare stresses in his comedies, where language and action relentlessly pursue logic into paradox. Questions of boundary, shape, language, and identity inevitably arise when men become asses, woman become men through disguise, and solitary individuals confront their doubles. Moreover, these questions have a peculiar relevance to, or location in, the theater. Shakespeare's interest in metamorphosis was no doubt equally stimulated by Ovid's narratives and by Burbage's impersonations. Such paradoxes of boundary and identity begin to explain the appeal of metamorphosis to dramatist and audience—its fearful liberation, its implausible possibilities—but do not trap the chimera in its lair. Following the tracks all the way leads us to even more bracing contradictions.[3]

❧

In the chapters which follow, I will probe these central paradoxes of metamorphosis. The first chapter will review various explanations of metamorphosis and Renaissance attitudes toward this power, and then examine at greater length some of the issues raised above. The succeeding chapters will offer extended readings of Shakespeare's major comedies as specimens of transformation. The order followed is roughly chronological, according to the plays' supposed dates of composition, but in some of the chapters the plays have also been grouped according to the mode of metamorphosis most dominant. The organization of the chapters suggests in part my argument that Shakespeare found a variety of modes of metamorphosis attractive, that his comedies frequently turn on representations of one of these modes, and that his interest in metamorphosis continued until the end of his career—indeed, his interest seems if anything to have deepened and intensified. The theatrical result is something rich and strange.

Chapter One ❧ Metamorphosis

An obsession with the nature of change runs throughout Western thought, beginning, like most of our ideas, with the pre-Socratics. Stories of the explicit changes called metamorphoses seem equally ancient, their origins in folk-tale, their historical manifestation in such sophisticated narratives as those of Lucian and Apuleius. Ovid's was not the first collection of metamorphic tales. Yet, common as these stories are in earlier literatures, it is quite difficult to find systematic attempts to explain them. Christian analysts pursued the question perhaps most vigorously, since metamorphosis could not obviously be reconciled with the nature of God and the doctrine of creation. Yet here were all these stories, most of them pagan, to be sure, but some from the best authorities: the possibility of shape-changing and witchcraft is authorized by the Bible itself, in the stories of Nebuchadnezzar and the Witch of Endor. Metamorphosis was clearly an insistent and a dangerous concept, and therefore required explanation, for demons, perhaps even the devil himself, might be involved.

St. Augustine, for one, reports hearing many stories of metamorphosis, in all of which the mind "did not become bestial, but remained rational and human, just as Apuleius, in the books he wrote with the title of *The Golden Ass,* has told, or feigned, that it happened to his own self that, on taking poison, he became an ass, while retaining his human mind." Yet Augustine rejects the possibility of such metamorphoses *actually* occurring, for though God "can do whatever He pleases" (and the Bible's metamorphoses were therefore real), demons cannot create. And if the demons really do perform metamorphoses, still they "do not create real substances, but only change the appearance of things created by the true God so as to make them seem to be what they are not." Augustine goes on to imagine that the metamorph is really only "the phantasm of a man," which is released when a man sleeps, and is then embodied in the shape of some animal, which "may appear to the senses of others, and may even seem to the man himself to be changed, just as he may seem to himself in sleep to be so changed, and to bear burdens."[1]

Augustine argues, then, that the transformed thing is really two things, the thing itself ("created by the true God") and the more compelling changed appearance (the metamorph "may even seem to the man himself to be changed"). He resists the conclusion of a violated *corporeal* boundary, however. Morpheus may be the god of metamorphosis, but Augustine cannot be sure that sleep is the proper analogue either, for the process does (and does not) finally occur "in some indescribable way unknown to me." We will all find metamorphosis in some way indescribable, just because all transformed things will "seem to be what they are not" and because the mind/body transgression is so unimaginable. Augustine's evident uneasiness with the whole subject is typical, but his 'resolution' of the question became the orthodox explanation. In his own discussion, for example, Aquinas quoted this passage in Augustine, concluding: "Those transformations which cannot be produced by the power of nature cannot in reality be effected by the operation of the demons; for instance, that the human body be changed into the body of a beast, or that the body of a dead man return to life."[2]

Many of Shakespeare's contemporaries, even scoffers like Reginald Scot, agreed with Augustine's substance versus accident explanation of metamorphosis. In *The Discoverie of*

Witchcraft (1584), in a passage denying the existence of Robin Goodfellow among others, Scot maintains that "these bugs [shapeshifters] speciallie are spied and feared of sick folke, children, women, and cowards, which through weaknesse of mind and bodie are shaken with vaine dreames and continuall feare. The *Scythians,*" he argues stoutly, "never see anie vaine sights or spirits. It is a common saieng; A lion feareth no bugs." Scot concludes sarcastically:

> For right grave writers report, that spirits most often and speciallie take the shape of women appearing to monks, &c: and of beasts, dogs, swine, horsses, gotes, cats, hairs; of fowles, as crowes, night owles, and shrecke owls, but they delight most in the likeness of snakes and drag- ons. Well, thanks be to God, this wretched and cowardlie infidelitie, since the preaching of the gospell, is in part forgotten: and doubtles, the rest of those illusions will in short time (by Gods grace) be detected and vanish awaie.[3]

Scot's skepticism is bracing, especially after reading through endless and repetitive accounts from witchcraft trials. But even in his orthodoxy, he seems an isolated figure. Most would no doubt assent intellectually to his position; but belief is another issue. Scot's location of metamorphosis—in the minds of "sicke folke, children, women, and cowards"—resonates sugges tively with accounts of witchcraft rituals (see below).

King James I replied to Scot in his *Daemonologie* (1597), arguing the existence of witches, devils, and enchanters. (He replied in another way when he took the throne in 1603, by ordering Scot's book to be burnt.) For him, one kind of meta- morphosis clearly existed:

> And that the Divel is permitted at som-times to put him- self in the liknes of the Saintes, it is plaine in the Scrip- tures, where it is said, that *Sathan can trans-forme himselfe into an Angell of light.*

But only the wicked can be so deceived, for

> God will not permit him so to deceive his own: but only
> such, as first wilfully deceives them-selves, by running
> unto him, whome God then suffers to fall in their owne
> snares.[4]

Throughout his work, James refers without qualification to
various metamorphic powers, but he finally makes the same
qualification as Augustine—metamorphosis, like the other
powers of the magicians, cannot be *real* because of God's
nature:

> And yet are all these thinges but deluding of the senses,
> and no waies true in substance. . . . For that is the dif-
> ference betwixt Gods myracles and the Devils, God is a
> creator, what he makes appeare in miracle, it is so in
> effect. As *Moyses* rod being casten downe, was no doubt
> turned in a natural Serpent: where as the Devill (as Gods
> Ape) counterfetting that by his *Magicians,* maid their
> wandes to appeare so, onelie to mennes outward senses
> (pp.22-3).[5]

Some of the metamorphoses of the Bible were real, then, especially the Incarnation and Jesus' miracles, because they were
God's will; but miracles now are ceased, and only delusions—
or outright fictions—can be seen.

Philomathes (James's skeptical Scot-figure) dismisses stories
of witch metamorphosis "in likenes of beastes or foules" as
"like old wives trattles about the fire" while Epistemon (James's
spokesman) defends these powers' existence even while explaining them away as delusions. Another case in point is the
legend of werewolves, but Epistemon has a ready explanation,
beginning with a cautious hypothetical:

> if anie such thing hath bene, I take it to have proceeded
> but of a naturall super-abundance of Melancholie, which
> as wee reade, that it hath made some thinke themselves
> Pitchers, and some horses, and some one kinde of beast

or other: So suppose I that it hath so viciat the imagination and memorie of some, as *per lucida intervalla,* it hath so highlie occupyed them, that they have thought themselves verrie Woolfes indeede at these times: and so have counterfeited their actiones in goeing on their handes and feete, preassing to devoure women and barnes, fighting and snatching with all the towne dogges, and in using such like other brutish actiones, and so to become beastes by a strong apprehension (pp. 61-2).

Metamorphosis is thus a kind of disease, partly the creation of an imbalanced "imagination" which turns the victim into nothing less than an actor, *counterfoiting the actions* of of either real werewolves, or simply of real wolves. Such things, in any event, exist only in the mind: "but as to their having and hyding of their hard & schellie sloughes, I take that to be but eiked, by uncertaine report, the author of all lyes" (p. 62). No wonder the poets were so attracted to the topic. Even the author of all lies is still an author. Shakespeare took up such skepticism about the deluding imagination in, most spectacularly, *A Midsummer Night's Dream,* where Theseus, like James, laments the deceptiveness of "counterfeited" actions and makes a similar distinction between "strong apprehension" and the comprehension of cool reason.

Accounts of witch trials and witchcraft in the sixteenth century raise further questions about "belief" in metamorphosis, and in the mimetic complicity of the metamorph. On one level, many people no doubt believed in a witch's ability physically to metamorphose into an animal, and no doubt others refused to accept such a notion at all; James I and Scot debated the point. But much nervous space lies between these extremes. In her well-known study of European witchcraft, Margaret Murray summarizes several stories of witch to animal metamorphosis, and then concludes:

In the earlier cults the worshipper, on becoming an animal, changed his outward shape to the eye of faith alone, though his actions and probably his voice proclaimed the transformation. The nearest approach to an outward change was by covering the body with the skin of the animal, or by wearing a part of the skin or a mask. The witches themselves admitted that they were masked and veiled, and the evidence of other witnesses goes to prove the same.[6]

That this could be a description of what happens on stage, as a triumph of the actor's craft, is almost too obvious to state: an actor puts on a costume, and though all acknowledge the disguise, to the "eye of faith," to suspended disbelief, a transformation takes place. Murray's stress on *ritual* in witchcraft is equally applicable to theatrical custom: "That is to say the witches did not attempt to change their actual forms but called themselves cats, hares, or other animals" (p. 233). The suggestion is thus Pirandellian: you are transformed if you think you are, and if you can get others to agree with you. The "eye of faith" must in fact perform a transformation as difficult, as striking, as that claimed by the witches in the first place:

> The witch announced to her fellow that she herself was an animal, a fact which the second witch would not have known otherwise; the second witch at once became a similar animal and went with the first to perform the ritual acts which were to follow. The witches were in their own estimation and in the belief of all their comrades, to whom they communicated the fact, actually animals, though to the uninitiated eye their natural forms remained unchanged (p. 235).

This description bears a strong resemblance to rituals more familiar to us: the actress announces to her audience that she is a queen (or gypsy, or cat), a fact they would not have known otherwise; they at once agree, and become implicated in the fiction; all involved "believe" in the transformation, though to the uninitiated eye they are merely actress and audience. Murray's summary reflects the accounts of Henri Boguet (*Examen of Witches*, 1602), an experienced judge at witchcraft

trials, who after listing a whole series of transformations concludes that "the metamorphosis of a man into a beast is impossible," and argues that either Satan does the witch's evil
deeds or "it is the witch himself who runs about slaying: not
that he is metamorphosed into a wolf, but that it appears to
him that he is so."[7] Some stories of metamorphosis, then,
require a *complicity* of faith or imagination, an implied agree-
ment between participant and observer, or even a total self-
deception. The theatrical analogues are clear.

An incomplete instance of this complicity may be found in
the case of Duke Ferdinand, brother to the Duchess of Malfi
in Webster's play. He is stricken with lycanthropia in the final
act, after ordering the murder of his twin sister. A doctor
explains the disease:

> In those that are possessed with't there o'erflows
> Such melancholy humor, they imagine
> Themselves to be transformed into wolves,
> Steal forth to churchyards in the dead of night,
> And dig dead bodies up; as two nights since
> One met the Duke, 'bout midnight in a lane
> Behind St. Mark's church, with the leg of a man
> Upon his shoulder; and he howled fearfully,
> Said he was a wolf; only the difference
> Was, a wolf's skin was hairy on the outside,
> His on the inside; bade them take their swords,
> Rip up his flesh, and try.

(V.ii.8-19)

The doctor's explanation is of a metaphorical and internal
change, rather than a literal and outward one, so that the
onlookers in the play are not required to "believe" or credit
any more than Ferdinand's psychological degeneration after
the murder; still, Ferdinand's action and language at the end
do suggest that a more literal and desperate metamorphosis
has indeed taken place, and in the feral snarl of Ferdinand's
rhetoric we begin to hear a more physical transformation at

work. Had Ferdinand worn the proper disguise, hairy on the outside, the doctor might have gone further in his explanation.

The required complicity between the actor and the audience of metamorphosis reaches in several directions. Simply to recognize metamorphosis can be complex. A complicity exists, to begin with, in the acceptance of an announced metamorphosis, witch to observer. Since one must be an initiate in order to perceive metamorphosis, it seems that the coven establishes the boundary (defined by criteria of membership) at the same time that it transgresses it (by existing at all). This double movement is even more clearly the case with the audience at a theater. The audience's complicity is involved not only in an announced transformation (Oberon: "I am invisible"; or Quince: "Bless thee, Bottom! Bless thee! Thou art translated."); it was a factor as soon as the actors came on stage ("Answer as I call you. Nick Bottom, the weaver." "Ready.") But a significant difference exists between Bottom's metamorphosis or Oberon's invisibility and Will Kempe's (or any actor's) announcement that he is Bottom. In the latter case, we were not self-conscious of our complicity, because we were merely indulging in the minor kind of transgression we commit every moment of our lives, and especially when we walk into a theater, where we become the initiates of a theatrical coven. But when a metamorphosis is announced or observed, when the boundary between one state and the next is transgressed, then we suddenly mark both the boundary and the transgression. The boundary has become known only when it is too late to preserve it. Metamorphosis thus signals a loss which has just occurred, the loss of something which did not even seem a possession until it was gone, and has only now been noticed; this loss, in the case of human transformation, is the loss of coherence or identity of the self. At the same time, of course, a new but untraceable boundary springs up, and the gain of part or all of a new self is recorded. This double movement of loss and gain, of destruction and creation, begins the moment an actor steps on a stage before an audience of initiates—begins, in fact, when the initiates gather together with a common expectation.

It is one thing to read Ovid's or James's accounts of metamorphosis and quite another to see one, or see the representation of one. Renaissance playwrights would struggle mightily in their attempts to bring metamorphosis to the stage, and though some would rely on trick trees and ingenious property managers—anything to represent it—Shakespeare would eventually turn toward something like the witches' solution: metamorphosis takes place because I say it does.

❧

Renaissance poets and playwrights responded with a variety of attitudes to both the appearance and the fact of transformation. As in I Corinthians, the Christian response might be joy over the transcendent reversion that would lift the pious soul out of a fallen, mutable world into the realm of light and eternity. Many of Vaughan's poems, for example, celebrate such a vision. Here change is prized because it leads to the Unchanging, whereas change within the wheel of earthly life amounts to no more than the repetition of shifting appearances and unstable shapes. Donne's two Anniversary poems can be invoked here as the negative and positive poles of the Renaissance view of change. In the first poem the demonstration that the world has decayed "from the first houre" until it is now merely a "drie . . . Cinder" (I, 201, 428) can be set against the second poem's elucidation of the spiritual permanence of Elizabeth Drury, now changed beyond all change, elevated to the heavenly choir where "accidentall things are permanent" (II, 488) and she, "by making full perfection grow, / Peeces a Circle, and still keepes it so" (II, 507-8).[8] Nothing could be sharper than this contrast between mortal change in time and immortal change into eternity. Echoing this distinction, Walton recommended that we look first upon an early portrait, then upon a later portrait of Donne in his shroud, so that the full extent of mortal change, and the contemptus mundi reflections prompted, can be appreciated before the reader considers Donne's own eternal transfiguration.

Whether the final change of the Apocalypse was considered or not, the facts of earthly life remained: birth, growth, dissolution, death. Brightness falls from the air: beauty cannot last. Spenser went so far as to arraign the Titaness Mutability:

> What man that sees the ever-whirling wheele
> Of *Change,* the which all mortall things doth sway,
> But that therby doth find, and plainly feele,
> How *Mutability* in them doth play
> Her cruell sports, to many mens decay?
>
> (M.C., Vi.i)[9]

Her sway over Nature seems absolute, yet Nature is able to look forward to the end of Mutability's reign:

> But time shall come that all shall changed bee,
> And from thenceforth, none no more change shall see.
>
> (M.C., VII.lix)

Spenser grants us a consoling vision of "the pilloaurs of Eternity" at the last, praying for "that Sabaoths sight" (*M.C.*, VIII.ii).

In this sublunary world, however, all is mere change. For someone as sage as Montaigne, this inevitability was cause for contemplation and resignation. Such knowledge, taken to heart, forced some men to sharpen and weigh the values by which their lives must be lived. For others, the consequence might be as hysterical as Malevole's sermon, in *The Malcontent,* to the usurping Duke Pietro—a speech notable for the absence of any saving recognition of a life beyond all change: "Think this: this earth is the only grave and Golgotha wherein all things that live must rot; 'tis but the draught wherein the heavenly bodies discharge their corruption, etc." This horrific vision somehow convinces Pietro to renounce his Dukedom, call for the banished Altofront (i.e., Malevole), and pronounce, "O, I am chang'd."[10] And so, from hour to hour, we rot and rot.

Renaissance literature overflows with such commonplaces about mutability, but they are worth repeating to make the point that change was frequently seen as something negative—something unavoidable, occasionally a cause of poignance, but ultimately a cause for lamentation. Life was brief. No perfection could be sustained on this earth. Whatever the vision of the afterlife, the grave seemed to gape thrice wider for everyone.

These attitudes are not a celebration of process, of the natural cycles that make life interesting and complex to a Romantic; they manifest instead a spiritual and psychological resistance to mutability. Yet although few authors gloried in process for its own sake, some Renaissance philosophers and poets did see the possibility of change, especially self-willed human change, as neither negative nor neutral but as a blessing and heaven-sent possibility. And here I should re-emphasize the distinction between the two kinds of change we have been discussing throughout: the grinding process of mutability and the more radical act of transformation. The first implies change within the flux of time, a movement, as from birth through life to death, which is linear and irreversible. The second, transformation, suggests a translation from a lower to a higher state, as in Oliver's change of heart in *As You Like It*, or from higher to lower, as in Bottom's metamorphosis. Those Renaissance thinkers who considered transformation, rather than mere mutability, held out some hope: man might move up the Chain of Being, though he was more likely to move down it; his own nature remained the critical factor. The classic statement of this optimism is a much-quoted paragraph, still worth examining at length, in Pico della Mirandola's *Oration on the Dignity of Man*. There Pico shows God, who has placed man "in the middle of the world," speaking to Adam:

> "Neither a fixed abode nor a form that is thine alone nor any function peculiar to thyself have we given thee, Adam, to the end that according to thy longing and according to thy judgment thou mayest have and possess

17

what abode, what form, and what functions thou thyself shalt desire. The nature of all other beings is limited and constrained within the bounds of laws prescribed by Us. Thou, constrained by no limits, in accordance with thine own free will, in whose hand We have placed thee, shalt ordain for thyself the limits of thy nature. We have set thee at the world's center that thou mayest from thence more easily observe whatever is in the world. We have made thee neither of heaven nor of earth, neither mortal nor immortal, so that with freedom of choice and with honor, as though the maker and molder of thyself, thou mayest fashion thyself in whatever shape thou shalt prefer. Thou shalt have the power to degenerate into the lower forms of life, which are brutish. Thou shalt have the power, out of thy soul's judgment, to be reborn into the higher forms, which are divine."

O supreme generosity of God the Father, O highest and most marvelous felicity of man! To him it is granted to have whatever he chooses, to be whatever he wills. . . . Who would not admire this our chameleon? Or who could more greatly admire aught else whatever?[11]

In a strategy we will soon find quite familiar, Pico goes on to explain the standard myth of metamorphosis, that of Proteus: "It is man," he says, "who Asclepius of Athens, arguing from his mutability of character and from his self-transforming nature, on just grounds says was symbolized by Proteus in the mysteries."[12] If Proteus was really another name for man, then protean man might easily assume any shape he pleased, and in Pico's view it was as likely to be a higher shape as a lower one.

Yet many others believed that man was more likely to sink than to rise, to become a brute rather than an angel. Sir John Hayward's skepticism is perhaps more typical of the age than Pico's optimism:

Certainly of all the creatures under heaven, which have received being from God, none degenerate, none forsake their naturall dignitie and being, but onely man; Onely man, abandoning the dignitie of his proper nature, is changed like *Proteus,* into divers forms.

And this is occasioned by reason of the libertie of his will: which is a facultie that transformeth men into so many things, as with violent appetite it doth pursue. . . . And as every kind of beast is principally inclined to one sensualitie more then to any other; so man transformeth himselfe into that beast, to whose sensualitie he principallie declines. . . . This did the ancient wisemen shadow foorth by their fables of certaine persons changed into such beasts, whose crueltie, or sotterie, or other brutish nature they did express.[13]

Left to his own devices, in this view, man could not transcend himself; some divine touch of grace was still needed. This view of human possibility and its dangers reflects the theological understanding of man's history: the first change was a Fall, and most subsequent changes were therefore likely to be descents as well. Falstaff's very name suggests as much, and he himself admits, "I have a kind of alacrity in sinking." The same point was generally made of all men.

Thus the great human potential which, in effect, helped generate the Renaissance, and which was celebrated with fearless enthusiasm by some, could as easily be turned on its head and found to be a dark reversal indeed. Perhaps the proper opposite to Pico would be Spenser's Grill, one of Acrasia's victims:

Said [the palmer] These seeming beasts are men indeed,
Whom this Enchauntresse hath transformed thus,—
Whylome her lovers, which her lusts did feed,
Now turned into figures hideous,
According to their mindes like monstruous.

But when they are returned to their proper shapes, yet

> one above the rest in speciall,
> That had an hog beene late, hight *Grille* by name,
> Repined greatly, and did him miscall,
> That had from hoggish forme him brought to naturall.
>
> Said *Guyon,* See the mind of beastly man,
> That hath so soone forgot the excellence
> Of his creation, when he life began,
> That now he chooseth, with vile difference,
> To be a beast, and lacke intelligence.
> (*F.Q.*, II. xii.lxxxv-vii)

The palmer has seen enough: "Let *Grill* be *Grill,* and have his hoggish mind." But the possibility that any man could forget the excellence of his creation and choose his own deformation provides an unsettling backdrop to the poem, and to the idea of metamorphosis generally.

I have been conflating two *causes* of metamorphosis here: external causes, such as Acrasia's Circean power over Grill, and self-generated metamorphosis, as when Jove descends into a bull or when Rosalind tries to become Ganymede. Metamorphosis caused by some alien force must inevitably be frightening, which is one reason that Bottom's change is so eerie. But Pico celebrates self-generated metamorphosis, which could also be dangerous. Perhaps Janus, the two-faced god, is the proper emblem for this topic. We need not go as far as Satan, in any event, to find this unpleasant edge—Ben Jonson's Mosca stands for the same exhilarating yet sinister power when he glories in his own transformative energies:

> I fear I shall begin to grow in love
> With my dear self, and my most prosperous parts,
> They do so spring and burgeon. I can feel
> A whimsy i' my blood: I know not how,
> Success hath made me wanton. I could skip
> Out of my skin now, like a subtle snake,

I am so limber.
. . . .

. . . your fine elegant rascal, that can rise
And stoop, almost together, like an arrow;
Shoot through the air as nimbly as a star;
Turn short as doth a swallow; and be here,
And there, and here, and yonder, all at once;
Present to any humor, all occasion;
And change a visor swifter than a thought.

(*Volpone*, III.i.1-29)

But once such powers are unleashed, they may be difficult to control, as Volpone himself, a master of transformation and disguise, soon discovers; in spite of his own formidable powers, the Mosca that he has turned on the world soon turns back on him, and he will be forced to "lie in prison, cramped with irons," until he is "sick and lame indeed" (V.vii.123-4), at last imprisoned in the shapes he merely feigned earlier. Mosca's notorious predecessor, Shakespeare's Richard III, has already been cramped and lamed when we first see him, both ashamed of and determined to triumph over his shape; but Richard's famous invocation of man's self-transformative powers warps and twists every positive into a negative:

Why, I can smile, and murder whiles I smile,
And cry, "Content" to that which grieves my heart,
And wet my cheeks with artificial tears,
And frame my face to all occasions.
I'll drown more sailors than the mermaid shall;
I'll slay more gazers than the basilisk;
I'll play the orator as well as Nestor,
Deceive more slily than Ulysses could,
And, like a Sinon, take another Troy.
I can add colors to the chameleon,
Change shapes with Proteus for advantages,
And set the murderous Machiavel to school.

(*3H6*, III.ii.182-93)

21

Richard is the nightmare Pico did not remember having. But Richard finds even his own self too slippery, himself the nightmare from which he is trying to awake, and in the famous dream sequence before Bosworth he debates who and what he really has become, and may yet be:

> What do I fear? Myself? There's none else by.
> Richard loves Richard: that is, I am I.
> Is there a murderer here? No. Yes, I am.
> Then fly. What, from myself? Great reason why!
> Lest I revenge. What, myself upon myself?
> Alack, I love myself.
> . . . .
> I am a villain. Yet I lie, I am not.
> Fool, of thyself speak well. Fool, do not flatter.
> My conscience hath a thousand several tongues. . . .
>   (R3, V.iii.183-94)

It is an inner debate that is literally self-defeating. Shakespeare shows that all the self-transformations have finally collapsed into the dual roles of victor and victim, confessor and criminal. Richard falls into the dilemma of all shapeshifters: "I am I" but also "I am not." He is and is not himself. In becoming so many others, he can no longer affirm clearly what he truly is.

Antony discovers a similar but more complex treachery in self-transformation when, after suffering another defeat, he broods in a "Roman" vein. He begins his famous speech with a vision of the shapes of clouds shifting from "dragonish" to "bear or lion," sometimes becoming "A towered citadel, a pendant rock, / A forked mountain, or blue promontory / With trees upon't that nod unto the world / And mock our eyes with air." The mutability and instability of "black vesper's pageants" (it is highly significant that a theatrical metaphor should enter here) remind Antony all too poignantly of his own transformations, which he has usually blamed on Cleopatra:

22

That which is now a horse, even with a thought
The rack dislimns, and makes it indistinct
As water is in water.
. . . .
My good knave Eros, now thy captain is
Even such a body: here I am Antony,
Yet cannot hold this visible shape, my knave.
                              (*A&C*, IV.xiv.1-14)

Antony has made a career out of denying he is anything but
Antony, but we have seen him drifting to and fro between the
Roman and the Egyptian worlds. Now the watery instability
of his own shape strikes him numb, though in a few moments
he will hasten back to his old serpent of Nile.

The capacity to change necessarily implies the capacity to
be changed. Shape-shifters cannot always maintain a desired
shape; once such energies are released, only the gods seem
able to control them. The greatest danger in this power has
been dramatized, again, by Spenser in the perversions of Archimago:

He then devisde himselfe how to disguise;
For by his mightie science he could take
As many formes and shapes in seeming wise,
As ever *Proteus* to himselfe could make:
Sometime a fowle, sometime a fish in lake,
Now like a foxe, now like a dragon fell,
That of himselfe he ofte for fear would quake,
And oft would flie away. O who can tell
The hidden power of herbes, and might of Magicke spell?
                              (*F.Q.*, I.II.x)

So fearful is this power that the magician even frightens himself. Moreover, Spenser fills his poem with other sinister manifestations of this power, such as Duessa ("For she could d'on
so manie shapes in sight, / As ever could Cameleon colours
new" [*F.Q.*, IV.I.xviii]), and Proteus himself, who assaults
Florimell in various forms:

23

To dreadfull shapes he did himselfe transforme,
Now like a Gyant, now like to a feend,
Then like a Centaure, then like to a storme,
Raging within the waves: thereby he weend
Her will to win unto his wished end.

(*F.Q.,* III.VIII.xli)

In Book Five, Malengin appears as yet another evil shape-shifter with a repertory even larger than Proteus'. But in each case we should note how promiscuous and unstable the transformations can be, for the power to change is itself helplessly inconstant.

By now the reader will have been asking, quite properly, "Where is Ovid in all this?" The answer is, everywhere. The preeminent text of metamorphosis in the Renaissance was of course Ovid's *Metamorphoses,* a text Shakespeare knew both in the original and in translation.[14] No greater repository of fables of transformation was known. The restless world Ovid described, especially in Pythagoras's speech in Book XV, struck a responsive chord among the Elizabethans toward the end of the century. But the Ovidian metamorphic world was without limit, and so un-Christian; change simply continued forever. And no change seemed—if I may invoke the paradox—permanent, as Christian revelation promised. If Ovid's system of metamorphosis was a conservative one, in which no energy was ever lost and each change simply led to another, then the Christian system of metamorphosis might be termed entropic, since all would one day hear the trumpet and come to the End of Change.

Renaissance poets and playwrights, as the preceding examples suggest, celebrated the capacity for self-fashioning, as Stephen Greenblatt has called it in a recent book,[15] but they also feared this power, not only because it seemed fundamentally a chaotic energy, and not only because they might sink down the scale of being, but also because no matter what the nature of their transformation—self-controlled or ran-

24

dom, higher or lower, celestial or bestial—man's essential identity is put to risk.

THE SHADOWS OF IDENTITY

Above all, metamorphosis prompts questions of identity. The boundaries transgressed, the shapes dissolved, may be physical and external—man to wolf, woman to water—but the equally frequent inner transformations may be more significant than the outward ones. In this respect, the whole idea of metamorphosis is subversive, for it undermines the traditional belief in a stable, fixed, and ordered self upon which much of Western thought, and in particular ethics, rests. As Sir John Hayward noted,

> in the creation of other things, God approved them, and saw that they were good; because hee gave them a stable and permanent nature. But of the goodnesse of man no mention at all. Mans goodnesse was left unapproved at the first because God gave him liberty of will; either to embrace vertue and bee like unto God, or to adhere to sensualitie and be like unto beasts.[16]

If the decision could go either way, then "no mention at all" can be made of man's essential goodness—or, as the passage also makes clear, his essential identity.

The psychoanalyst Heinz Lichtenstein has argued that "metamorphosis and identity are the two limits of human existence, incompatible with one another, but complementary in that human life exists in a movement between these two limits."[17] Elsewhere, Lichtenstein suggests that "identity is change arrested," an equation that reveals the difficulty in defining the self.[18] To describe one's identity is to reassert the transgressed law: change itself must first be "arrested." But the identity so defined is already obsolete, for it has continued to change. Nostalgia for the present motivates all such efforts.

The metamorphosis of the self, the reshaping of identity,

may release all of man's potential, from Pico della Mirandola's optimistic vision to Shakespeare's demonic Richard III. The freedom to become anything, whether ill or good, however, brings with it a troubling corollary: the freedom to become nothing. Every metamorphosis, as we have seen, is partly a loss. The double motion of metamorphosis therefore insures that it always contains a dark shadow; it becomes both a synonym for, and a version of, death, the ultimate change that awaits us all. Metamorphosis may make us queasy even as it exalts or liberates us, because it ultimately signifies hazard and loss.

The most graphic way of representing metamorphosis on the stage is through masking and disguise. This strategy dramatizes how identities can shift, collapse, and re-form: to put on a mask is to become someone else. Whatever the degree of intention, whatever the presumed distance between man and mask, disguise always constitutes an encounter with the metamorphic. Shakespeare's comedies are filled with clowns and courtiers who must but usually do not learn to distinguish between themselves and their roles. These poseurs range from the pedants and rude mechanicals who put on the Pageant of the Nine Worthies and the Tragedy of Pyramus and Thisby, through the noble Duke Orsino, still posturing even at the end of *Twelfth Night,* to Prospero laying aside his magician's robes forever. Ben Jonson suggests how far-reaching and dangerous this tendency of costume and role to become self can be: "*I have* considered, our whole life is like a *Play:* wherein every man, forgetfull of himselfe, is in travaile with expression of another. Nay, wee so insist in imitating others, as wee cannot (when it is necessary) returne to our selves."[19] Like many other writers of the time, Jonson will find it necessary to resort to a metaphor of the theater when he is describing mimetic metamorphosis; so Shakespeare, in representing metamorphosis on the stage, turns to the devices of mimickry as one mode of representation.

Yet masquerade does not merely represent metamorphosis: it *is* metamorphosis. In an essay on masks, whose implications may extend to every form of disguise, Mircea Eliade notes that in Greek drama, as well as in "primitive" minds, "the actor temporarily loses his identity: he becomes another, he *is* the character he enacts." Eliade explains the further implications of masking:

> Whether ritual, funerary, or for any spectacle, the mask is an instrument of ecstasy. He who wears one is no longer himself, since he is projected beyond his personal temporal identity. He becomes "other," even when the mask is his own portrait. . . . Whatever its type, every mask proclaims the presence of some being who does not belong to the everyday world.[20]

The testimony of characters in Shakespeare's plays who have assumed masks or disguises and find the experience at least partly transformational is plentiful, from Viola's recognition of the moral implications in disguise ("Disguise, I see thou art a wickedness / Wherein the pregnant enemy does much" [*TN*, II.ii.27-8]) through Rosalind's growing boldness as Ganymede and Hamlet's increasing distress over his "antic disposition," to Perdita's sense that her costume as Flora has altered her own nature until she is *becoming* Flora:

> Methinks I play as I have seen them do
> In Whitsun pastorals; sure this robe of mine
> Does change my disposition.
> (*TWT*, IV.iv.132-4)

Earlier in the scene, she has been embarrassed by her promotion to divinity— "and me, poor lowly maid, / Most goddesslike pranked up"—and distressed by Florizel's demotion to shepherd—"so noble, / Vilely bound up." But she is set at ease by Florizel's Ovidian rationalization:

> Apprehend
> Nothing but jollity. The gods themselves,
> Humbling their deities to love, have taken
> The shapes of beasts upon them. Jupiter

Became a bull, and bellowed; the green Neptune
A ram, and bleated; and the fire-robed god,
Golden Apollo, a poor humble swain,
As I seem now. Their transformations
Were never for a piece of beauty rarer,
Nor in a way so chaste, since my desires
Run not before mine honor, nor my lusts
Burn hotter than my faith.
                (*TWT*, IV.iv.24-34)

Contrary to his examples, Florizel maintains that his disguise
has not changed him, that the erotic spurs of transformation
have not made him bellow, bleat, or burn. Taking on trans
formation is a proof of a lover's sincerity, according to him.
Florizel thinks he can still control it, but Perdita knows better.
Like every metamorph, Florizel will find his identity being
tested in the play—he will temporarily become a shepherd,
don the clothes of the comic thief Autolycus, and eventually
confirm his identity as a son; the audience realizes, as the
allusion to Ovid confirms, that all these metamorphoses, and
perhaps *all* metamorphosis, are caused by "my desires," by
the power of love. As we will see in the next section, desire
and metamorphosis are invariably linked together.

Amor and Metamorphosis

The duality of metamorphosis—both destroyer and creator—
encompasses the extremes and paradoxes of life itself. If it
figures a kind of death, or dissolution of identity, leading to
oblivion, it also leads to the enchantments of love. Loss itself
can be gain, once we understand the peculiar and insistent
connection between metamorphosis and erotic love. Stories
of metamorphosis are of course often stories *about* love; the
association is conventional and widespread. Northrop Frye
calls metamorphosis "the central symbol of divine love as the
pagans conceived it," linking heaven and earth alike, and
Brooks Otis, writing on Ovid, refers to love as "the final secret

of metamorphosis" and terms Ovid's poem "an epic of love."[21] Yet even as a symbol of love, metamorphosis may frighten and threaten.

It is a clinical fact that some people fear to love because it signifies for them a surrender of their identity to another, and hence a loss of psychological shape. Anna Freud has written of what can be an engulfing identification with the love object which "implies a threat to the intactness of the ego, i.e., a loss of personal characteristics which are merged with the characteristics of the love object. The individual fears this regression in terms of the dissolution of the personality." For some, "to love signifies therefore not a gain, but a loss, against which the individual defends himself."[22] This fear of love proceeds partly, I think, from a failure to discern the *full* functioning of metamorphosis—the establishing of the very boundaries it violates, the defining of the ego that is changed, the loss that is also a gain. In much of Shakespearean comedy, success in love requires some submission to transformation, with a richer, stronger self resulting in the end; when the lover's "characteristics . . . are merged with the characteristics of the love object," two have become one. This fusion through transformation seems to be an inevitable result of love in Shakespeare's comedies, and to some extent their very goal.

Above all other emotions or energies, love generates metamorphosis in man. As *agape,* love might prompt the ecstasy of St. Teresa, or the divine transfiguration of Christ. Moreover, the descent of god into man, in the person of Jesus, was granted through divine love for man; the descent of Jove into a bull, on the other hand, was prompted by divine lust for woman. As *eros,* love might produce ennobling transformations (the chivalric ideal of service at its best) or, more dangerously, transformations into mere bestiality. On the other hand, transformation can itself also function as an escape from the demands of love. The nymphs who flee their erstwhile lovers in Ovid, as Daphne does Jove, may in their desperation turn into a laurel tree, a reed, or a pool of water, but they

29

rarely succeed in escaping; in Shakespearean comedy, the lovers are never so skittish.

The most humiliating of love's transformations, from a masculine point of view, is that which turns the lover, after marriage, into a horned beast—a cuckold. The apparently infinite number of joking allusions to the "horn" in Shakespeare, even in the tragedies, suggests the insecurity of all male lovers, who have as it were already lost their shapes and risked their identity by loving in the first place. The possibility of this risk—of the failure of marriage and its necessary transformation—leads to the corollary grotesque fear of a mocking transformation. Coppelia Kahn has described the irony of the cuckold wearing the horns, traditional emblems of virility, rather than the cuckolder: the part of the cuckold "that is at once his pride and his vulnerability, that makes him godlike in sexual power, but bestial in blind appetite, is exposed as his nemesis, his fatal flaw. Its power is mocked and its dumb bestiality confirmed in horns."[23] Clearly, falling in love will lead to one form of metamorphosis or another, and in some particularly deluded men—such as Ford in *The Merry Wives of Windsor* or Othello or Leontes—there is an inevitable connection (marriage becomes *equivalent* to cuckoldry) between the transformations generated by love.

One powerful, recurring emblem of ambivalent sexual energy is the figure of Circe. Charles Segal has noted how Ovid, departing from Homer, has removed "Circe's gentler and more benevolent qualities," making her far more active and enlarging her scope of influence until her power of passion and magic "seems limitless and irresistible."[24] The conjunction in a single figure of these two powerful and related energies—desire and metamorphosis—must have seemed at once inevitable and awesome in the Renaissance. Certainly Spenser's Acrasia and Duessa are especially dangerous temptations in their various false shapes. The first thought of Shakespeare's bewildered Antipholus of Syracuse, confused by his experiences in Ephesus, is that some dark enchantress has seized him, one of those "dark-working sorcerers that change the

30

mind, / Soul-killing witches that deform the body" (*CE*, I.ii.99-100). He will later invoke the "siren . . . mermaid" twice, once in delight as Luciana approaches him, once in confusion as he considers the changes being wrought in him. At the end of the play the Duke will explain the confusing errors by asserting that "you all have drunk of Circe's cup" (*CE*, V.i.271).

As these Circean fears suggest, one inevitable stage in the metamorphic process of love is the transformation of the lover, who becomes "other" for some period of time before (in comedy at least) returning to a replenished self. Each of Shakespeare's comic lovers is transformed: some become more generous, some more foolish, some more dangerous, one becomes literally an ass, dozens become figurative asses, a few become, finally, themselves, their best selves. We may find Bottom "translated" into an ass, hear that Armado will become a votary for Jacquenetta, watch skeptically as Angelo suddenly turns toward Isabella, applaud as Orsino and Olivia are altered by the beneficent influence of Viola—but in each case the *primum mobile* is love, erotic or platonic, selfish or selfless, carnal or comic. Desire leaves no one unchanged. Indeed, the changes wrought by love embody the governing principle of Shakespearean comedy, nowhere summed up as well as in Benedick's confused recognition: "I will not be sworn but love may transform me to an oyster" (*MA*, II.iii.23). It is this essential connection between love and metamorphosis which I will trace through the individual plays in later chapters.

In Shakespearean comedy, real love cannot remain unfulfilled; an endless and unsatisfied longing would mean a one-way metamorphosis, a suspension in otherness or self-alienation which would never cease. Rather, love is always harnessed, as Proteus was by Menelaus, into a single shape—into marriage, the final cause of comedy. Those Shakespearean lovers who have shown themselves capable of, and receptive to, metamorphosis, not only achieve their loves, but at the same time regain their lost shapes; yet at the end they are no longer the same as at the beginning of the play. Only a humors character like Malvolio or Jaques goes without completed love; they do not change essentially since they cannot love, and they cannot love because they are unable to change. Marriage, in Shakespearean comedy, is the paradoxical state in which two become one but also remain two; in which the self is given and so lost, but miraculously received back; in which transformation leads to permanence. The peculiar urgency toward completion sensed in the endings of Shakespeare's comedies derives in part from this need to slake the thirst of desire, to harness its shapes, to make Proteus stand and answer our questions.

The Liberation of Language

Transformations in language, as the poets know, can be as powerful as any other shape-shifting. Bacon laments that "even definitions cannot cure this evil in dealing with natural and material things; since the definitions themselves consist of words, and those words beget others," thus voicing the impossible hope that language itself will somehow be immune to the virus of transformation, when language seems more and more to be the virus itself.[25] For part of the Renaissance, at any rate, language was more than the relation of signifier to signified. Metamorphosis and dissolving boundaries occur not only to people but also to their language; words can lose their shape as easily as lovers, and, like them, exchange identities with close cousins and unexpectedly trip over the erotic. All of Shakespeare's plays, but especially the comedies, rest on a semi-magical linguistic energy, in which words can shift sound, meaning, and shape, malapropisms become mythopoetic, and puns perform triple duty. Two meanings in one word is the linguistic equivalent of Cesario in *Twelfth Night*, two identities in one name.

If any linguistic feature ought to resist transformation, it is the proper name. To the extent that a name, magical or otherwise, identifies some essence, naming and metamorphosis stand in a dialectical relationship. As Kenneth Burke notes, the "idea of locating, or placing, is implicit in our very word for definition itself: to *define*, or *determine* a thing, is to mark its boundaries."[26] But who can mark the boundaries of Proteus, or Archimago, or even Falstaff? Liberation of the self must also mark the liberation of naming. So even names are subject to revision in Shakespeare, as when the prince changes from Hal to Harry Monmouth to the Prince of Wales and finally to King Henry the Fifth; or names may already be figures of speech (Dull, Bottom) or multiple puns (Falstaff, Moth, Jaques). The liberation of all language from fairly fixed meaning is an inevitable corollary to metamorphosis.

A further crisis of language often results during or after metamorphosis; Ovid's characters, for example, frequently suffer the loss of public speech. In Book One of the *Metamorphoses*, Io, changed into a heifer, finds her altered state imprisoning:

And had she had hir speach at will to utter forth hir thought,
She would have tolde hir name and chaunce and him of helpe
  be sought.
But for bicause she could not speake, she printed in the sande,
Two letters with hir foote, whereby was given to understande
The sorrowful chaunging of hir shape.
                    (*Met*, I.802-6)

The human impulse towards articulation remains unchanged, then, but a different language must be employed. Io loses speech but turns to writing, as Lavinia does in *Titus Andronicus*, when her mutilated arm writes in the dust the names of her violators (not to mention a little Seneca); some "tragic alphabet" will thus be sought to satisfy the compulsion to speak. When Io's metamorphosis is later reversed, she "gladly would have spoke: yet durst she not so do, / Without good heede, for feare she should have lowed like a Cow. / And therefore softly with hir selfe she gan to practice how / Distinctly to pronounce hir wordes that intermitted were" (*Met*, I.935-8). Because speech is one proof of humanity, recovery of language signals the return to human boundaries. Examples of this sort may be readily multiplied throughout Ovid.

Metamorphosis can thus deny articulation altogether. Although it may liberate language in some cases, it can suppress it completely in others. For poets especially, the need to articulate by whatever systems of signs and gestures may be available is the impulse most radically human. The Renaissance truism that man differs from the animals by his faculty of rational discourse suggests how frightening, indeed, must have been the surrender of that power to an animal shape. Here as elsewhere, loss is more poignant than possession.

The most verbal of all our poets rarely deprives his transformed characters utterly of speech, however. Lear may howl and Lavinia write in the dust, but most transformations, certainly those in the comedies, are followed not by a loss of language but by a further transformation of it. The lover's rhetoric may collapse into convention (Proteus' vows to Julia) or become inspired (Berowne's Promethean Fire speech); it may turn suddenly Petrarchan (Titania on first seeing Bottom) or caustic and witty (Benedick and Beatrice). These romantic and rhetorical transformations in the overplots are inevitably accompanied by more bizarre and comical verbal deformations in the underplots, where dense malaprops, witty punsters, and rhetorical onanists rule. When love releases the energies of metamorphosis, the linguistic aftershocks are felt everywhere.

※

I return to Ovid for help in making a final point. Among the deepest mysteries of metamorphosis is its connection with the philosophical question of the One and the Many. Fully recognizing the paradoxes of transformation, Pico della Mirandola cryptically summarizes them thus: "He who cannot attract Pan approaches Proteus in vain."[27] Presumably he means by this that there is an underlying unity to the world—Pan—which permits us to see and to interpret its multiplicity—

Proteus. In the *Oration*, Pico had said that Proteus was a symbol for man in the ancient mysteries. For Pico, according to Edgar Wind, transformation "is the secret gate through which the universal invades the particular."[28] Pointing out the apparent "law of self-contrariety" belonging to the gods, Wind summarizes Pico's insight that in this self-contrariety "the gods reveal their Protean nature: but the very fact that each god contains his opposite in himself, and can change into it when occasion demands, makes him shadow forth the nature of Pan in whom all opposites are one."[29] Such inner contradictions will prove troubling indeed to those Shakespearean characters who don antithetical disguises only to find them imprisoning, so that they are and are not themselves. The natural perspective of the comedies, which paradoxically "is and is not" (*TN*, V.i.216), will be seen again and again.

Pico's understanding provides a useful commentary on the gods as Ovid depicts them, but suggests as well what happens to those mortals in Shakespeare who suffer or embrace change. Beneath the multiplicity remains a unity, for those who are changed are also unchanged. In a narrow sense, transformation often serves merely as a physical confirmation of what is already the case. The usual strategy is to transform the metaphorical into the literal: thus Bottom becomes an ass, Volpone will be warped by corporal punishment until his physical and spiritual deformities coincide, and Satan will become the serpent he already is. But in all these transformations, there remains a *residue* of the self, of whatever is characteristically human, after the change. When Lycaon metamorphoses into a wolf, he attacks the sheep,

> thirsting still for bloud as heretofore,
> His garments turnde to shackie haire, his armes to rugged
> pawes:
> So is he made a ravening Wolfe: whose shape expressely
> drawes
> To that the which he was before: his skinne is horie
> graye,

His looke still grim with glaring eyes, and every kinde of waye
His cruell heart in outward shape doth well it self bewraye.

(Met, I. 274-9)

When Daphne becomes a tree she escapes Apollo only in a narrow sense; all is changed for her, and yet

Remayned nothing in the worlde, but beautie fresh and greene.
Which when that Phoebus did beholde (affection did so move)
The tree to which his love was turnde he coulde no lesse but love.

She has not even fully escaped erotic possession:

he softly layde his hande upon the tender plant,
Within the barke newe overgrowne he felt hir heart yet pant.
And in his armes embracing fast hir boughes and braunches lythe,
He proferde kisses to the tree, the tree did from him writhe.
Well (quoth Apollo) though my Feere and spouse thou can not bee,
Assuredly from this tyme forth yet shalt thou be my tree.

(Met, I.676-84)

Even in Ovid, few changes are radically absolute, as the case of the transformed Actaeon shows:

He sighde and brayde: for that was then the speach that did remaine,
And downe the eyes that were not his, his bitter teares did raine.
No part remayned (save his minde) of that he earst had been.

(Met, III. 239-41)

Metamorphosis may thus amount to a change that is no change. The loss of human shape may sometimes paradoxically confirm what the shape ought to be, and what the essence is. Shakespeare's comic characters will find, in a similar manner, that their transformations are both liberating and constricting, that they are drastically but often not essentially changed, that there is an aptness to their changes even as they seem most surprising. Many of these comic characters will discover that Pico is right, but that the reverse of his statement is just as correct: he who cannot attract Proteus approaches Pan in vain. We must embrace the metamorphic multiplicity of the world before we can understand its underlying unity. The way to triumph in Shakespearean comedy will be found through metamorphosis rather than stasis.

COMEDY AND METAMORPHOSIS

Through these paradoxes of love, identity, and language, metamorphosis inherently lends itself to comedy, and especially to Shakespearean comedy. Metamorphosis is not exclusively a comic theme, of course, as the more brutal moments in Apuleius or Ovid will confirm. Nor is this the place to lament the fact that so few critics have considered metamorphosis as central to a definition of comedy. But Bergson's classic essay *Laughter* offers an interesting parallel. He argues there that "a sudden dissolution of continuity" with custom must occur before the comic can occur, and in one of his formulations offers a "general law": "Any incident is comic that calls our attention to the physical in a person, when it is the moral side that is concerned." Later, he says that what incites laughter is "the momentary transformation of a person into a thing. . . . We laugh every time a person gives us the impression of being a thing."[30] In some ways, this formulation coincides with the phenomenon I have been describing: the "momentary transformation of a person into a thing" exactly characterizes metamorphosis as it generally occurs. Yet metamorphosis as comic theme and structure frequently inverts

Bergson's formula. Though the imposition of the mechanical upon the living may indeed cause laughter, so does the animation of the inanimate (as in *The Winter's Tale*), or the energizing of the inert.

We might equally connect metamorphosis with that theory of comedy which establishes links with fantasy and dream-fulfillment. The traditional happy endings of comedy, for example, may stem not so much from any inherent logic in their plots, as from a collective wish-fulfillment; such wishes are pre rational, perhaps, and may stem from childlike projections. Thus the unrealistic moments in comedy are explained away by the logic of the unconscious. Metamorphosis corresponds with such a theory rather nicely. If nothing else, transformation seems supernatural, and may generate any number of happy endings. In many ways metamorphosis itself is the purest fantasy: it incarnates the belief not only that man can change, but also that man can change himself, and few ideas now seem as wishful as that.

Perhaps the most useful theorizing about literary metamorphosis has been conducted by Northrop Frye, who makes it an integral part of the structure of romance. For Frye, "most romances exhibit a cyclical movement of descent into a night world and a return to the idyllic world, or to some symbol of it like a marriage."[31] Frye investigates themes of both "descent" and "ascent." Romance tends to begin with a descent:

> Every aspect of fall or descent is linked to a change in form in some way, usually by associating or identifying a human or humanized figure with something animal or vegetable. Daphne becomes a laurel and Syrinx a reed; Adam and Eve in Genesis, on losing their original preternatural gifts, become the rational animals symbolized by the "coats of skins" they receive from God. Even Daphnis and Chloe are almost assimilated to the animals they are brought up with. (p. 105)

During the descent phase, this loss of shape, which may amount to nothing but assuming a disguise, predominates, but it is

38

inevitably attended by familiar images: "pictures or tapestries or statues or mirrors" which suggest "the exchange of original identity for its shadow or reflection" (p. 155).

But the way down is also the way up. Romance always provides a compensating ascent, and here, as Frye argues, the opposite themes prevail: "escape, remembrance, or discovery of one's real identity, growing freedom, and the breaking of enchantment" (p. 129). In romance, metamorphosis reverses itself, something which happens only rarely in Ovid but far more frequently in Shakespeare. Frye sees the major theme as

> the growing of identity through the casting off of what-ever conceals or frustrates it. The simplest form of such ascending metamorphosis is the removal of enchantment, in which an animal disguise or something parallel is re-placed by the original human form. The frog becomes the prince; Lucius the ass, in Apuleius, becomes Lucius the initiate of Isis; the Wife of Bath's loathly lady, having got what she wanted, becomes a beautiful lady. Closely related is the comic theme of release from a humor, where a character with a mechanical pattern of behavior is able to become free of it. (p. 140)

In a typical application of his theory, Frye terms the structure of A Comedy of Errors "a metamorphosis structure, a descent into illusion and an emergence into recognition. The main action takes place in a world of illusion and assumed madness; the imagery of the final recognition scene suggests a passing through death into a new world."[32]

My purpose in citing Frye here is to record one way in which metamorphosis may be applied to a particular theory of genre and thereby reveal structural connections among all kinds of transformations. But in the chapters ahead, I will focus more on the fact of metamorphosis than on the genre to which it may be assigned. I happen to agree with Frye that romance is the bedrock of drama and that, in general, the structure of Shakespeare's comedies, no less than that of his last plays, reflects the typical structure of romance. But my aim here is to discover how metamorphosis works in the comedies rather than to prove that they all coincide with a certain structural pattern. My muse is Proteus, not Pan.

Shakespeare seems to have been attracted to metamorphosis in part because of the paradoxes it provokes—the loss that is a gain, the man who can both be and not be himself, the double complicity between participant and witness. Stated this way, metamorphosis is not simply a power read about in Ovid but the condition of all life and, most interestingly, the condition of the theatrical experience. Although I will argue that in his comedies Shakespeare was deeply attracted to metamorphosis, the fact is that he rarely attempted to represent directly the most prevalent literary type (the Ovidian), even though he showed that he could, with Bottom, and even though he had seen or read of the magical Ovidian transformations dramatized by his theatrical colleagues in England and Italy. Lyly engineered a conventional transformation in almost every play, from the spiritual changes of his moonstruck lovers, through the man-into-ass formula in *Midas,* to the promised sex-change in *Gallathea.*[33] Shakespeare seems to have been drawn with equal power to alternate modes of transformation such as miming, marriage, and doubling. Virtually every comedy, in my view, reflects a *dramatic* investigation of another mode of transformation. Behind the manifestations, the individual transformations, lies metamorphosis itself, the force that propels the surge of waves or the shattering of the cocoon. Metamorphosis is not the wave or the cocoon, the surge or the shattering, but the force out of which they grow. Only a poet could make sense of it.

Chapter Two ❧ The Taming of the Shrew and Marriage

The Taming of the Shrew serves effectively as an introductory specimen of comic metamorphosis in Shakespeare. It contains, in some form, virtually every mode of metamorphosis found in the later plays, and its central question is the psychological transformation, the "taming" of a shrew into a wife. The question of metamorphosis in *The Taming of the Shrew* can be most directly confronted by dealing with the play's most remarkable and controversial instance of it—Kate's transformation, or at least her speech announcing it, at the conclusion. Yet that final scene, as everyone has noticed, is amply anticipated (with much else) in the play's Induction.[1] We might begin, then, by examining the changes detailed there for whatever light they may throw on Kate's exchange of her worst nature for her best.

The Induction to *The Taming of the Shrew* alerts us to the fact that the play will involve not only play-acting but all forms of metamorphosis. It clearly foreshadows much of the play to come. But the exact nature of Kate's final transformation is by no means made clear here, for the Induction offers several different kinds of transformation as possible models. First of all, we witness a transformation by disguise

41

in the Lord's trick on Christopher Sly. Sly's clothing and physical world will be radically altered: he is to be

>   conveyed to bed,
> Wrapped in sweet clothes, rings put upon his fingers,
> A most delicious banquet by his bed,
> And brave attendants near him when he wakes—
> . . . .
> Carry him gently to my fairest chamber
> And hang it round with all my wanton pictures;
> Balm his foul head in warm distilled waters
> And burn sweet wood to make the lodging sweet.
> Procure me music ready when he wakes
> To make a dulcet and a heavenly sound.
>   (Ind.i.37-40,46-51)

And so on, through every sybaritic fantasy, including a "Lady."
It should be so convincing that Sly will dismiss the real world
"as a flatt'ring dream or worthless fancy" (1. 44), and even
go so far as to "forget himself" (1. 41). Of course it doesn't
go quite so far as this, for Sly proves essentially irremediable.
He tries to rise to the challenge, musters some blank verse
now and again, and demands his lordly rights with his Lady,
but Sly finally remains Sly, lapsing back into prose, ordering
but small ale, and falling asleep at the play. His change is all
on the surface, as Bottom's will be. It is a model of a mimetic
metamorphosis which fails in part because of unbreachable
boundaries. Like many of Shakespeare's comic "actors," Sly
is entirely unable to "forget himself" and allow his own identity to dissolve sufficiently to *become* another. We will see
more successful instances of this mode of transformation in
the cases of Julia, Portia, Rosalind, and Viola, each of whom
will "forget to be a woman" and in so doing win true love.

A second instance of mimetic metamorphosis occurs when
the Lord's page dresses like a lady to go with Sly. This attempted transformation differs from Sly's in that it is self-
conscious, and the boundary between androgynous page and
young woman is not as impossible to bridge. The Lord's in-

structions for the boy suggest as well the terminology of Kate's last speech:

> Such duty to the drunkard let him do
> With soft low tongue and lowly courtesy,
> And say, "What is't your honor will command
> Wherein your lady and your humble wife
> May show her duty and make known her love?"
> And then, with kind embracements, tempting kisses,
> And with declining head into his bosom,
> Bid him shed tears, as being overjoyed
> To see her noble lord restored to health.
>
> (Ind.i.113-21)

In effect, Sly will enjoy a perfect male fantasy—entirely feigned and exempt from reality. If the boy can't mime properly, the Lord continues,

> And if the boy have not a woman's gift
> To rain a shower of commanded tears,
> An onion will do well for such a shift,
> Which in a napkin being close conveyed
> Shall in despite enforce a watery eye.
>
> (Ind.i.124-8)

This actor's trick reminds us of contrivance in the very play we are watching, and implies that if Sly is gullible enough to trust his "Lady," so are we to "believe" in Kate and Bianca. As an audience, we may not go so far as Sly—who prepares to ravish his lady without further ado—does but our belief in the actor's metamorphosis is similar. Throughout the comedies, moreover, Shakespeare will explore at every chance the implications of the self-disguising actor as a figure embodying transformation, and in referring to transformation will almost inevitably invoke theatrical language in order to describe it. Shakespeare's recurring and often-noted "metadramatic" interests[2]—especially those characters who are described as or refer to themselves as "actors" in some fashion—therefore seem designed not simply to express artistic self-consciousness

43

for its own sake, but rather continually to erect and then dissolve the boundaries of the theater. Such self-consciousness functions as a reminder of the theatricality of life as well as the life of theatricality. Every play, after all, takes place in a twilight zone created by the constant resurrection and transgression of boundaries. The theater is itself such a place, though in the case of Christopher Sly nothing has worked.

Another form of metamorphosis, invoked to ease Sly's own change, is found in the several allusions to Ovid in the Induction. These allusions to the *Metamorphoses* do not occur in the anonymous play, *The Taming of A Shrew*—one of Shakespeare's major sources for *The Shrew*—nor do others cited elsewhere in the play. They seem to be Shakespeare's self-conscious addition to his sources. To make Sly more susceptible to the change, for example, the Lord invokes a host of fantasies, including the beautiful Semiramis (whose Babylon is the city in which Pyramus and Thisby live—*Met*, IV), and one of the servingmen then offers to show Sly a series of erotic metamorphic paintings straight out of Ovid:

> We will fetch thee straight
> Adonis painted by a running brook
> And Cytherea all in sedges hid,
> Which seem to move and wanton with her breath
> Even as the waving sedges play with wind.
> LORD. We'll show thee Io as she was a maid
> And how she was beguiled and surprised,
> As lively painted as the deed was done.
> 3RD. SERVINGMAN. Or Daphne roaming through a thorny
>   wood,
> Scratching her legs that one shall swear she bleeds,
> And at that sight shall sad Apollo weep,
> So workmanly the blood and tears are drawn.
>   (Ind. ii.49-60)

These are changes of a different sort, and although they indicate the possibilities of love and metamorphosis, in fact their deep connection, Sly would have done well to think about these three stories more carefully, for happiness does not figure conspicuously in any of them. Each picture elides the real pain of the legend, offering a freeze-frame just before the subject's metamorphosis and, in Adonis' case, death. But the promise is too great for Sly to resist, and who can blame him? The powerful transformations of art itself, moreover, promise to work psychological alterations in the viewer. These pictures are "as lively painted" and "so workmanly" done that, ironically, the very boundaries between art and life seem bridged in the verbal descriptions, though not in Sly, and these feigned fictions turn into apparent realities even as others are failing.

Yet another type of transformation suggested in the Induction is the salubrious reformation experienced by an audience watching a play. A cry of players, the true masters of mimetic metamorphosis, appears, and the Lord insures that they not break the transformative effect, but remain safely on the other side of the boundaries they are about to cross:

> But I am doubtful of your modesties,
> Lest over-eyeing of his odd behavior—
> For yet his honor never heard a play—
> You break into some merry passion
> And so offend him.
>   (Ind.i.94-8)

The boundary between actor and role will remain firm in at least this case. The effect, Sly is told, will be life-giving:

> For so your doctors hold it very meet,
> Seeing too much sadness hath congealed your blood,
> And melancholy is the nurse of frenzy.
> Therefore they thought it good you hear a play
> And frame your mind to mirth and merriment,
> Which bars a thousand harms and lengthens life.
>   (Ind.ii.130-5)

Of course, the metamorphosis fails to take, and Sly, quickly bored, is soon fast asleep. His return at the end of *A Shrew,*

45

moreover, shows there that he hasn't learned anything any-how. In Shakespeare's *Shrew,* he simply falls into silence.

Is it possible to say what *kind* of metamorphosis the In-duction predicts for Kate? I think not. The Induction gives too many possibilities: transformations that are incomplete, transformations that are of clothes only, transformations that are both physical and emotional, transformations that are either erotic and desirable or frightening, transformations that are resisted and then accepted, mimetic transformations that are strictly the result of a suspension of disbelief, transfor-mations that thin the blood and triumph over disease. Kate's change at the end partakes of all these possibilities. Many readers have analyzed the methods Petruchio uses on Kate during the play—he "kills her in her own humor" (IV.i.169), he verbally creates an image of her as the tamed haggard, he shows her in himself a horrific male shrew, and so on. But the problem of her attitude, and Shakespeare's, persists at the end.[3] Alexander Leggatt has shown how the famous sun/moon scene (IV.v) with Vincentio completes the play's emphasis on games and sport, and the sheer pleasure derived from playing. In Kate's final transformation, he argues, "her sporting nature is not crushed but redirected." Leggatt finds a middle ground, moreover, between the traditional interpretive extremes of the ending:

> The fact that Katherina relishes her speech as a perform-ance does not necessarily mean she is ironic or insincere. She is simply enjoying herself. Her submission to her husband is not something to be admitted with shame, or rationalized, but celebrated—particularly in the presence of women who have just failed the test she has so trium-phantly passed.[4]

Though many would argue with this reading, still Leggatt redirects our attention to the ludic, and therefore indetermi-nate, possibilities of the ending from another point of view. Like all transformations, we might say, Kate's is total but necessarily incomplete. If she is undergoing transformation, as she seems to be, then her identity cannot be arrested.

Kate begins her speech with an exhortation to the other ladies to deshrew themselves, to undo a transformation that has unpleasant effects—"Fie, fie, unknit that threatening unkind brow" (V.ii.138). Such an effect is comparable to a natural mutation: "It blots thy beauty as frosts do bite the meads, / Confounds thy fame as whirlwinds shake fair buds" (ll. 141-2). She offers as a counterexample to the others her own transformation into apparent humility:

> My mind hath been as big as one of yours,
> My heart as great, my reason haply more,
> To bandy word for word and frown for frown.
> But now I see our lances are but straws,
> Our strength as weak, our weakness past compare,
> That seeming to be most which we indeed least are.
>
> (ll. 172-7)

That last line bears some further inspection, given the fact that a boy actor is portraying a woman who claims to have been a shrew but now is radically altered. Kate's insistence that one must seem what one has become was matched earlier in the speech by her equal insistence that one must become what one seems:

> Why are our bodies soft and weak and smooth,
> Unapt to toil and trouble in the world,
> But that our soft conditions and our hearts
> Should well agree with our external parts?
>
> (ll. 167-70)

These assertions and rhetorical questions are designed to "prove" nothing, but rather to call into question the very nature of metamorphosis, and Kate's in particular.

The end of the play shows above all, as the Induction had, that the essential quality of metamorphosis is its very indeterminacy, the mysterious way in which even apparent solidity proves momentary and newly announced identities fade into doubt: it is the sun, then the moon; it is Kate, then Katherina. Baptista claims at the end of the play that Kate "is changed as she had never been" (l.117), but the ambiguity of the syntax—she is changed as if she had never been a shrew; changed into what she had never been; changed as if "she" had never existed; and changed as she has never been changed before—defeats the assertion and simply reflects the problem. The final lines of the play offer yet another doubt, as Hortensio's assertion to the departing and victorious Petruchio—"Now, go thy ways; thou hast tamed a curst shrow"—is countered by Lucentio's quizzical doubt, "'Tis a wonder, by your leave, she will be tamed so" (ll. 191-2). We may recall here that the first sign of Kate's transformation was the dispute over sun and moon, and as she said to Petruchio,

> . . . the moon changes even as your mind.
> What you will have it named, even that it is,
> And so it shall be so for Katherine,
> (IV.v.20-2)

But as the Induction shows, even the naming of "Katherine" (though it linguistically suggests the transformation from "Kate") is an act of transformation.

Lucentio, meanwhile, is well on his way to horns with the suddenly changed Bianca. The irony of his allusion—

> I saw sweet beauty in her face,
> Such as the daughter of Agenor had,
> That made great Jove to humble him to her hand
> When with his knees he kissed the Cretan strond
> (I.i.167-9)

—becomes clear at the end when the other husbands must humble themselves in an unexpected way. After kissing the strond, after all, Jove turned into a bull, whereas Lucentio is made an ass. The play suggests that it is far preferable for Kate to *choose* to "become" a version of Petruchio, or her antithesis, than to be a passive victim of metamorphosis, like Sly. Thus she is among the first of Shakespeare's characters to embody the necessity of self-willed transformation, in contrast to the unnatural rigidity which she had displayed earlier, and which other characters still manifest at the end. The worst thing about a shrew, it seems, is her inability *not* to be a shrew, her Bergsonian inflexibility. So it is with every comic character that approaches the stiffness of an automaton.

The central cause of Kate's willing transformation is her growing love for Petruchio, strange as it is. And love motivates many of the other characters as well. Tranio's advice to his master, Lucentio—Close thy Aristotle; open thy Ovid—seems to epitomize the central impulse in the entire play:

> Let's be no stoics nor no stocks, I pray,
> Or so devote to Aristotle's checks
> As Ovid be an outcast quite abjured.
> (I.i.31-3)

This is not to be the outcast Ovid of the Pontic epistles, then, but the poet of love and metamorphosis. Later, Lucentio, in disguise as Cambio (the name means "exchange," one of many switches in the play), will deliver a reading-list for Bianca which contains only "books of love" (I.ii.145), and especially "the Art to Love" (IV.ii.8), or *Ars Amatoria*. In one comic scene, Lucentio even woos her between the words of a passage from the *Heroides*:

> Hic ibat, as I told you before, Simois, I am
> Lucentio, hic est, son unto Vincentio of Pisa,
> Sigeia tellus, disguised thus to get your love,
> Hic steterat etc.
> (III.i.31-3)

This is truly the interlinear text of love. Honest Ovid would have applauded, though his text is appropriate only ironically for this context.[5]

The obvious Ovidian context of *The Taming of the Shrew* has frequently been well-documented, but the different forms of transformation have too often been lumped together, in my view. Metamorphosis is neither a simple nor a single thing in

49

this play, but its recurring cause remains romantic love. At the end of the play Lucentio will explain what has happened:

> BIANCA. Cambio is changed into Lucentio.
> LUCENTIO. Love wrought these miracles. Bianca's love
> Made me exchange my state with Tranio
> While he did bear my countenance in the town.
> (V.i.120-3)

In fact, most of the play's famous "supposes" are generated by this power of love, or the intrigue to achieve it, and some even become self-generating, as Tranio explains:

> I see no reason but supposed Lucentio
> Must get a father, called "supposed Vincentio,"
> And that's a wonder. Fathers commonly
> Do get their children, but in this case of wooing
> A child shall get a sire if I fail not of my cunning.
> (II.i.400-4)

Each "suppose" is a temporary transformation which is usually also an "exchange" with someone else; a similar effect is generated by the mode of doubling in *The Comedy of Errors* and *Twelfth Night*. The "suppose" also suggests yet another kind of transformation at work, as Gascoigne indicates in his Prologue to *Supposes*, one of the play's sources:

> But understand, this our Suppose is nothing else but a mystaking or imagination of one thing for an other. For you shall see the master supposed for the servant, the servant for the master: the freeman for a slave, and the bondslave for a freeman: the stranger for a well knowen friend, and the familiar for a stranger.[6]

Exchanges such as these, of an almost metronomic regularity, not only are themselves transformations but may require a transformation of complicity in the onlooker as well. The total reversal of each category into its opposite, moreover, is a simplicity of conception which in Shakespearean comedy is frequently suggested and invariably undermined.

🦎

"Love wrought these miracles": the taming of the shrew, the "supposes" that come true, the mimetic transformations that temporarily succeed in their feigning. Yet Petruchio's objective in the taming, and the objective of most Shakespearean comedy, is not simply the expression of romantic love, but the fulfillment and culmination of it in marriage. Petruchio points out that "To me she's married, not unto my clothes" (III.ii.116), though he chiefly presents his clothes and other feigned roles to her until the end of the play, when she is ready for his essential identity. I find it significant that Kate and Petruchio's official marriage is held offstage, in the middle of the play, bracketed by wooing in the first half and growing mutual acceptance in the second. The marriage ceremony itself is reported as a hugely comic affair, with the priest dropping the book and then as he stoops to pick it up, "This mad-brained bridegroom took him such a cuff / That down fell priest and book and book and priest" (III.ii.162-3). Petruchio celebrated with a drunken carouse, pandemonium reigned, and then "he took the bride about the neck / And kissed her lips with such a clamorous smack / That at the parting all the church did echo" (III.ii.177-8). All in all, Grumio concludes, "Such a mad marriage never was before." Nor is one, yet, for a wedding there may be but a marriage there is none. The actual ceremony is suppressed on the stage, and its consummation delayed, until a marriage of true minds has occurred. Only at the end of the play, after the wager has been won and Kate and Petruchio have played out their game, does Petruchio confirm the marriage and announce the real consummation:

> Come, Kate, we'll to bed.
> We three are married, but you two are sped.
> 'Twas I won the wager, though [Lucentio] hit the white,
> And, being a winner, God give you good night.
> (V.ii.186-9)

51

The usual formula, that comedy ends in marriage, requires revision in considering Shakespearean comedy, for it is frequently the *completion* of marriage, not the wedding itself, which heralds the end of the play, as in *The Taming of the Shrew*. In *The Comedy of Errors,* marriages are restored as well as made, though in *Love's Labour's Lost* a tremendous surprise awaits those expecting a Jack-shall-have-Jill ending. We shall see, in the chapters following, how Shakespeare varies the details and extends his investigation of marriage in each succeeding comedy. He is clearly interested in the idea of marriage as a transformative process, and in its three constituent elements: the courtship, the wedding ritual, and the physical consummation or symbolic completion of the marriage. These three elements, which were legally distinct though logically connected,[7] are often widely separated in time in the course of a play, as in the spacing between marriage and mating in *The Taming of the Shrew*.

The gap between wooing and ceremony, or ceremony and completion, is frequently the space in which much of the play itself occurs—as in *Measure for Measure* and *All's Well That Ends Well,* or in the play-within in *A Midsummer Night's Dream*. Marriage cannot be completed until the end of the play because, of course, it is the goal of the play, but more importantly because completion cannot occur *before* but only after the full transformation of one or both of the lovers; thus Sly is never permitted to take his "wife" to bed because he has not been able to surrender to transformation.

Put another way, the process of marriage cannot be completed until at least one of the lovers has metamorphosed into the other: two must become one. All the comic marriages in Shakespeare resemble, to some degree, the embrace of Amoret and Sir Scudamore, in the first ending of Book III of *The Faerie Queene,* in which the two lovers embrace and melt into one another, "as growne together quite," as if "they had been that faire Hermaphrodite" (*F.Q.* III.xii). Kate may be "madly mated," but "Petruchio is Kated'" at the same time; he has turned himself into her for a time, until she can in turn become

her own antithesis. He must possess her through transformation before he can possess her as a wife.

One model of this kind of possession and transformation
is Ovid's story of Salmacis and Hermaphroditus, who is changed
by the gods in answer to Salmacis' prayer:

The bodies of them twaine
Were mixt and joyned both in one. To both them did remaine
One countnance: like as if a man should in one barke beholde
Two twigges both growing into one and still togither holde.
Even so when through hir hugging and hir grasping of the
 tother
The members of them mingled were and fastned both togither,
They were not any lenger two: but (as it were) a toy
Of double shape. Ye could not say it was a perfect boy
Nor perfect wench: it seemed both and none of both to beene.
                                                        (*Met,* IV.462-70)

In Francis Beaumont's version (1602) of the myth:

Nor man nor mayd now could they be esteem'd:
Neither, and either, might they well be deem'd,
When the young boy Hermaphroditus sayd,
With the set voice of neither man nor mayd.[8]

"Two twigges both growing into one," "a toy of double shape,"
"both and none of both," "neither, and either": we shall meet
these transformative paradoxes of union and difference
throughout our examination of Shakespeare's lovers, for whom
marriage is frequently described in similarly paradoxical terms.

In the Renaissance, even the common love of friendship
could cause this transformative two-into-one paradox, as Helena tells Hermia:[9]

We, Hermia, like two artificial gods,
Have with our needles created both one flower,
Both on one sampler, sitting on one cushion,
Both warbling of one song, both in one key;
As if our hands, our sides, voices, and minds,

Had been incorporate. So we grew together,
Like to a double cherry, seeming parted,
But yet an union in partition;
Two lovely berries molded on one stem;
So, with two seeming bodies, but one heart;
Two of the first, like coats in heraldry,
Due but to one, and crowned with one crest.
(*MND*, III.ii.203-14)

Metaphors of art and nature come naturally to such descriptions, as we see again much later in *The Winter's Tale*: "We were as twinned lambs, that did frisk i' th' sun, / And bleat the one at th' other" (I.ii.67-8). Yet both these perfect friendships, these symbolic unions in partition, inevitably divide and metamorphose. Separation and difference intrude. The cause in both plays is in part natural growth and mutability—"there rooted betwixt them then such an affection, which cannot choose but branch now" (*TWT*, I.i.24-5)—but more importantly the power of romantic love. The recognition of sexual difference, of new boundaries, enforces changes in same-sex friendship. Crossing the boundary to become one with a different sex proves inevitably desirable in Shakespeare, but inevitably destructive of old boundaries as well. Helena senses a sharp betrayal in these terms: "And will you rent our ancient love asunder, / To join with men in scorning your poor friend?" (*MND*, III.ii.215-16). And Polixenes muses on the change that was no change:

what we changed
Was innocence for innocence; we knew not
The doctrine of ill-doing, nor dreamed
That any did; had we pursued that life,
And our weak spirits ne'er been higher reared
With stronger blood, we should have answered heaven
Boldly, "Not guilty"; the imposition cleared,
Hereditary ours.

His meditation is by turns in the past tense and in contrary to fact subjunctive, and thus Hermione's conclusion is our own: "By this we gather / You have tripped since" (*TWT*, I.ii.68-76). These unions in partition between friends of the same sex are asserted in the strongest terms, either nostalgically as in *A Midsummer Night's Dream* and *The Winter's Tale,* or defiantly as in *As You Like It,* where Celia declares

> If she [Rosalind] be a traitor,
> Why, so am I. We still have slept together,
> Rose at an instant, learned, played, eat together;
> And wheresoe'er we went, like Juno's swans,
> Still we went coupled and inseparable.
>
> (I.iii.71-5)

Employing Rosalind's favorite "if" construction, Celia then asks her "sister," "thou and I am one. / Shall we be sund'red, shall we part, sweet girl?" (I.iii.96-7). It is not a rhetorical question, as it turns out. All these fraternal and sororal unions, like those of the actual twins in *The Comedy of Errors* and *Twelfth Night,* undergo a division, a re-forming, and finally a metamorphosis into the eternal two-in-one of marriage.

❧

Shakespeare takes up the idea of marriage as a form of transformation in almost every comedy; in *The Shrew,* as we saw, the union of Kate and Petruchio requires an essential alteration in both before the culmination of their marriage. This metamorphic power to blend identities is described in both the Old ("Therefore a man leaves his father and his mother and cleaves to his wife, and they become one flesh"—Genesis 2:24) and the New Testaments ("A man shall leave his father and mother and be joined to his wife and the two shall become one"—Ephesians 5:31). In the latter case, Paul offers this interpretation: "This is a great mystery, and I take it to mean Christ and the church." For some poets, and evidently for Shakespeare, this symbolic and actual fusion was still a great mystery, one without any obvious explanation. Hamlet's sarcasm to Claudius echoes the tradition while it mocks Claudius's debasement of it:

HAMLET. But come, for England! Farewell, dear Mother.
KING. Thy loving father, Hamlet.
HAMLET. My mother—father and mother is man and
wife, man and wife is one flesh, and so, my mother.

(IV.iii.49-53)

Shakespeare frequently refers to this doctrine in his plays; the
Friar's promise to Romeo and Juliet that "you shall not stay
alone / Till Holy Church incorporate two in one" (II.vi.36-7)
is representative.[10]

The straightforward but "mysterious" formulations of the
Bible received expansive commentary from the Neoplatonists.
In his *Dialoghi d'Amore,* for example, Leone Ebreo elabo-
rately describes the perfect union of friendship:

> Such union and conjunction must be based on the mutual
> virtue or wisdom of both friends; which wisdom, being
> spiritual, and so alien to matter and free from corporeal
> limitations, overrides the distinction of persons and bod-
> ily individuality, engendering in such friends a peculiar
> mental essence, preserved by their joint wisdoms, loves
> and wills, unmarred by divisions and distinctions, exactly
> as if this love governed but a single soul and being, em-
> bracing, —not divided into,— two persons. In conclu-
> sion I would say that noble friendships make of one
> person—two; of two persons—one.[11]

An even more powerful, and mystical, union is created between two persons who love each other mutually, who, Ebreo
says, "are not really two persons" but "only one or else four,"
since

> each one being transformed into the other becomes two,
> at once lover and beloved; and two multiplied by two
> makes four, so that each of them is twain, and both
> together are one and four.[12]

In *The Courtier,* Castiglione has Bembo make a similar comment, in the famous "kiss" passage; the perfect courtier

hath a delite to joyne his mouth with the womans beloved with a kisse: not to stirre him to any dishonest desire, but because hee feeleth that that bonde is the opening of an entrie to the soules, which drawne with a coveting the one of the other, poure them selves by turne the one into the others bodie, and bee so mingled together, that each of them hath two soules.

And one alone so framed of them both ruleth (in a manner) two bodies.[13]

Perhaps the fullest revelation of mystical marriage on the Renaissance stage may be found in Ben Jonson's masque *Hymenaei* (1606), where love, marriage, and union operate on many vast, symbolic levels. Juno, goddess of marriage, is also, anagramatically, *Unio* or Union, who according to Reason is

> She that makes souls with bodies mix in love,
> Contracts the world in one, and therein Jove,
> Is spring and end of all things: yet, most strange!
> Her self nor suffers spring nor end nor change.
>
> (ll.124-7)

The happy bride and bridegroom "must both make one / Blest sacrifice to Union" (ll. 145-6). The cosmic and political significance of this act is magnificently expanded throughout the masque, as D. J. Gordon has noted in his important study: "The union of marriage consummated in love typifies the harmonious ordering of man's nature and man's society that follows when reason is obeyed: this is perfection. . . . The circle is eternity, perfection, God . . . [and] also the girdle of Venus: marriage that is a bond of union through love"[14].

Shakespeare is at *his* most mystical and Neoplatonic in "The Phoenix and the Turtle," where the paradox of two-in-one through love provides the poem's central experience:

> So they loved, as love in twain
> Had the essence but in one;
> Two distincts, division none:
> Number there in love was slain.

. . . .

Property was thus appalled,
That the self was not the same;
Single nature's double name
Neither two nor one was called.

Reason, in itself confounded,
Saw division grow together,
To themselves yet either neither,
Simple were so well compounded;

That it cried, "How true a twain
Seemeth this concordant one!
Love hath reason, reason none,
If what parts can so remain."
(ll. 25-8, 37-48)

This is only the most cryptic description of what seems a dominant force throughout the comedies—where, as we will see, "the self was not the same" and the "double name" of single nature confused the onlookers. The object of love is finally always a "concordant one." No wonder Reason is "in itself confounded." Even Bottom is smart enough to know that "reason and love keep little company together nowadays; the more the pity, that some honest neighbors will not make them friends" (*MND*, III.i.142-5).

My intention is not to launch a vast survey of Renaissance Neoplatonism and Neoplatonic raptures on mystical love—a considerable task—but merely to suggest something of what ideal love and marriage might have meant in Shakespeare's time. Of course, no matter how exalted and ethereal the mystical theory of marital union might be, Shakespeare's comedies also clearly understand marriage to be not only this spiritual condition but also something quite down to earth and material, from Petruchio's concern with Kate's dowry and Bassanio's need for financial backing before he goes to Belmont, to Touchstone's even franker explanation to Jaques:

As the ox hath his bow, sir, the horse his curb, and the
falcon her bells, so man hath his desires; and as pigeons
bill, so wedlock would be nibbling. (*AYLI,* III.iii.77-81)

Touchstone's straightforward argument—"We must be married, or we must live in bawdry" (III.iii.95)—recalls that other Pauline comment about marriage and burning, and reminds us that Shakespeare, neither Neoplatonic nor stoic in his comedies, knows that marriage is or ought to be a transformative fusion of *all* the energies of life, carnal and spiritual. Shakespeare's comedies register and pursue a drive toward marriage on both these levels, and the comedies suggest, in several different ways, how marriage itself is a type of metamorphosis, both in the sense that the lovers necessarily undergo transformation as part of the process of marriage, and in the sense that the final, completed state of marriage is itself a metamorphic fusion of two identities into each other. It is an ironic fact that rarely if ever does Shakespeare show us a truly happy marriage in progress; we hear about them, in the past or future, but even the few obvious exceptions cannot lay to rest the biographical ghosts lurking around this omission. Still, the comedies show us what marriage ought to be, for better or worse, for richer or poorer.

Part Two ❧ Doubling and Mimesis

"*Plinie* reporteth to have seene *Lucius Cossitius* upon his marriage day to have beene transformed from a woman to a man. *Pontanus* and others recount the like Metamorphosies to have hapned in *Italie* these ages past: And through a vehement desire of him and his mother.

> *Vota puer solvit, quae faemina voverat Iphis.*
>
> OVID
> *Metamorphoses*, XV. 794

> *Iphis* a boy, the vowes then paid,
> Which he vow'd when he was a maid.

My selfe traveling on a time by *Vitry* in *France*, hapned to see a man, whom the Bishop of *Soissons* had in confirmation, named *Germane*, and all the inhabitants thereabout have both knowne and seene to be a woman-childe, untill she was two and twentie yeares of age, called by the name of *Marie*. He was, when I saw him, of good yeares, and had a long beard, and was yet unmarried. He saith, that upon a time leaping, and straining himselfe to overleape another, he wot not how, but where before he was a woman, he suddenly felt the instrument of a man to come out of him; and to this day the maidens of that towne and countrie have a song in use, by which they warne one another, when they are leaping, not to straine themselves overmuch, or open their legs too wide, for feare they should bee turned to boies, as *Marie Germane* was. It is no great wonder, that such accidents doe often happen, for if imagination have power in such things, it is so continually annexed, and so forcibly fastened to this subject, that lest she should so often fall into the relaps of the same thought, and sharpnesse of desire, it is better one time for all, to incorporate this virile part unto wenches."

MONTAIGNE
"Of the Force of Imagination"

PHILLIDA. Suppose I were a virgine, (I blush in supposing my selfe one) and that under the habite of a boy were the person of a mayde, if I should utter my affection with sighes, manifest my sweete love by my salte teares, and prove my loyaltie unspotted, and my griefes intollerable, would not then that faire face pittie thys true hart?

GALLATHEA. Admit that I were as you woulde have mee suppose that you are, and that I should with intreaties, prayers, othes, bribes, and what ever can be invented in love, desire your favour, would you not yeeld?

PHILLIDA. Tush, you come in with "admit."

GALLATHEA. And you with "suppose".

PHILLIDA. [aside] What doubtfull speeches be these?

JOHN LYLY
Gallathea, III. ii. 17-28

Chapter Three ❧ To Be and Not to Be: The Comedy of Errors and Twelfth Night

In *The Comedy of Errors* and *Twelfth Night*, Shakespeare stretches the possibilities of transformation from the "offered fallacy" of *Errors* to the more complex "natural perspective" of *Twelfth Night*, by subtle and ingenious manipulations of the apparently hackneyed formulae of doubling and twins. Two familiar topoi of doubling are reanimated in these comedies. The first is the Plautine convention of lost or separated twins, unknown to each other or anyone else, brought to the same location. The consequences include considerable confusion, questions of identity, and challenges to perspective and knowledge; the Shakespearean prototype is found in *The Comedy of Errors*, where we meet not one but two sets of twins. A second motif, broadly Plautine but also associated with romance, has a girl disguised as a boy (occasionally but rarely the reverse) and disguised parties of the same sex falling in love with one another.[1] The resulting "errors" or "supposes" become sexual as well as epistemological. The typical resolution of these confusions is found in the encounter of the separated twins, unexpected by everyone but the audience: the Antipholi and Dromii in *The Comedy of Errors* finally meet, as do Sebastian and Viola in *Twelfth Night;* or the disguised maiden reveals her identity and gender, as do Julia

63

in *The Two Gentlemen of Verona,* Portia and Nerissa in *The Merchant of Venice,* Rosalind in *As You Like It,* and, again, Viola in *Twelfth Night.* The hallmarks of these Plautine motifs are intrigue, disguise, and mechanical plotting—nothing very magical at all. Moreover, the prosaic urban setting of the Plautine tradition, with its obsessive concern with money and commerce, seems an unlikely location for metamorphosis to take place. No enchanted forests flourish on the Rialto.

Both *The Comedy of Errors* and *Twelfth Night* nevertheless offer alternative versions of the Isola Encantada or magical forest. Ephesus and Illyria represent, in varying degrees, removed spaces where anything might happen because boundaries are breached and identities are fluid. So, rejecting overt nymph-to-tree or man-to-stag metamorphoses, Shakespeare manipulates alternative modes—doubling, disguise, and mistaken identity—to do double duty. These conventions function in the normal way, as devices of intrigue plots, but also work simultaneously as new and subtle versions of transformation. The result is a sustained revelation of what it means to be and not to be, when a single identity splits into two, and two fuse back into one.

Ben Jonson saw one problem with stage twins right away: he had intended, he told Drummond of Hawthornden, "to have made a play like Plaut[us']Amphitrio but left it of, for that he could never find two so like others that he could persuade the spectators they were one."[2] Minor technical difficulties like this rarely stopped Shakespeare, of course, who was not only less literal-minded than Jonson but also fond of twins out of all proportion to their occurrence in nature (in spite of his own), or even in literature. The richest literary source of twins was the Plautine-Terentian tradition, which Shakespeare's contemporaries instantly recognized as the dramatic precursor of two of his plays. The famous *Gesta Grayorum* of 1594 reported that after various "sports, a *Comedy of Errors* (like to Plautus his *Menechmus*) was played by the players."[3] In very similar language, John Manningham in 1602 recorded the Middle Temple production of *Twelfth Night,* which was "much like the *Commedy of Errores,* or *Menechmi* in Plautus, but most like and neere to that in Italian called *Inganni.*"[4] In several ways, *The Comedy of Errors* and *Twelfth Night*—Shakespeare's two most Plautine comedies—represent his deepest explorations into metamorphosis.

The Comedy of Errors

The rhetoric and terminology of metamorphosis are everywhere overt in *The Comedy of Errors,* but the physical process itself has been carefully sidestepped; the dramatist employs instead doubling and an ingenious manipulation of what might be termed "situational" point of view to achieve the same effects. Shakespeare also changes the play's location from Epidamnum (in Plautus's *Menaechmi*) to Ephesus, presumably to take advantage of the suspicious connotations of Ephesus, biblical and otherwise. Antipholus of Syracuse finds Ephesus immediately threatening, in the first of many similar comments:

> They say this town is full of cozenage:
> As nimble jugglers that deceive the eye,
> Dark-working sorcerers that change the mind,
> Soul-killing witches that deform the body,
> Disguised cheaters, prating mountebanks,
> And many suchlike liberties of sin.
> (I.ii.97-102)

It is partly legend ("They say"), but frightening enough; in any list of urban dangers, disguised cheaters and changed minds are as much to be feared as is a deformed body. The transformations of Ephesus are partly mere fictions that "deceive," partly deep psychological alterations, perhaps even real physical changes; and the twisted language of the "mountebanks" as well as the "disguised" illusionists also suggest that these transformations are akin to those of the theater itself. The common denominator throughout the passage is a fear that loss of control leads to loss of shape. This

65

is unwilled metamorphosis, a nightmare of helpless passivity as eye, mind, body, and soul are worked upon by forces both mundane ("cheaters") and magical ("sorcerers").

Antipholus' servant, Dromio of Syracuse, has an earthier, more rustic view, which anticipates the world of *A Midsummer Night's Dream:*

> This is the fairy land. O spite of spites!
> We talk with goblins, owls, and sprites;
> If we obey them not, this will ensue:
> They'll suck our breath, or pinch us black and blue.
>
> (II.ii.190-3)

After Luciana calls him "thou drone, thou snail, thou slug," Dromio asks his master to confirm his sense of metamorphosis:

> I am transformed, master, am not I?
> S. ANTIPH. I think thou art in mind, and so am I.
> S. DROMIO. Nay, master, both in mind and in my shape.
> S. ANTIPH. Thou has thine own form.
> S. DROMIO.   No, I am an ape.
> LUCIANA. If thou art changed to aught, 'tis to an ass.
> S. DROMIO. 'Tis true, she rides me and I long for grass.
>   'Tis so, I am an ass.
>   (II.ii.196-202)

To think that your outward form has been altered when it hasn't is itself a transformation, as we saw in Chapter One with the witches' metamorphoses; yielding to the illusion as Christopher Sly could not, Dromio already seems less human. Appropriately enough, this comic identification is duplicated within forty lines by the Ephesian doubles:

> E. ANTIPH. I think thou art an ass.
> E. DROMIO.   Marry, so it doth appear
> By the wrongs I suffer and the blows I bear.
>   (III.i.15-16)

But Bottom's forest change is not appropriate to this urban world, and so the asinine metamorphoses remain internal, felt as psychological transformations, though the changes of these alternate modes seem no less drastic or traumatic to the victims.[5] In this play, Shakespeare makes the perfectly mundane seem absolutely magical—no mean transformation in itself.

Applying the language of physical change to interior changes becomes a *modus operandi* in *The Comedy of Errors*. Shakespeare incarnates metamorphosis within his characters in such a way that both its mysterious powers and skepticism about its existence are felt simultaneously. The odyssey of Antipholus of Syracuse reflects both possibilities. He is, to begin with, the stranger in a strange land. Virtually every recent commentator on the play has seized on his melancholy and near-suicidal self-reflections in the first act—"I will go lose myself"—and has noted the image of the

> drop of water
> That in the ocean seeks another drop,
> Who, falling there to find his fellow forth,
> Unseen, inquisitive, confounds himself
> (I.ii.35-8)

later echoed by Adriana (II.ii.126-30). The question of identity, as Harold Brooks and others have noted, looms throughout the play.[6] Metamorphosis is the quintessential loss of self, and doubling, the Shakespearean mode here, offers an ironic and unsatisfying way of finding that lost self. The physical reunion of the separated twins will thus constitute only one part of a complex re-forming of the self.

The kind of experience Antipholus of Syracuse undergoes serves as a model of transformation by doubling. He begins the play in what we deduce is an altered state: he has fallen from his customary state to being "dull with care and melancholy" (I.ii.20). This change is unexplained and troublesome, and will be reversed by the end of the play; but melancholy is soon forgotten when madness seems to enter. As he falls into the plot's manifold errors, Antipholus will alternate between two theories to explain what is happening: first, that some force external to him, in Ephesus, deceives his eye and deludes his senses; second, that he has in fact gone mad. The two explanations are by no means exclusive. His long-lost twin, Antipholus of Ephesus, will undergo a similar transformative dislocation, made perhaps even worse because the "familiar" everyday world he has lived in becomes completely strange. He too enters the play already changed—estranged from his wife Adriana, who accuses him (in the person of his brother) of being "strange to me," and taunts him that she has been unfaithful, because he has supposedly avoided her for another:

> For, if we two be one, and thou play false,
> I do digest the poison of thy flesh,
> Being strumpeted by thy contagion.
>   (II.ii.143-5)

The ideal of two becoming one, which takes on increasing suggestiveness in the play, marks only an unfortunate dislocation here. Antipholus' reply is confused, and Luciana exclaims, "Fie, brother, how the world is changed with you" (l. 153). The other inhabitants of Ephesus decide more simply that no matter which Antipholus is present, the poor fellow is mad.

As the scene proceeds, Antipholus of Syracuse lights upon a third explanation, that he lives a dream: "What, was I married to her in my dream? / Or sleep I now, and think I hear all this?" (ll. 183-4). He accepts this transformation for the time being, in a spirit of adventure, for something in him sympathetically recognizes that error (in the root sense of wandering) is what his own life has been, and is still the way to new revelation:

> What error drives our eyes and ears amiss?
> Until I know this sure uncertainty,
> I'll entertain the offered fallacy.
>
>   . . . .

68

> Am I in earth, in heaven, or in hell?
> Sleeping or waking, mad or well-advised?
> Known unto these, and to myself disguised?
> I'll say as they say, and persever so,
> And in this mist at all adventures go.
>   (II.ii.185-7, 213-17)

Mist, water, error: metamorphosis thrives in unstable regions, and it takes some courage to step into "this mist"—here, not the obliviousness of Bottom, but something self-conscious and risk-taking. Antipholus also understands his position as existence in some kind of fiction, wondering at the paradox that he may be "to myself disguised," that he can be not himself and yet know it at the same time.

Both Antipholi are increasingly startled by unexplained transformations in everyday language. Faces are the same, names the same, but nothing fits: *S. Antiph.*: "How can she thus then call us by our names, / Unless it be by inspiration?" (II.ii.167-8). His brother's servant echoes him, in a now familiar trope, when he confronts his unseen twin:

> O villain, thou hast stol'n both mine office and my
>   name.
> The one ne'er got me credit, the other mickle blame.
> If thou hadst been Dromio today in my place,
> Thou would have changed thy face for a name, or thy
>   name for an ass.
>   (III.i.44-7)

Later, he rudely remarks, "A man may break a word with you, sir, and words are but wind; / Ay, and break it in your face, so he break it not behind" (ll. 75-6). Words are but wind (as unstable as water) in this play because Shakespeare has taken special pains to create a symbolic world in which language itself, among other things, is constantly transformed and so "fails" in the strict constructionist sense. Nothing could be more disorienting than a world which precisely resembles the ordinary one except for the fact that customary language no longer operates there. The Antipholi and Dromii believe, alternatively, that they are transformed; that everyone else is transformed; and that their mere words have been mysteriously transformed.

Of all the words that have once been effectual but are now without stable meaning, that ordinarily establish the boundaries of identity, none is more important than one's name:

> There's not a man I meet but doth salute me
> As if I were their well-acquainted friend;
> And everyone doth call me by my name.
> Some tender money to me, some invite me;
> Some other give me thanks for kindnesses;
> Some offer me commodities to buy.
> Even now a tailor called me in his shop
> And showed me silks that he had bought for me,
> And therewithal took measure of my body.
> Sure, these are but imaginary wiles,
> And Lapland sorcerers inhabit there.
>
> (IV.iii.1-11)

The method of creating this linguistic and social dislocation—twins with the same name—is quite mechanical, as the play's detractors are always pointing out; but the effects created are anything but mechanical. The linguistic transformations are both cause and effect of the extensive psychological changes. Small wonder that at the end of the play Emilia asks everyone to "Go to a gossips' feast, and joy with me / After so long grief such nativity" (V.i.406-7). These people need not only a re-birth but also the re-naming that a christening party will provide. Antipholus of Syracuse especially needs a new beginning, his last one having failed in all ways:

> In Ephesus I am but two hours old,
> As strange unto your town as to your talk;
> Who, every word by all my wit being scanned,
> Wants wit in all one word to understand.
>
> (II.ii.149-52)

70

The new names at the gossips' feast will, of course, be the same as they always were, but the people, paradoxically the same outwardly, will change once again. So the gossips' feast is both renewal and repetition, since the names—what started the confusion in the first place—are and are not unique.

As identity and language begin to transform, and comfortably familiar boundaries collapse, the inevitable erotic obligato begins to sound. Pleading for her neglected sister, Luciana succeeds only in making the wrong brother (Antipholus of Syracuse) fall in love with her:

> Sweet mistress, what your name is else, I know not;
> Nor by what wonder you do hit of mine;
> . . . .
> Are you a god? Would you create me new?
> Transform me, then, and to your pow'r I'll yield.
> But if that I am I, then well I know
> Your weeping sister is no wife of mine,
> Nor to her bed no homage do I owe;
> Far more, far more, to you do I decline.
> (III.ii.29-30, 39-44)

Like every other Renaissance annotator faced with the powerful combination of woman, water, and metamorphosis, Antipholus next resorts to the legend of the siren to represent his experience:

> O, train me not, sweet mermaid, with thy note,
> To drown me in thy sister's flood of tears.
> Sing, siren, for thyself, and I will dote;
> Spread o'er the silver waves thy golden hairs;
> And as a bed I'll take them, and there lie,
> And, in that glorious supposition, think
> He gains by death that hath such means to die.
> Let Love, being light, be drowned if she sink!
> (ll. 45-52)

Antipholus is not much of an Odysseus, to be sure, but the audience knows what he means. The Renaissance fascination with metamorphosis finds a perfect culmination in the related myths of Circe and the sirens—the figure of the female temptress who could transform a warrior into a Gryll or, conversely, a naive young man into a mature and worthy lover. If she was a fleshly temptress for some, she could also be (as for Antipholus) a kind of muse. She might signify lust for Homer or Ovid, or the "glorious supposition" of romantic love. This stereotyped double nature—virgin or whore—may be partly seen in Antipholus of Syracuse's two references to the siren. The first, above, is one of rapture. But near the end of the same scene, after a little more thought about his "wife" Adriana and his new love for Luciana, it all seems more difficult:

> There's none but witches do inhabit here,
> And therefore 'tis high time that I were hence.
> She that doth call me husband, even my soul
> Doth for a wife abhor. But her fair sister,
> Possessed with such a gentle sovereign grace,
> Of such enchanting presence and discourse,
> Hath almost made me traitor to myself.
> But, lest myself be guilty to self-wrong,
> I'll stop mine ears against the mermaid's song.
>
> (ll. 157-65)

He is already *not* himself in this situation; but his determination to hang onto his inner self of honor, his last shred of identity, insures that his metamorphosis will remain incomplete. Clearly, the audience recognizes that there is nothing in *fact* wrong with his love for Luciana; somewhat less clearly, we see that there is something wrong instead with the entire situation. Antipholus of Syracuse will not *become* someone else, though he is mightily tempted as a way of fulfilling desire; what he doesn't realize is that he has *already* been transformed into someone else by his situation.

The Plautine convention rarely leads as deeply as Shakespeare is about to take us. He seems, in short, to have rejected the basic assumption that identical twins are identical. For

72

dramatic purposes, the most important fact about identical twins is that they are and must be finally different. If they were *completely* identical, there would be no play. Their overwhelming similarity allows the playwright to construct a complex transformational situation, but only their difference allows it to come to dramatic life. The situation is a vivid illustration of one we will see again and again: a man resists transformation, though attracted to it; he resists it even though it could never, in human imagination, be easier to accept; and even though he resists it, it still happens. Metamorphosis appears as both change *and* stasis, then; it manifests itself simultaneously as being (remaining the same) and not-being (the metamorphosed other). The "comic horror" attached "to the notion of the *complete* identity of two human beings," as G. R. Elliot notes,[7] underlies the play's doubling, but like any metamorphosis, which is and is not, absolute identity is only asymptotically approached, and difference, the "is not," is preserved. That Antipholus blames local "witches," finally, reminds us from Murray's accounts that the complicity of the viewing audience (onstage for now) is also required.

Antipholus of Syracuse's existential predicament finds a comic mirror in his servant's. Dromio's transformation similarly derives not only from his situation in Ephesus but also from the power of love:

> s. DROMIO. Do you know me, sir? Am I Dromio? Am I your man? Am I myself?
> s. ANTIPH. Thou are Dromio, thou art my man, thou art thyself.
> s. DROMIO. I am an ass; I am a woman's man, and besides myself.
>
> (III.ii.73-8)

That love transforms one, makes Dromio both himself and "besides myself," is by now a commonplace, though Dromio's capture at the hands of Nell (or Luce) seems rather desperate. After his famous comic blazon of her parts ("She is spherical, like a globe. I could find out countries in her"—ll. 114-5),

Dromio leaves with the familiar animalistic fears on his mind: "And, I think, if my breast had not been made of faith, and my heart of steel, / She had transformed me to a curtal dog, and made me turn i' th' wheel" (ll. 146-7). As she is a "globe," so engulfment by her would be a total loss of self, as complete as a drop of water falling into the ocean. As in *A Midsummer Night's Dream,* the characters in *The Comedy of Errors* fear the impingement of the animal, and the lowering or abolition of human boundaries. To stop one's ears is all a mariner can do. Not to be oneself, to be an "other," is as much as being an ass or a curtal dog.

As the play progresses and the "errors" multiply, the characters experience more and more transformations through situational changes in vision. Hearing that her husband's brother has wooed Luciana, Adriana begins to find her "husband"

> deformed, crooked, old and sere,
> Ill-faced, worse bodied, shapeless everywhere:
> Vicious, ungentle, foolish, blunt, unkind,
> Stigmatical in making, worse in mind.
>
> (IV.ii.19-22)

This description of course applies to her as well. From the start her shrewishness has been a given from which, we expect, she will be changed by the end of the play. The madness spreads rapidly, for S. Dromio soon describes a simple jailor as "A devil . . . a fiend, a fairy . . . a wolf . . . a hound that runs counter" (IV.ii.32-9). His master sees a routine courtesan as "the devil. . . . Avoid, then, fiend!" (IV.iii.65-6). But for all its strange occurrences, local eccentrics, and ambiguous reputation, Ephesus is after all a fairly conventional Renaissance city of commerce. The chief citizens are all merchants, and money remains their chief interest. Gold chains (and prompt payment) still take precedence over questions of the supernatural. The courtesan is not a witch but a local merchant herself; the brilliance of the play is to make her *both* things, depending—and this is crucial—on one's point of view.

The final act of *The Comedy of Errors* offers a series of

contrasting perspectives. Adriana, for example, attributes her husband's sudden transformation to demonic possession (the infamous Dr. Pinch is brought in): "This week he hath been heavy, sour, sad, / And much different from the man he was" (V.i.45-6). Emilia, however, explains his changes as the result of "the venom clamors of a jealous woman . . . his sleeps were hind'red by thy railing . . . thy jealous fits / Hath scared thy husband from the use of wits" (ll. 69-86). The Abbess's version is not necessarily the whole story, though, for S. Antipholus's history shows that melancholy is widespread. Emilia, at any rate, intends to nurse him, like a mother, "With wholesome syrups, drugs, and holy prayers, / To make of him a formal man again" (ll. 104-5), as if he had in fact lost his form; to be normal is to be formal here. As the competing stories are offered, Antipholus and Dromio of Ephesus suddenly burst in with an hysterical account of their escape from Dr. Pinch. Confusion, accusation, and denial increase, and the Duke resorts, for the third time in the play, to the myth of the sorceress: "Why, what an intricate impeach is this! / I think you all have drunk of Circe's cup" (ll. 270-1). At the moment of maximum confusion on stage, when transformations and dislocations have generated the greatest chaos, discovery begins. Appropriately, the discovery must be not only an uncovering of error but also a recovery of lost names, normal perspectives, and secure boundaries to identity.

Egeon ironically initiates the discoveries with still another error: "Is not your name, sir, called Antipholus? / And is not that your bondman Dromio?" (ll. 287-8). He is both right and wrong. When E. Antipholus fails to recognize him, Egeon refers to his own transformation as an explanation:

> O, grief hath changed me since you saw me last,
> And careful hours with time's deformed hand
> Have written strange defeatures in my face.
> . . . .
> Not know my voice! O, time's extremity,
> Hast thou so cracked and splitted my poor tongue

In seven short years, that here my only son
Knows not my feeble key of untuned cares?
(ll. 298-300, 308-11)

Time's hand, itself both deformed and deforming, may produce metamorphoses as great as any magic; the ravages of
simple mutability, "winter's drizzled snow," can change one
as greatly as the pangs of jealousy or the raptures of love.
Mutability may slowly achieve what transformation gains in
an instant.

In trying to outdo the Plautine conventions, Shakespeare
has shown remarkable ingenuity, multiplying the twins, the
complex situations, and the consequent errors as much as is
dramatically feasible. To engineer the resolution of his complications, Shakespeare need only bring the twins together
before everyone, and then neatly "explain" all. But he has
other questions on his mind, not to be disposed of mechanically, and so the ending takes some odd turns. With both sets
of twins on stage, the following exchange occurs:

ADRIANA. I see two husbands, or mine eyes deceive me.
DUKE. One of these men is genius to the other;
    And so of these, which is the natural man,
    And which the spirit? Who deciphers them?
S. DROMIO. I, sir, am Dromio; command him away.
E. DROMIO. I, sir, am Dromio; pray let me stay.
(ll. 332-7)

This kind of recognition scene is modeled partly on Lylyesque
or Italian pastoral drama, as I will argue more fully in discussing the ending of Twelfth Night. What stands out here
are the rich implications of these lines. Adriana has indeed
seen "two husbands," one of them mis-seen as "deformed,
crooked, old and sere." The Duke makes the understandable
assumption that one of the Antipholi cannot be real, but a
"genius" or "spirit," with possibly sinister overtones; only
one can be "the natural man." Of course, nature has given
us both men—just as she will give us the "natural perspective"

76

at the end of *Twelfth Night*—but the achievement of this play allows each Antipholus to feel that he has an attendant spirit, or perhaps is himself such a spirit. The Duke's final question, "Who deciphers them?" leads even further. No one on stage can answer him nor do the deciphering, and in fact the Dromii immediately make rival but identical nominal claims and self-assertions, as if to reveal the impossibility of answering the Duke. We might say that only the audience can decipher them, but if the actors are indeed identical twins, as in Komisarjevsky's famous production,[8] and they are dressed the same, then how can the audience ever decipher them? In practice, they will appear as different. But we know they are different chiefly from their asides and what they say in given situations—they are different because they say they are. To "decipher" them is to be able to "read" them in a special way. The difficulty in doing this recurs throughout the final scene:

> DUKE. Antipholus, thou cam'st from Corinth first.
> S. ANTIPH. No, sir, not I; I came from Syracuse.
> DUKE. Stay, stand apart; I know not which is which.
>
> (ll. 363-5)

But standing apart won't help much. The crucial difference between them, the key to deciphering them, lies in their language; only that finally marks them apart.[9] If the Antipholi had lost the power of speech, as Lucius and Apuleius do when metamorphosed, then they would have been, for all intents, completely identical. Here is an anomalous case where the retention of speech becomes ironic cause for further transformation. And yet names, and all language, have been revealed as generically susceptible to metamorphosis. To say "I, sir, am Dromio," is to announce and to undermine one's identity at the same time, because our names uniquely mark us and yet do not mark us. Words are but wind—our own breath and the world's.

Shakespeare turns the Plautine conventions back upon themselves, then, and in the process of challenging the tradition raises much larger questions. For the play shows us what it is like—in large part what it must *feel* like—to be and not to be at the same time. Each man acknowledges his own self, yet feels his own self violated, slipping away, its normal boundaries gone; each experiences the paradoxes of duality. On the one hand, Antipholus becomes Antipholus; on the other hand, Antipholus becomes Antipholus. When Egeon and Emilia speak of their long separation and present reunion, each twin (and certainly the audience) must recall his departure from being into not-being and his return. Amid the other reunions and re-namings in the play, this re-formation of the self is essential.

Even then, the reunion cannot be entirely unambiguous. "I know not which is which," the Duke says even now. "And are not you my husband?" Andriana wonders. Even the life-long servants remain confused:

S. DROMIO. Master, shall I fetch your stuff from shipboard?
E. ANTIPH. Dromio, what stuff of mine hast thou
    embarked?
S. DROMIO. Your goods that lay at host, sir, in the
    Centaur.
S. ANTIPH. He speaks to me. I am your master, Dromio.

(ll. 409-12)

Still, even S. Antipholus' assertion is ambiguous, for it could refer to either master or either servant. The entire complication of the plot serves to focus our attention on questions of language and intention, specifically on the linguistic loss that so often accompanies metamorphosis and makes it more fearful. It is hardly a coincidence that the inn in question is the Centaur—half man, half animal, yet another example of the metamorphosed human shape.

The doubling of doubles, so baroque in its excess, represents more than a display of mechanical virtuosity on Shakespeare's part. This situational confusion also allows Shakespeare to link speech and identity, and to dramatize how this link may be served, or at least called into question, through metamorphosis. Moreover, if we identify with either Antipholus, or through some fluke of nature happen to undergo a similar experience, we will understand how, in this play at least, metamorphic doubling leads to self-alienation. In a technical sense, the Antipholi are both literally beside themselves and "mad," since the referents of their speech become dislocated from their words, and their own names and identities seem to be appropriated by some Other.

The Dromii end the play by going off "hand in hand, not one before another," E. Dromio explaining that "We came into the world like brother and brother" (l. 426). But of course they came into the world not side by side, but one after the other, not only the same but also different. Chronology therefore becomes an issue:

E. DROMIO. Will you walk in to see their gossiping?
S. DROMIO. Not I, sir, you are my elder.
E. DROMIO. That's a question; how shall we try it?
S. DROMIO. We'll draw cuts for the senior; till then, lead thou first.
        (ll. 420-4)

E. Dromio then rejects this motion of difference, bidding them instead to go out together. It seems a quixotic effort. A great deal of the play has gone to show that even minimal difference and boundary become crucial to human identity. At the moment of metamorphosis, when S. Dromio becomes E. Dromio or vice versa, one or both will temporarily cease to exist. Shakespeare has put such a case quite flamboyantly here, with two sets of twins. And though the re-naming of the christening feast will go far toward sorting out the "sympathized one day's error," we will still recall that the sheerest linguistic thread maintained the margin of difference. Two almost became one, or one none.

The round of marriages—new or restored—that ends the play suggests yet another way in which two can become one. The traditional endings of comedy—marriages planned, consummated, or restored, harmful changes reversed, separations bridged, families reunited—move toward the elimination of difference and separation; yet these very forces of division are equally shown, in Shakespearean comedy, to be a human necessity. Consequently, the endings of Shakespearean comedies will increasingly feature some element that refuses to be transformed, reunited, psychologically altered, or made two in one by marriage. Something there is which loves a boundary.

Twelfth Night

The multiple powers of metamorphosis govern the action throughout *Twelfth Night:* mysterious energies which turn two into one and one into two, and mimetic impulses which lead people to become actors, donning disguises and willingly turning themselves into what they are not. Shakespeare again adopts the Plautine mode in this play, but broadens and complicates his borrowings until he has produced something quite new and strange. Uncertainty and mutability are the very essence of this play's world, as we see in the opening scenes; against this instability stands the loving constancy of Viola for Orsino and her lost brother Sebastian.[10] Orsino's first lines suggest the restless cyclical motion typical of the play, where appetite grows, surfeits, sickens, dies, and begins again. The "spirit of love . . . receiveth as the sea," that all-purpose symbol of generation and change. Whatever enters a lover's capacity "But falls into abatement and low price / Even in a minute" (I.i.13-14). Falling and rising, music, appetite, love— all is liquid and unstable. Orsino himself has already experienced a metamorphosis:

> O, when mine eyes did see Olivia first,
> Methought she purged the air of pestilence.
> That instant was I turned into a hart,
> And my desires, like fell and cruel hounds,
> E'er since pursue me.
> (I.i.19-24)

The allusion to Actaeon is conventional, and Orsino's pun on hart/heart is routine, but the truth of what he says is undeniable: he describes what it is to fall in love. One experiences metamorphosis, and finds that part of one's self has taken on an independent life: desire has turned one's former self into a stranger. Orsino has become the other that he always was. Olivia experiences something similar, in another version of love at first sight, though she likens her transformation to catching a disease (Orsino had her purging the air for him), rather than turning into an animal:

> How now?
> Even so quickly may one catch the plague?
> Methinks I feel this youth's perfections
> With an invisible and subtle stealth
> To creep in at mine eyes.
> (I.v.292-6)

Water—the central element of transformation—from tears and from the sea, engulfs most of the characters in *Twelfth Night*. Olivia "water[s] once a day her chamber round / With eye-offending brine" (I.i.30-1), and Sebastian in turn will mourn his lost Viola: "She is drowned already, sir, with salt water, though I seem to drown her remembrance again with more" (II.i.30-1). Viola has been washed ashore by the sea, believing her brother drowned. But the Captain offers a kind of hope: after the shipwreck, he saw Sebastian tie himself

> To a strong mast that lived upon the sea;
> Where, like Arion on the dolphin's back,
> I saw him hold acquaintance with the waves
> So long as I could see.
> (I.ii.14-17)

The Captain's glimpse of Sebastian overcoming flux and peril in the metaphoric guise of Arion—like Orpheus, a familiar figure of the poet, triumphing over mutability and raising himself, through his powers, above the elements—offers an emblem of how one can surrender to and still triumph over the mere elements.

Throughout the opening scenes of *Twelfth Night*, questions

of constancy and order, and images of the sea, receive special emphasis. Toby Belch, a smaller but noisier version of Falstaff, is ordered by Maria to "confine yourself within modest limits of order" (I.iii.9), as if that were possible. But Toby is only the most extreme of those characters in the play who defy conventions, resist limits, and spill over boundaries. Feste links together all in the play who are done in by liquids:

> OLIVIA. What's a drunken man like, fool?
> CLOWN. Like a drowned man, a fool, and a madman. One
> draught above heat makes him a fool, the second mads
> him, and a third drowns him.
> (I.v.129 32).

Even his language partakes of the play's typical oscillating rhythm, as he works a triple transformation on a single idea, each version of the drunken man revealing yet another kind of transformation, which "makes . . . mads . . . [and] drowns him."

Feste's most common rhetorical tool—the figure of anti-metabole (or *commutatio*), in which sentence elements are glibly reversed—reflects a verbal metamorphic capability which matches the other changes in the play. Here, for example, he quotes a non-existent authority:

> For what says Quinapalus? "Better a witty fool than a foolish wit." . . . For give the dry fool drink, then is the fool not dry. Bid the dishonest man mend himself: if he mend, he is no longer dishonest; if he cannot, let the botcher mend him. Anything that's mended is but patched; virtue that transgresses is but patched with sin, and sin that amends is but patched with virtue. (I.v.36-7, 44-50)

If this "simple syllogism" won't do, he goes on, "what remedy?" Certainly Viola puts up more resistance to these verbal gymnastics:

> VIOLA. Dost thou live by thy tabor?
> CLOWN. No, sir, I live by the church.

VIOLA. Art thou a churchman?

CLOWN. No such matter, sir. I do live by the church; for
I do live at my house, and my house doth stand by
the church.

VIOLA. So thou mayst say, the king lies by a beggar, if
a beggar dwell near him; or, the church stands by thy
tabor, if thy tabor stand by the church.

(III.i.1-10)

Resisting such glib reversals of language or of love is one of
Viola's chief functions (though she experiences her own radical changes), and this pattern of change versus constancy is
seen repeatedly. Feste ironically agrees with Viola in this case:
"You have said, sir. To see this age! A sentence is but a chev'ril
glove to a good wit. How quickly the wrong side may be
turned outward!" (ll. 11-13). He goes on to lament that "words
are grown so false I am loath to prove reason with them"
(l. 25) and describe himself, not as Olivia's fool, "but her
corrupter of words" (l. 37). One of Shakespeare's constant
interests in the comedies is the instability of language, its
power to change, and its own plasticity. To transform a sentence into its opposite meaning is, like all change, both wonderful and fearful. The deep connection between metamorphosis
and unstable language is everywhere stressed, and emphasized
in Viola's ability to do anything with words, but to be wise
about which changes in them are truly significant.

Between Orsino's instability in love and Olivia's obstinancy
in continuing to mourn her brother stands Viola. In her disguise as Cesario she represents a loving, clear-sighted constancy more sensible and endearing than Olivia's rigid devotion
to—as the line so ambiguously reads—her "brother's dead
love" (I.i.32). In her disguise-taking and common sense about
her own lost brother, Viola exhibits a capability for intelligent,
willed change that the others would do well to imitate. Orsino
describes himself as the typical changeable lover:

> For such as I am all true lovers are,
> Unstaid and skittish in all motions else

83

Save in the constant image of the creature
That is beloved.
(II.iv.17-20)

Orsino goes on to say, first, that men's fancies are "more giddy and unfirm" than women's are and, second, to the contrary, that women "lack retention" (l. 96) in love. He attributes to them the cyclical motion found throughout the play, with an unwitting irony in his image of the sea, and a dramatic irony in that he is saying this to Viola:

Alas, their love may be called appetite,
No motion of the liver but the palate,
That suffer surfeit, cloyment, and revolt;
But mine is all as hungry as the sea
And can digest as much.
(ll. 97-101)

Against this confused self-consciousness, or rather self-obsession, Viola offers two models: herself, as Cesario, an embodiment of fidelity, service, and love; and the story of her "sister" who

never told her love,
But let concealment, like a worm i' th' bud,
Feed on her damask cheek. She pined in thought;
And, with a green and yellow melancholy,
She sat like Patience on a monument,
Smiling at grief. Was not this love indeed?
(ll. 110-15)

To Olivia she offers, in the name of Orsino but also in proof of her own powers of love, a vision of how steadfast and unchanging she would be as a lover:

Make me a willow cabin at your gate
And call upon my soul within the house;
Write loyal cantons of contemned love
And sing them loud even in the dead of night;
Hallow your name to the reverberate hills

And make the babbling gossip of the air
Cry out "Olivia!"
(I.v.266-72)

Even more importantly, Shakespeare takes special pains to
show Viola's sense of honor and fidelity to duty, by creating
a situation in which Viola/Cesario must vigorously woo Olivia
for the man she herself loves. Her disguise creates complications of self-betrayal which Rosalind, for example, is spared,
but the apparent self-betrayal, in which she will employ but
not reveal her own desire, turns out to be redemptive.

Viola's ability to change when she will and yet also to be
constant to be and not to be distinguishes her from all
others in the play. Shakespeare suggests in her energies, as he
does earlier with Julia in *The Two Gentlemen of Verona*, a
distinction between active and passive metamorphosis, between a willed embrace of flexibility and the kind of rigidity
which Olivia displays at the beginning of the play. But Viola's
decision to disguise herself is, as in many of the comedies,
vague in its reasoning; Shakespeare seems to bow to the convention without bothering to explain it, but we can also see
something urgent and compulsive in the repeated urge to conceal one's self, to become someone else:

Conceal me what I am, and be my aid
For such disguise as haply shall become
The form of my intent. I'll serve this duke.
Thou shalt present me as an eunuch to him.
(I.ii.53-6)

The form of her intent is never made clear—she wishes not
to "be delivered to the world, / Till I had made mine own
occasion mellow, / What my estate is" (ll. 42-4)—but once
the plot begins we turn toward the results of such change.
Still, there is something appropriate to this vagueness; Viola
shows herself to be adventurous and vital, entertaining the
offered fallacy as Antipholus does, and we are no doubt sup-

posed to believe that playing a role has appealed to these qualities. But why a eunuch?

Shakespeare's initial choice of the eunuch role may have been for pragmatic reasons. "Cesario" would not be sexually identified and as a neutral figure could more easily become a confidant of Olivia. But somewhere along the way, Shakespeare changed his mind and dropped the idea, perhaps because Viola is already a eunuch as far as Olivia goes; and a *man* playing a eunuch affords comic possibilities, but a woman playing a eunuch—nothing. As the play continues, we see that Cesario must in fact be essentially bisexual, not neuter, as Viola is both firm and flexible, both deliberate and careless, both committed and disengaged. No matter the gender, though, for Viola perceives (and she is the first of Shakespeare's comic heroines to do so) that disguise can be dangerous. Becoming someone else entails remaining in character at all times, or being judged "insane," as happened in *The Comedy of Errors.* When Olivia falls in love with Cesario, Viola marvels:

> I am the man. If it be so, as 'tis,
> Poor lady, she were better love a dream.
> Disguise, I see thou art a wickedness
> Wherein the pregnant enemy does much.
> How easy is it for the proper false
> In women's waxen hearts to set their forms!
> (II.ii.25-30)

This speech wittily registers transformation on several levels— as male actor to girl to "man" again, as love, as dream, as disguise, as wax set in a form; and, in its ironic self-consciousness, it reminds the audience once again of its own complicity in helping to create a mimetic transformation. Viola's assertion "I am the man" is true and false at once, a pointed rendering of the complex and paradoxical process of transformation at work here: of being (woman) and not-being (man). Her self-consciousness about all this marks a sharp difference between her and the helpless protagonists of *The Comedy of Errors,* moreover. In every comedy following *Er-*

rors, Shakespeare makes at least one character, usually female, aware of the powers of change, even if she can't fully control or understand them. But even Viola is unaware that she herself is doubled by a living brother. Thus Shakespeare doubles the possibilities of transformation, by mirroring Viola's mimetic transformation with the situational transformation engendered by doubling. The complexities of *The Comedy of Errors* increase exponentially in *Twelfth Night*.

Viola calls herself a "poor monster," because as Cesario she is neither female nor male, neither Viola nor Sebastian, but a fusion of both.[11] Like the Antipholi, too, Viola feels her own linguistic identity threatened by her situational transformation. She can no longer, in her role, make nominal assertions, but must describe herself as something Other, all potential forms of being, and yet also nothing:

> I am all the daughters of my father's house,
> And all the brothers too, and yet I know not.
> (II.iv.121-2)

As is appropriate for a fiction, she begins to speak of herself, in both her identities, in the conditional:

> My father had a daughter loved a man
> As it might be perhaps, were I a woman,
> I should your lordship.
> (ll. 108-10)

When (or if) the audience begins to think about the still larger transformative fiction—boy to woman to man—it can see the mimetic impulse as another form of metamorphosis, and wonder about its own role in all this.

Viola at one point sees no way out of what she has willingly become—Cesario, who is "what you will," all things to all people. "As I am man," she says, "My state is desperate for my master's love." But "as I am woman (now alas the day!), / What thriftless sighs shall poor Olivia breathe?" (II.ii.36-9). She leaves this difficult "knot" for time to "untangle." This knot has been less mechanically tied than the similar one in

The Comedy of Errors, but is more complicated because it grows so much more out of human will as well as out of pure accident. But taking the risks that accompany metamorphosis leads to the multiple resolutions and happiness of the ending.

Malvolio has no interest in taking such risks, however. His anti-festive "virtuousness" has been described by C. L. Barber "as a self-limiting automatism. . . . He is not hostile to holiday because he is a Puritan; he is like a Puritan because he is hostile to holiday."[12] One of Malvolio's least attractive traits is his maniacal resistance to transformation, his refusal to allow boundaries to give way (unless the ones between him and Olivia), especially the social boundaries which supposedly divide him from Toby Belch and set him apart from the rest of mankind. The more strongly he resists change, the more rigid his stance, the more certain it is to happen. His objections to Andrew and Toby's festivity turn in large part on the social and chronological boundaries of decorum:

> Have you no wit, manners, nor honesty, but to gabble like tinkers at this time of night? Do ye make an alehouse of my lady's house, that ye squeak out your coziers' catches without any mitigation or remorse of voice? Is there no respect of place, persons, nor time in you?
>
> (II.iii.87-93)

Toby's reply—"We did keep time, sir, in our catches"—suggests the kind of harmonious rhythms which Malvolio sees only as "disorders" (l. 97). He cannot allow anyone to *make* "an alehouse of my lady's house" because his own identity is fixed and stable only in relation to the house's boundaries. Malvolio stands opposite Feste in yet another way, then, beyond the familiar and frequently discussed range of attributes suggested by their names: Feste would become almost anyone (indeed, as a fool he is technically no one, but only a reflection) but Malvolio would remain only himself. Between these two poles of human identity—the many and the one, multiplicity and singularity—most of us live; certainly Viola does.

The plot against Malvolio creates great irony, for though

its success springs from his correctly diagnosed "self-love" (I.v.90) and from what Barber calls his "secret wish . . . to violate decorum himself,"[13] the nature of the plot is more complex: it is designed to make him release the few transformative powers he has so earnestly suppressed. The plot will, Andrew affirms, "make him an ass" (II.iii.167)—the metamorphosis the comedies are so frequently contriving in one way or another. Malvolio will be forced into several transformations—first, an inner change wrought by desire and (self-) love; second, a physical change in his clothing and appearance; and third, a "possession" or "madness" like the one which brought forth Dr. Pinch in *Errors*.

We should also remember that the plot against Malvolio involves language which is and is not Olivia's. Maria will forge "some obscure epistles of love" (II.iii.154), and the conspirators will "observe his construction of it" (l. 174). Olivia's true writing will be doubled by Maria ("on a forgotten matter we can hardly make distinction of our hands"—l. 160), eventually producing from Malvolio a second or doubled Malvolio—the "mad" one, the one made an ass. Malvolio shows himself all too susceptible to this doubling when it is reported that "he has been yonder i' the sun practicing behavior to his own shadow this half hour" (II.v.14-15), and he enters the scene quoting from his own imagined dialogue. So he is quite prepared to recognize or "read" false writing as true:

> By my life, this is my lady's hand. These be her very C's,
> her U's, and her T's; and thus makes she her great P's.
> It is, in contempt of question, her hand. (ll. 84-7)

Malvolio's failure to make the letters and sounds cohere, much less to catch the double entendre, is quickly followed by another linguistic conundrum, which he does try to resolve. The letter's mysterious line, "M.O.A.I. doth sway my life" (l. 109) helps reveal Malvolio's motives in reading: "If I could make that resemble something in me!" (l. 117). Reading thus becomes an effort to double oneself, to find in letters something that "resemble[s]" oneself—a willed transformation that is, however, quite unlike Viola's, but more like Narcissus's. As if in mockery of the very attempt, Toby phonetically mirrors Malvolio: "O, ay, make up that." Eventually Malvolio will "read" the letter enough to transform it into his own reflection:

M,O,A,I. This simulation is not as the former; and yet, to crush this a little, it would bow to me, for every one of these letters are in my name. (ll. 135-7)

There must be a text behind the text, then, but the other text is still just one's own reflection. Malvolio cannot escape this "simulation" because he is so completely solipsistic. His "love" turns out to be another manifestation of his self-love, his surface transformations revealed as not essential ones.

The forged letter releases what meager powers of transformation lie within Malvolio and therefore makes possible his adoption of the outward changes: "Be opposite with a kinsman, surly with servants. Let thy tongue tang arguments of state; put thyself into the trick of singularity" (ll. 145-7). He is also to appear in yellow stockings, cross-gartered, and perpetually smiling. Like any metamorph, he must become the other that he already is: in this case, a fool. The "trick of singularity" is usually glossed as something like the "affectation of eccentricity" but the phrase also reminds us of Malvolio's problems with doubling. "Singularity" is a kind of role which one must "put thyself into." Thus "singularity" in the narrowest sense is impossible. He can't get out of himself.

The play will suggest on a number of occasions how Malvolio's changes have the appearance of any lover's. So, on hearing of his transformation, Olivia will say, "I am as mad as he, / If sad and merry madness equal be" (III.iv.13-14). But Olivia's vision of Malvolio makes her diagnose his case as "very midsummer madness" (l. 59). And why not? Because in speaking to Olivia, Malvolio quotes from a text which is a forgery; thus his words have (to her) no referents. His situation now parallels that of Antipholus of Ephesus: the names and faces are the same, but he stands alienated from his own

language. Therefore he is "mad" or "possessed" (i.e., transformed), and will be locked up and exorcised; Dr. Pinch in
Errors anticipates Feste's role as Sir Topas here. In a few
moments Sebastian will begin to experience the same self-
estrangement as Malvolio, but through a different kind of
doubling; Andrew will even dare to strike him, believing him
to be the less courageous Cesario. Sebastian then enjoys the
experience Malvolio is denied: Olivia takes him by the hand
and full of love leads him into her house. Sebastian's response
is filled with familiar tropes—"Or I am mad, or else this is a
dream. / Let fancy still my sense in Lethe steep; / If it be thus
to dream, still let me sleep!" (IV.i.62-4)—but unlike Antipholus of Syracuse he succumbs to, even welcomes, this metamorphosis. He is not exactly in control of it, but yielding to
it is the right thing.

Whereas Sebastian wonders if he is mad, Malvolio wonders
if everyone else is. He is exorcised from society but not from
himself. His further exorcism will be painful and complex,
because a linguistic correction is also needed; but it will ultimately fail. Presiding over the exorcism in the guise of Sir
Topas, Feste promises to "dissemble myself in 't" (IV.ii.4);
that is, he will dis-resemble himself, he will metamorphose.
His self-consciousness in becoming someone else contrasts
with Malvolio's obtuseness. Feste gives Toby a sample of this
new self:

> Bonos dies, Sir Toby; for, as the old hermit of Prague,
> that never saw pen and ink, very wittily said to a niece
> of King Gorboduc, "That that is is"; so, I, being Master
> Parson, am Master Parson; for what is "that" but that,
> and "is" but is? (IV.ii.13-17)

Toby applauds him: "the knave counterfeits well" (l. 20).
Thus Feste begins his dis-resembling, his counterfeiting, with
a fiction about an old hermit "that never saw pen and ink"—
one who could not forge, or even write; a linguistic innocent.
When Feste drops the voice of Sir Topas, and re-assembles
himself, Malvolio asks for "a candle, and pen, ink, and paper"

(ll. 84-5); he will prove his sanity by the act of writing, of doubling himself. Feste replies ironically to his request: "I will help you to 't. But tell me true, are you not mad indeed, or do you but counterfeit?" (ll. 115-16). To speak to Malvolio of counterfeiting, of false acting and writing, reminds us if not him of his own hypocrisy and rigidity. And now he is other than himself, transformed: "how fell you besides your five wits?" (l. 88).

It is especially appropriate, moreover, that Feste/Topas uses the following catechism as the proper test of Malvolio's sanity:

> CLOWN. What is the opinion of Pythagoras concerning wild fowl?
>
> MALVOLIO. That the soul of our grandam might happily inhabit a bird.
>
> CLOWN. What think'st thou of his opinion?
>
> MALVOLIO. I think nobly of the soul and no way approve his opinion.
>
> CLOWN. Fare thee well. Remain thou still in darkness. Thou shalt hold th'opinion of Pythagoras ere I will allow of thy wits, and fear to kill a woodcock, lest thou dispossess the soul of thy grandam. (ll. 50-60)

The irony here is that Malvolio gives the "right" answer in terms of the experts and the orthodox, but the wrong one in terms of the play, where metamorphoses of various kinds flourish.[14] And the theory of metempsychosis, whether derived from Pythagoras's speech in Book XV of Ovid's *Metamorphoses* or from any number of popular accounts, is a related version of metamorphosis—the soul changing bodies rather than the body changing shape.

The exorcism scene ends with Feste's ironic question to Malvolio, "do you but counterfeit?" bringing to the surface one more time the idea of forgery. In his own self-conscious role-playing, Feste has exemplified the possibility of the multiple self in contrast to Malvolio's single-mindedness.[15] Shakespeare closes that scene by making Feste compare himself "to the old Vice" (l. 126). To invoke the Vice is to remind the audience of yet another clever shape-shifter, and to hint again at the dangers as well as the pleasures of self-transformation.

❧

The final scene of *Twelfth Night* brings together all the questions about metamorphosis raised earlier in the play. Feste, for example, explains to the puzzled Orsino how he can be "the better for my foes, and the worse for my friends" (V.i.12-13); this explanation is itself a figure of metamorphosis:

> Marry, sir, they [his friends] praise me and make an ass of me. Now my foes tell me plainly I am an ass, so that by my foes, sir, I profit in the knowledge of myself, and by my friends I am abused; so that, conclusions to be as kisses, if your four negatives make your two affirmatives, why then, the worse for my friends, and the better for my foes. (ll. 17-23)

Turning "negatives" into "affirmatives," or men into asses, is all one. Orsino misses the point, even when Feste responds to the gift of a gold coin, "But that it would be double-dealing, sir, I would you could make it another" (ll. 29-30). But when he gives the other coin, Orsino can joke that he "will be so much a sinner to be a double-dealer" (ll. 34-5). This is a minor moment in a long scene, but these parables of transformation and doubling anticipate much of what is to come.

When the confusion mounts, Olivia must call in the Priest to prove her marriage to Cesario, and his description of the marriage suggests that a yet more profound kind of transformation has occurred:

> A contract of eternal bond of love,
> Confirmed by mutual joinder of your hands,
> Attested by the holy close of lips,
> Strength'ned by interchangement of your rings;
> And all the ceremony of this compact

Sealed in my function, by my testimony.

(ll. 155-60)

Already two have become one. The two lovers are never distinguished in this description—"your hands," "lips," and "your rings" represent a single figure. A subtle alliteration—contract, confirmed, compact—stresses the union of two into one. The language of the passage, by turns legal and formal—contract, bond, joinder, attested, interchangement, testimony—witnesses the ritualistic joining together symbolized by this ceremony. Such a reminder of the meaning of marriage and its transfigurative power has an emblematic status in this scene; so complete and so carefully crafted a description is certainly unnecessary for the plot alone. The final scene of *Twelfth Night* moves through this revelation of two-in-one—marriage—to the discovery of still another two-in-one—Cesario. Sir Andrew, for example, complains of the double nature of "one Cesario," not realizing there are two of him: "We took him for a coward, but he's the very devil incardinate" (ll. 179-81). The pun accentuates the notion of incarnation, of two-in-one which best describes Cesario himself, and possibly even means incardinate – without number. Perhaps we should remember here as well that Twelfth Night marks the Eve of Epiphany, the announcement of yet another incarnation.

At the greatest moment of confusion, threatened harm, and accumulated paradox, Sebastian enters and the twins confront each other and the rest of the troupe. Orsino's famous words gather up associations from this play and from earlier works as well:

One face, one voice, one habit, and two persons—
A natural perspective that is and is not.

(ll. 215-16)

In some plays contemporary with Shakespeare's, a simple discovery scene suffices to clarify confusion and reveal identity; in others, such as Lyly's *Gallathea,* a full metamorphosis will be required. In *Twelfth Night,* the discovery scene must reveal the paradoxes of past transformations—and represent them linguistically as well as dramatically—even as it presses the audience with new metamorphoses.

Sebastian and Viola question each other as if they had been separated a lifetime. As Anne Barton says, they "put each other through a formal, intensely conventional question and answer test that comes straight out of Greek New Comedy."[16] Viola even for a moment wonders if Sebastian is a ghost, but he explains to Olivia the nature of the dual paradox:

> So comes it, lady, you have been mistook.
> But nature to her bias drew in that,
> You would have been contracted to a maid;
> Nor are you therein, by my life, deceived:
> You are betrothed both to a maid and man.
>
> (ll. 258-62)

"Incardinate," "maid and man," "one habit, and two persons": the paradoxes all point to a mysterious transformation in which two become one and one becomes two. Marriage itself, as we have seen, is one paradigm of this process, and Cesario's fission another: a maid for Orsino, a man for Olivia, one for the master, one for the mistress. As has been pointed out, this fission is the perfect fulfillment of the play's subtitle, "What you will."[17] The fission is also a translation of earlier and even contemporary magical resolutions in other plays. But the magic here is all Shakespeare's. What *Twelfth Night,* and especially its ending, offers us are successive moments of fusion and fission.

Much recent criticism has rightly focused on the question of "perspective," natural or unnatural, both as a specific optical instrument and as a more generalized way of seeing.[18] Such perspective instruments or paintings are of course themselves metamorphic, or anamorphic. The position and disposition of the viewer are necessarily crucial to a proper viewing, and Shakespeare alludes to the audience's complicity in such viewing when Feste asks Toby and Andrew, "Did you never see the picture of We Three?" (II.iii.16-17), a picture in which the spectator becomes the missing third of three asses. As Walter King, Ernest Gilman, and others have shown, the play as a whole offers a series of perspectives to the audience, which can view it in a number of different ways. Gilman goes on to an even greater claim: "The exercise and refinement of that double vision [which is exemplified in the "natural perspective"] is one of the main tasks Shakespearean comedy imposes on its audience."[19]

I would like to shift the emphasis, however, to the second half of Orsino's famous words, from the "perspective" to the paradox "that is and is not."[20] In one sense, the two halves of the sentence are not synonymous, for the "double" perspective shows two identical figures, neither of which "is not." Rather, the whole tableau may seem something "that is and is not," something evident to the sense but impossible to credit. But the paradox also epitomizes the whole mystery of two-in-one. Sebastian and Viola are and are not themselves; Cesario is and is not Cesario. The strangeness of all metamorphosis is revealed in this cryptic phrase, which we heard in Chapter One in Augustine's puzzled comments. Throughout the play, moreover, similar paradoxes have been expressed. Viola/Cesario has twice given Olivia a similar veiled warning: "I am not that I play" (I.v.182); "I am not what I am" (III.i.143). And she has said of Olivia, "you do think you are not what you are" (III.i.141). Mistaking Sebastian for Cesario, Feste will parody the full exent of the confusion:

> No, I do not know you; nor I am not sent to you by my
> lady, to bid you come speak with her; nor your name is
> not Master Cesario; nor this is not my nose neither.
> Nothing that is so is so. (IV.i.5-9)

Feste's speech in one sense merely reflects the conventions of the usual appearance/reality theme, yet his speech has deeper resonances; his explanations and definitions proceed strictly by negation, as if to reflect our sense that metamorphosis is no thing. There is a logical difficulty, moreover, in the structure of the sentence "Nothing that is so is so" which seems curiously self-canceling and tautological at the same time: that which is so is also not so. These cryptic references gain even more force from Feste's "old hermit of Prague" parody of them in the fourth act:

"That that is is" . . . for what is "that" but that, and "is" but is? (IV.ii.15-17)

The reply comes in the fifth act: something "that is and is not." These enigmatic formulations all reflect the central mystery of metamorphosis we have been following, and suggest as well the role language plays in transformation. If antimetabole, one of the favorite figures of this play, reflected the possibilities of reversed transformation, these gnomic utterances of negation seem the verbal form, perhaps even one cause, of transformation. Their duplicity is further doubled when the audience understands them even more ironically as the actors' allusions to their own counterfeiting.

Few characters in *Twelfth Night* have been merely themselves; they have also become not-themselves through transformation—through disguise, trickery, situation, and love. We find another confirmation of this duality when Malvolio's long-delayed letter defending his sanity is finally read. It doesn't matter when it is read, Feste says, because "a madman's epistles are no gospels" (V.i.286), as if only the Word need immediately find an audience. What follows is another demonstration of metamorphic powers as a species of mimesis:

OLIVIA. Open't and read it.
CLOWN. Look then to be well edified, when the fool delivers the madman. [*Reads in a loud voice.*] "By the Lord, madam"—
OLIVIA. How now? Art thou mad?
CLOWN. No, madam, I do but read madness. And your ladyship will have it as it ought to be, you must allow *vox.*

OLIVIA. Prithee read i' thy right wits.
CLOWN. So I do, madonna; but to read his right wits is
    to read thus. (ll. 289-300)[21]

To read a text is necessarily to *become* the author, then, as
well as the reader. Thus Feste is and is not himself here, and,
in a simpler version of this verbal mimesis, Malvolio has become the forgery he has read, cross-gartered and in yellow
stockings. Viola too has become the fiction of counterfeit
"Cesario", and as she tells us earlier, she consciously "imitate[s]" her brother (III.iv.387). Still, beyond the characters
there are the actors themselves, the technicians of the mimetic,
who read a text in *vox* and take on another shape.

The next circle of discovery is to reveal Maria's forged letter
to Malvolio, a *vox* that has been persuasive enough not only
to fool Malvolio but also to make Toby marry its author
Maria. But the spirit of forgiveness and the whirligig of time
cannot lessen Malvolio's rage. His eruption into the final scene,
after the "natural perspective" has been created, reminds us
of everything that refuses to be transformed, of that obstinate
streak of vindictiveness that will not change and so is less than
human (as Bergson might argue) but at the same time is all
too human. Malvolio has been shown throughout to be unable
to see—that is, he sees only his own reflection wherever he
looks, whether in writing or in "practising behavior to his
own shadow." When he looks in a glass, he sees only himself;
but when Viola looks in the "perspective" glass, she sees both
herself and also a loving other. To show Malvolio imprisoned
within himself, unable to change essentially, and finally locked
in a dark room and his blindness confirmed, marks the sharp-
est difference from Viola and Sebastian; Malvolio's inflexibility registers the necessity for their flexibility. The capacity
for self-transformation marks one sign of human health, and
Malvolio seems completely closed off from any possibility of
redemptive doubling.

I would like to return to Ben Jonson, who did not write plays such as *Twelfth Night* or *The Comedy of Errors* in part because "he could never find two so like others that he could persuade the spectators they were one." Northrop Frye reports an even more pedantic anecdote of this sort: "A doctor once remarked to me that he was unable to enjoy a performance of *Twelfth Night* because it was a biological impossibility that boy and girl twins could resemble each other so closely."[22] In *Twelfth Night*, Shakespeare had Antonio call attention to how like the two are: "An apple cleft in two is not more twin / Than these two creatures" (V.i.222-3). But Jonson was, in a narrow sense, right, which is undoubtedly why Shakespeare went ahead and wrote these plays. No two actors, perhaps not even twins, could be "so like." The *difference* between Sebastian and Viola is as important as the similarity. It allows Cesario to be two different things, depending on one's "perspective." But it also requires a critical transformative act by the audience, presumably not wholly consisting of geneticists, to bridge the difference. Shakespeare has displaced the metamorphic principle from the stage itself into the mind of the audience.

As a beginning dramatist Shakespeare must have found the plays of Plautus and Terence a tempting model; in terms of plot alone, *The Comedy of Errors* shows its source quite openly. By the time of *Twelfth Night*, on the other hand, Shakespeare had written something like twenty plays; after the brilliance of *A Midsummer Night's Dream, As You Like It,* and the Henriad, he hardly needed to return to Plautus just to filch another plot. He seems to have been drawn to these plots because of the problems they could produce and the manner, through doubling, in which these problems could be resolved. I have stated that the Plautine tradition was inhospitable to the representation of physical metamorphosis on the stage, but doubling, situational transformation, and mimetic transformation, the traditional staples of intrigue drama, provided Shakespeare with suggestive metamorphic alternatives. In the endings of the two Plautine plays, with the discovery of doubling by the characters, we may also detect a specific acknowledgement and revision of an earlier kind of metamorphic play (see the Appendix for some examples).

Doubling is a particularly apt species of transformation.[23] It is "naturalistic," broadly speaking, but the effects may be remarkable. Only in a narrow sense is it "mechanical" or "merely farcical." But doubling, through twins or through mimetic impulse, also becomes an emblem for "writing" and "reading" in these two plays. "Who deciphers them[?]" asks *The Comedy of Errors*. To read a text properly, "you must allow *vox*." The actor's craft is to double the author, or rather the author's words; and the audience must imaginatively perform difficult transformative acts as well. "Did you never see the picture of We Three?" A writer may be said to double himself when he writes. He transforms himself through writing so that he is and is not. His writing is no longer a part of himself but still is himself. Something of this self-consciousness operates in these plays, where Shakespeare pays insistent attention to the kind of character who declares "I am not what I am."

The endings of these two plays are constructed so as to reveal similarity: twinship, the harmony of marriage, forgiveness, an unexpected achievement of common interests. But in addition to establishing what "is," these endings insist as well on what "is not," on the differences. In *Twelfth Night* Malvolio, puffed full of injured merit, will separate himself from the vulgar. Moreover, when Viola comes to swear her own love to Orsino, she invokes an image of astronomical separation:

> DUKE. Boy [though he now knows Cesario to be a woman]
>   thou hast said to me a thousand times
>   Thou never shouldst love woman like to me.
> VIOLA. And all those sayings will I over swear,

And all those swearings keep as true in soul
As doth that orbed continent the fire
That severs day from night.
                    (V.i.266-71)

The principle of separation seems rather ironic here, for Viola
is still dressed as a boy (through the end of the play) though
now known by Orsino to be a girl, and further known by the
audience to be a boy actor. The scene thus ends with that
peculiarly Shakespearean tension between images of division
and identity. Orsino's pledge that "A solemn combination
shall be made / Of our dear souls" (ll. 384-5) cannot be fulfilled
literally. The rule of transformation yet lingers so powerfully
that Viola has still not quite returned, as Orsino admits:

              Cesario, come—
For so you shall be while you are a man,
But when in other habits you are seen,
Orsino's mistress and his fancy's queen.
                    (ll. 386-9)

Thus Viola leaves the stage at the end with her identity known
but neither her proper shape nor her name restored.

Feste's song concluding the play offers us not only a vision
of the Four Ages of Man but also yet another moving if somewhat cynical vision of mutability, suggesting the inevitable
nature of change and the great final metamorphosis that awaits
us all. It has been frequently noted that in the song Feste
breaks character: he seems to be both clown and, toward the
end, actor ("our play is done"). This fusing could have been
predicted: Feste is and is not Feste. As Feste, the singer of the
epilogue presents a distant, even bleak view of human life,
marked by foul weather, drunkenness, "knaves and thieves."
But as an actor, the singer concludes with the cheerfully dis-
missive "But that's all one, our play is done," while announcing that this melancholy song, and the whole play, forms a
part of the actor's creed: "And we'll strive to please you ev-

eryday" (l. 409). Both visions can be encompassed in the song because the singer offers in himself yet another natural perspective, by being Feste *and* someone else, and by enfolding his vision of natural mutability in a sophisticated verbal form. Shakespeare does no less.

Chapter Four ❧ "Forget to Be a Woman"

The actor's knowledge of metamorphosis is necessarily first-hand, for each working moment on the stage requires an act of self-transformation; and that act must be accompanied (*pace* Bottom) by a self-immolating transgression of apparent boundaries. Yet neither act can ever be complete. It is one thing, moreover, for an Elizabethan actor to become a Bottom or a Iago, and something else again to switch sexes and become a Rosalind; and when Rosalind asks us to pretend that she is not a woman, and she isn't, vertigo sets in. Shakespeare was aware of the inherent thematic possibilities of his own craft from the very beginning of his career, but he seems to have grown increasingly self-conscious, in the comedies, of women disguising and therefore transforming themselves; as actors and as "women," they become two (or more) things in one.

The women in Shakespeare's comedies often assume conventional disguises for various practical or symbolic reasons. The four ladies in *Love's Labour's Lost* assume masks and exchange "favours" so as to confuse the men. A similar exchange and confusion occurs in *Much Ado About Nothing*, with the further complication that Hero's face remains veiled during her second marriage to Claudio. In *Measure for Measure* and *All's Well That Ends Well* certain signs are exchanged between Diana-Helena and Mariana-Isabella so that the bed tricks will work with the exchanged bodies. But in many of the comedies, Shakespeare pushes the dramatic possibilities even further, to their mimetic limit, making the central women undergo metamorphosis to become someone else. In several cases, the woman must temporarily become her psychological and sexual antithesis, a man, and so we find a shadow-cast of "male" players: "Sebastian" (Julia in *The Two Gentlemen of Verona*), "Balthasar" (Portia in *The Merchant of Venice*), "Ganymede" (Rosalind in *As You Like It*), "Cesario" (Viola in *Twelfth Night*), and "Fidele" (Imogen in *Cymbeline*). Each of them, as Pisanio tells Imogen, "must forget to be a woman" (*Cym*, III.iv.155). Only by passing through this forgetting can each woman truly be a woman.

Recent critical studies of role-playing in Shakespeare have provided useful commentary on this female- to male-phenomenon.[1] Yet Shakespeare's recurring interest in women's becoming men, and its confinement to the comedies and romances, is perhaps better illuminated through the larger and even more obsessive question of metamorphosis in general, and the power of love to generate change in particular. Only when a woman is trying to get a man must she become a man. Julia, Portia, Rosalind, and Viola achieve marriage only after the necessary detour through transformation; like all lovers in Shakespearean comedy, they will become something other, and *then* return to themselves and their men. The details vary in the different cases, but Shakespeare takes the usual lover-into-loved-one transformation even further, turning the women into images of their men, so that two become one in a rather literal sense. This cross-dressing produces effects similar to those of doubling (both are available in *Twelfth Night*), but with greater paradoxical moments of illusion and belief. Shakespeare will not hesitate to invoke the metadramatic possibilities either, for the woman-to-man transformation mirrors the man-to-woman illusion the actor has already generated. All the paradoxes of cross-dressing, like those of doubling, represent the constant resurrection and transgression of specifically *theatrical* boundaries—self-willed change in its most protean mode—but these paradoxes also represent an inves-

104

tigation of sexual boundaries, of androgyny *as* metamorphosis.

Mircea Eliade has offered one useful way of thinking about this obligatory Shakespearean androgyny through transvestism. The ritual significance of such initiatory androgyny, he argues, is clear (he is speaking here of a male's experience): "One cannot become a sexually adult male before knowing the coexistence of the sexes, androgyny; in other words, one cannot attain a particular and well-defined mode without first knowing the total mode of being." Shakespearean comedy, it seems, enacts a similar ritual for certain of its female characters and, vicariously, for its audience; the end result, in Eliade's terms, is

> a coming out of one's self, a transcending of one's own historically controlled situation, and a recovering of an original situation, no longer human or historical since it precedes the foundation of human society; a paradoxical situation impossible to maintain in profane time, in a historical epoch, but which it is important to reconstitute periodically in order to restore, if only for a brief moment, the initial completeness, the intact source of holiness and power.[2]

We need not subscribe to all Eliade's points to recognize immediately that the transcendence of one's self, the contact with some source of holiness and power, flows naturally from Shakespearean sexual disguise, and that these sexual disguises seem to stand mysteriously at the heart of each play's experience.

Although female sexual disguise may be traced back to Greek and Roman comedy, through the miracle play, and to such romantic plays as *Clyomon and Clamydes* (c.1570), Lyly's *Gallathea* (c.1584), and Greene's *James the Fourth* (c.1591),[3] in none of these instances does the play's central vision come to be so embodied in the heroine and her disguise as in Shakespeare, nor does anyone return to the motif as frequently as Shakespeare does. The mere fact of a sexual disguise was savaged by the theater's Puritan critics, who denounced the players' very existence, and they surely would have extended their net to include Rosalind and Viola; as one critic argued, "Player's practices can hardly be warranted in religion: for a man to put on woman's apparel, and a woman a man's, is plain prohibition."[4] As Jonson's Zeal-of-the-Land Busy echoes to the puppets: "my main argument against you is that you are an abomination, for the male among you putteth on the apparel of the female, and the female of the male" (*Bartholomew Fair*, V.v.101-4). Phillip Stubbes fulminated, in a familiar allusion, against what he implies was an everyday occurrence on the streets: "*Proteus*, that Monster, could never chaunge him self into so many fourmes & shapes as these women doo . . . these Women may not improperly be called *Hermaphroditi*, that is, Monsters of bothe kindes, half women, half men."[5] To find so many boys playing women, and so many "women" disguised as men in Shakespeare, in comparison with his dramatic predecessors and in opposition to the moral policemen of the day, suggests that Shakespeare quite deliberately came to employ such moments as preeminent instances of metamorphosis, as literal embodiments of two-in-one.

In four of his romantic comedies, Shakespeare requires his heroine to cross-dress and change sex temporarily, while her man remains essentially the same. In some instances, the woman in fact doubles the appearance or behavior of her love—Portia becomes harsh and judging, as Bassanio was of Shylock; Rosalind feigns being foolish and "romantic," like Orlando—though in other cases she becomes the opposite of her man, an emblem of loving constancy and devotion—like Julia and Viola. In every case, though, it is the woman who must change. The reasons for this are complex. In one sense, only the women are *capable* of such self-transformation. Moreover, the men have already changed, by falling in love, though they usually must be "cured" of it, as Orlando is by Rosalind, and transformed to some further state where they can see more clearly and are fully worthy of their women.

It seems, finally, that the woman becomes the man not only to get the man but also more importantly for the sake of the man: her embodied changes run parallel with some process of change within him. At the same time, though the woman changes name, sex, and costume, her disposition and personality are altered to a much lesser degree. In these transformations through disguise, the salient features of character come out more sharply: there was always something reserved, cool, orderly, and dispassionate about Portia in the first place; there was always something playful, clever, and quickwitted about Rosalind before she ever climbed into trunkhose; and something sad, silvery, and elegiac about Viola even though she didn't lose her brother and has to fence with Toby. The women go *through* the changes but without essentially changing, whereas the men, always and ever themselves, come out the other end looking different, altered in shape and point of view by what the women have done in their stead. The women are doing for the men what the men can't do for themselves.

Every lover must be, and inescapably is, transformed by love; as we have seen, this transformative process must be fully worked through before the completion of marriage can occur. In *The Taming of the Shrew,* Kate must be kated and de-shrewed; in *A Midsummer Night's Dream,* the human lovers must confront the otherness of their own desires, embodied in comic monsters, before repairing to the best bride-bed. In *Twelfth Night,* we saw, Viola must become Cesario in order to survive her own disappointments, and to transform Orsino and Olivia from their self-imprisonments. Viola's method was to become male *and* female, lover and beloved; her close cousins—Julia, Portia, and Rosalind—employ similar guises, as we will now see. It is the lesser blot, as Julia tells us, for "Women to change their shapes than men their minds."

JULIA

At the center of an unstable, mutable world, in which one character is named after the supreme shape-shifter Proteus, stands a constant moral presence, Julia, who will paradoxically change shape and gender, don disguise and role, in her effort to be steadfast. She is Shakespeare's first comic heroine to become a man. The other characters in *The Two Gentlemen of Verona* experience transformations that are frequently compulsive and frightening when they aren't comic; few have any control over the power. Because Julia's transformations are mostly self-willed, they seem more complex than those forced on Kate, and more beneficent than other changes in this play. Yet the central impulse of *Two Gentlemen*'s plot stems not from Julia's flexibility but from her initial rigidity, one not foolish like Malvolio's but naive rather than knavish. Julia's misplaced confidence in her beloved Proteus stems from her belief that

> His words are bonds, his oaths are oracles;
> His love sincere, his thoughts immaculate;
> His tears pure messengers sent from his heart;
> His heart as far from fraud as heaven from earth.
>
> (II.vii.75-8)

Julia is not so much foolish as utopian here, and her own rhetoric too rigidly insists on rigidity. This is the way things ought to be but aren't, as her own simile in line 78 reveals, for if heaven and earth were not so distant, there might be less fraud in man's heart. "Were man / But constant, he were perfect! That one error / Fills him with faults" (V.iv.111-13): such is Proteus's lame defense. Francis Bacon, among others, might have added, Were words but constant, they were perfect. Julia's faith that "his words are bonds, his oaths are oracles" describes a pre-Babel linguistic relation, an identity of word with deed, of intention with action, that can never again exist in this age of iron. Words have been liberated from their "bonds," to both their glory and their shame. The relentless instability experienced by the figures in this play—the transformations of character, the shifting of allegiances, the erosion of resolve—is not only mirrored by their unstable language, but to some extent caused by it. Much of the characters' difficulty and unhappiness result from a failure to recognize that everything that exists is "a kind of chameleon" (II.iv.25).

As it does in all the comedies, love constitutes the great agent of transformation in *Two Gentlemen*. Characters who assert some selfish inflexibility toward love soon find their positions undermined. In scene one, Proteus rhapsodizes, "I leave myself, my friends, and all, for love. / Thou, Julia, thou hast metamorphized me" (I.i.65-6), and Speed notes of Valentine, "now you are metamorphized with a mistress, that, when I look on you, I can hardly think you my master" (II.i.31-3). The iterated verb calls attention to the drastic perceptual changes in the play. Even the comic dialogue affirms the power of love to alter vision (II.i.45-76). Appropriately the chameleon is twice invoked (II.i.171; II.iv.25), not only as a central emblem of change but also for its alleged ability to live on air as a spurned lover lives on nothing. Love, we are told, is like the changeable weather:

> O, how this spring of love resembleth
> The uncertain glory of an April day,
> Which now shows all the beauty of the sun,
> And by and by a cloud takes all away!
>
> (I.iii.84-7)

Everyone talks about it, but no one can predict it. Like clouds on the wind the characters in the play, and their language, change helplessly.

Yet there *are* centers of constancy in the two women, Julia and Silvia, whose loves burn with steady flames, allowing us to see that the Duke's easy confidence in Silvia's malleability is badly misplaced:

> This weak impress of love [for Valentine] is as a figure
> Trenched in ice, which with an hour's heat
> Dissolves to water, and doth lose his form.
> A little time will melt her frozen thoughts,
> And worthless Valentine shall be forgot.
>
> (III.ii.6-10)

That is the theory, of course, and the metamorphic power which elsewhere governs this play. But the Duke's very "figure" of rhetoric is itself "trenched in ice," too coolly schematized to explain flesh and blood. Enough people have melted and lost their resolves that we do find some truth in the comparison, yet the very neatness of the image betrays its inadequacy, especially when it so closely resembles the rigid oaths and vows continually being sworn, and soon being betrayed.

Like Mark Antony, Proteus "cannot hold his visible shape." *The Two Gentlemen of Verona* insistently explores the relation between "visible shape" and love, and the relation between the "flexibility of the self," as Thomas M. Greene has described it[6], and the flexibility of language. The characters in the play are all granted a "goodly shape" (IV.i.57), like Valentine, though too many of them begin sacreligiously "to worship shadows and adore false shapes" (IV.ii.130). The characters, like Proteus, who believe their shapes fixed, their selves inert, are of course the first to suffer loss, and the Proteus who "needs must lose myself" if he can't have Silvia, "cannot now prove constant to myself" (II.vi.20, 31) soon after unless he betrays his former friend. Valentine feels just as strongly that "Silvia is myself. Banished from her / Is self from self. . . . She is my essence" (III.i.172-3, 182), though he too will undergo a transformation in the final act and offer "all that was mine in Silvia" (V.iv.83)—his very essence—to Proteus in the name . of friendship.

As so often in Shakespearean comedy, the women point the way for us, Silvia by her perfection and constancy, Julia by her resourcefulness and boldness. Julia, in particular, shows how flexibility is the only way for the self, how the shape can be deliberately but not permanently altered through transforming disguise. She assumes her disguise as "some well-reputed page" named "Sebastian" in order to "prevent / The loose encounter of lascivious men" (II.vii.40-1). As usual, the reasons for the disguise are less important than the need to exercise a new self, or openly to reveal one's secret self. Disguise almost always enables liberation. Although Shakespeare elaborates this insight more complexly in Rosalind and Viola, we ought to acknowledge how much has been achieved here. Now Julia must also prove "false traitor to myself" (IV.iv.105) as she plays "Sebastian" and delivers Proteus's letter to Silvia; Viola performs a similar role for Orsino in *Twelfth Night*. Only because Julia assumes such a disguise will she ever receive Proteus back as her lover. What seems roundabout is actually the shortest distance between two points.

Although she is playing the role of "Sebastian," Julia reveals even more self-consciousness as she describes "herself" to Silvia:

> SILVIA. How tall was she?
> JULIA. About my stature: for, at Pentecost,
>   When all our pageants of delight were played,
>   Our youth got me to play the woman's part,
>   And I was trimmed in Madam Julia's gown
>   Which served me as fit, by all men's judgments,
>   As if the garment had been made for me.
>   Therefore I know she is about my height.
>   And at that time I made her weep agood,
>   For I did play a lamentable part.
>   Madam, 'twas Ariadne passioning
>   For Theseus' perjury and unjust flight,
>   Which I so lively acted with my tears
>   That my poor mistress, moved therewithal,
>   Wept bitterly; and would I might be dead
>   If I in thought felt not her very sorrow!
>   (IV.iv.158-72)

"Pageants," "trimmed," "play," "part," "acted"—the entire network of references to theater suggests an acceptance of the mutable self which parallels similar discoveries about language. Julia's assumption of the role of Ariadne is the prototypical act of distancing the self, of crossing a boundary to step outside oneself. Nor can we ignore the involuted complexity of the context: a boy actor is playing the "lamentable part" of a young Italian Ariadne, abandoned by her lover;

the girl Julia is disguised as Sebastian, a male page; "Sebastian" describes how he once disguised himself as Julia, "trimmed in Madam Julia's gown," which fit perfectly; and then "Sebastian," playing a double woman's part, acted the role of Ariadne "passioning / For Theseus' perjury and unjust flight." Even Ariadne might be unable to retrace all these steps. Of course, Julia is not acting now even as she was then, for here she too weeps over her lover's perjury and flight. Just as her mistress, supposedly "moved therewithal, / Wept bitterly" in the Pentecost pageant, so does Silvia now "weep myself to think upon thy words" (l. 175). To act is not to act, then; to be oneself one must first become not oneself. Metamorphosis offers the only road to self-knowledge as well as self-revelation.

The baroque complications of Julia's situation are familiar enough to readers of other Shakespearean comedies, and no doubt Rosalind has an even more difficult role to sustain for a longer stretch. But Julia's predicament here completely epitomizes the concern running through *Two Gentlemen*—the question of metamorphosis versus rigidity, the need to diversify as opposed to the need to consolidate the self. Even more than Proteus, who *cannot* make himself act differently, Julia is the true "chameleon" in this play, able to don disguises, invent and describe still others, thereby defining and fixing her self by first being able to release and transform it at will. Who is Julia? Apparently anyone she desires to be. After Silvia leaves the stage, in tears over "Sebastian's" story, Julia is already trying to change her shape once more, to metamorphose herself into Silvia in order to win back Proteus' love. Holding up a picture of Silvia to her own face, Julia anticipates more melodramatic mirror-gazers—Richard II, Hamlet—as she envisions the next transformation:

> If I had such a tire, this face of mine
> Were full as lovely as is this of hers.
> . . . .
> Her hair is auburn, mine is perfect yellow:

If that be all the difference in his love,
I'll get me such a colored periwig.
. . . .
What should it be that he respects in her,
But I can make respective in myself,
If this fond Love were not a blinded god?
Come, shadow, come, and take this shadow up,
For 'tis thy rival.
　　　(IV.iv.185-98)

To turn herself into Silvia will not quite be necessary, however, for Proteus will (under pressure) return to his former self. But Julia is ready to "make respective in myself" virtually any quality, to "take this shadow up," assuming a whole new self; in one sense, as Sebastian, she already is the "shadow" or shade, a ghost of an actor. A critical difference exists between Julia's "shadow" and Valentine's "essence," for Julia might be anything, but Valentine only one thing. The connotations of "shadow" elsewhere in Shakespeare, especially as actor ("Lest we shadows have offended"), and dream-fantasy ("the king of shadows"), link up with the suggestions of "portrait" or "art" here. Julia is the Queen of Shadows in all these senses.

But Julia's supposed king, Proteus, her perjured and flown Theseus, leaves much to be desired. As most readers of the play have seen, and as A. Bartlett Giamatti has carefully demonstrated[7], Proteus receives his name from the sea god who changes shape at will and so incarnates the metamorphic qualities of the element he lives in. Ordered by his father to the Emperor's court, Shakespeare's Proteus laments, "Thus have I shunned the fire for fear of burning, / And drenched me in the sea, where I am drowned" (I.iii.78-9). He must part in a flood: "The tide is now:—nay, not thy tide of tears; / That tide will stay me longer than I should" (II.ii.14-15). So he begins yet another journey across water, after which he will drown his former self and undergo a sea-change not so rich as strange. Immersed in the destructive element, confronted with Silvia's beauty, Proteus begins to dissolve:

113

> now my love [for Julia] is thawed,
> Which, like a waxen image 'gainst a fire,
> Bears no impression of the thing it was.
>
> (II.iv.200-2)

This metaphor of transformation anticipates the Duke's "fig-ure / Trenched in ice" which "dissolves to water" that we have already seen; fire or ice—it makes no difference—love's powers to alter cannot be evaded. In his long soliloquy in II.vi, Proteus tries to rationalize his unwilling transformation, but the falsity of his position and the artifice of his rhetoric insure our disapproval. Some changes are better than others, it is clear, and the very self-consciousness of Julia's metamor-phoses seems a far healthier shift than the helpless compul-siveness of Proteus, who will hypocritically tell Valentine of Silvia's mourning,

> she hath offered to the doom [of banishment]—
> Which, unreversed, stands in effectual force—
> A sea of melting pearl, which some call tears.
>
> (III.i.223-5)

We are beginning to learn, however, that few things in this play will ever be allowed to stand "unreversed." This procla-mation has no more final authority than any of the vows and oaths sworn by the lovers.

In a passage which anticipates Julia's reflections on the "shadow," and augurs his own eventual reformation, Proteus swears allegiance to Silvia:

> Madam, if your heart be so obdurate,
> Vouchsafe me yet your picture for my love,
> The picture that is hanging in your chamber.
> To that I'll speak, to that I'll sigh and weep;
> For since the substance of your perfect self
> Is else devoted, I am but a shadow,
> And to your shadow will I make true love.
>
> (IV.ii.119-25)

Julia's wry aside displays the awareness in her the audience comes to admire: "If 'twere a substance, you would, sure, deceive it, / And make it but a shadow, as I am" (IV.ii. 125-7). It turns out that "shadows" necessarily have more substance than would first appear, because the Platonic relationship between essence and shadow has been subtly reversed. Proteus' malleability is both his vice and the means of his regeneration, for he can return as quickly as he fell. His sudden repentance—"My shame and guilt confounds me. / Forgive me, Valentine" (V.iv.73-4)—is psychologically absurd, but Shakespeare rarely interests himself in simple verisimilitude. Proteus' conversion works thematically, resolving for once and all (presumably) the fluctuations in his self. Julia shakes her disguise at him—"let this habit make thee blush!" (V.iv.105)—and drives home the moral:

> It is the lesser blot, modesty finds,
> Women to change their shapes than men their minds.
>
> (ll. 108-9)

Julia's greatest paradox—constancy in metamorphosis—is revealed just after we hear the song "Who is Silvia" and she complains that the musician "plays false" and the music "jars so":

> HOST. Hark, what fine change is in the music!
> JULIA. Ay, that change is the spite.
> HOST. You would have them always play but one thing?
> JULIA. I would always have one play but one thing.
>
> (IV.ii.68-71)

From music to men, modulation and change are inevitable; were music or man but constant, no variety, no life could exist. Ironically, in a touching moment, the chief shape-shifter of the play, even now in a many-layered disguise, asks that "one play but one thing." Of course she is the living proof that to "play" is always and inevitably to be at least two things and possibly more. The mimetic impulse to play a part, as we have seen before, leads one to be (oneself) and not to be (the disguised or metamorphosed other). Julia's desire for a theatrical monogamy is undermined by her own complex existence.

Some question remains about the extent of Julia's influence on Proteus. The distinction between changing shapes and changing minds summarizes much of the conflict in the play, and turns upon the same distinction between mutability and rigidity traced in the language of the play. In the men, stilted syntax and formulaic epigrams became unwitting disguises, expressions of an impossibly constrained self. Valentine's sudden renunciation of Silvia is even more disturbing than Proteus's easy born-again attitude, at least psychologically. It must be admitted that Shakespeare has not engineered the resolution of *Two Gentlemen* as imaginatively as he would that of *The Winter's Tale,* where the artifice, the impossibility, the evident magic, are precisely the goal. The artifice at the end of *Two Gentlemen* is partly the point, but it is also partly awkwardness—an uneasy balance which also mars the end of *Much Ado About Nothing.*

The Two Gentlemen of Verona concludes, as most comedies do, with a restoration of order. Decorum returns with the repeal of a harsh and unnatural law (Valentine's banishment), the exorcism of an imbalanced humor, the round of marriages, the sweet penance for past wrongdoing, and the achievement of *discordia concors:* "one feast, one house, one mutual happiness" (V.iv.174). The unity receives further emphasis with the restoration of the rings exchanged between Proteus and Julia as the emblem of concord becomes the agent of reunion. The use of rings, or similar tokens, is a standard New Comedy recognition device, and recurs to even greater effect in *The Merchant of Venice.* Here the rings returned herald the self returned to its former, "natural" stage; they also suggest how metamorphoses have run full circle, as change closes upon itself in restoration. Transformation has brought even the outlaws in the forest to be "reformed," their original "worthy qualities" recovered, their noble shapes re-formed; they are now "civil, full of good, / And fit for great employment" (V.iv.157-8). At its worst in this play, metamorphosis is a kind of disease, comic in Valentine, almost demonic in Proteus, whose helplessly metamorphic condition represents a terrifying triumph of pure unconstrained desire, in which the self dissolves under the pressures of its own insatiable hungers. One name for this condition was Actaeon. But Julia intervenes in the hunt before Proteus' desires can completely destroy him, revealing the possibilities of, and the necessity for, benign metamorphosis, in the willed self-consciousness of redemptive change. She at least has learned that glory is uncertain and clouds may take all away.

In *The Taming of the Shrew*, Kate sees the grotesqueness of her own shrewishness once it is embodied in a man, and changes in part by relinquishing her own rigidity and taking on some of Petruchio's playfulness and some of the flexibility so evident elsewhere in the play. Julia, on the other hand, is quite ready to reveal her wisdom to others, but rather than seeing herself *in* a man, she *becomes* one. As Sebastian, her sexual disguise serves the mechanics of the romance plot, but more importantly represents a detoxified version of the poisonous energy of desire which rules Proteus. His attempt to rape Silvia not only reveals this chaotic power but suggests how it perverts the ordered transformative process of marriage. Only once the disrupted courtship and the "natural" relations among the lovers have been re-formed can we look toward marriage and its proper completion. Proteus must first change his mind before Julia can change her shape, for good, back into that of a woman. She has gained her man only because she first became one.

PORTIA

Portia is neither the Merchant nor the Jew of Venice, but the play is also her story. In order to transform the harsh law of justice into the forgiving spirit of mercy, the dead letter into the living word, Portia has to transform herself into a man, Balthasar, so that she may enter into and act on the implacable world of men. Shylock's forced conversion from Jew to Christian is at one end of a continuum of conversions and willed transformations—Antonio out of his melancholy, Bassanio into a new seriousness, Jessica from the house of "hell" to the house in Belmont—while Portia's change, fully self-willed, is at the other end. She, or what she represents, is Shylock's real enemy.

Portia is, to begin with, the object of masculine desire, the origin of a quest, as Bassanio explains to Antonio:

> Nor is the wide world ignorant of her worth,
> For the four winds blow in from every coast
> Renowned suitors, and her sunny locks
> Hang on her temples like a golden fleece,
> Which makes her seat of Belmont Colchos' strond,
> And many Jasons come in quest of her.
> (I.i.167-72)

Portia is not only the object of the quest, the fleece, but also a kind of domesticated Medea, falling in love with her Jason, rebelling at her father's will, ready to help her lover with the much tamer but still effective magic she has at her disposal.[8] Portia's ending will be far happier than Medea's, and Bassanio presumably a more faithful husband than Jason proved to be, but remnants of Medea's powers of transformation linger on in Portia.

The three ritualistic tests in *The Merchant of Venice*—the casket scene, the pound-of-flesh trial, the rings at the end—have been most frequently discussed from the point of view of Antonio, Bassanio, or Shylock, but I should like to examine them as tests also of Portia, which indicate her own change in the play from one who bristles because "the will of a living daughter [is] curbed by the will of a dead father" (I.ii.23-4) to one who "drop[s] manna in the way / Of starved people" (V.i.294-5), and suggest why she must at one point become a man in order to win her man. It is important to be a man in this play, in part because power is vested in men, but that power badly needs humanizing as well. To influence the outcome of Antonio's trial, Portia must take on the shape of a participant, and that is male.

But first, because of her father's will, Portia must endure a trial of patience and passivity of her own—"I may neither choose who I would nor refuse who I dislike" (I.ii.22-3). This limbo makes her "aweary of this great world" (I.ii.2) as the play begins, but she regains her energy and wit quickly when Nerissa names over the list of her suitors and Portia comments on each. It is a wonderful comic scene, with a European cast of suitors all come to Belmont; each suitor suffers some stereotyped national flaw—the German is a drunkard, the Neapolitan prince can talk only of his horse—but each of the flaws is also a traditionally masculine flaw. If Portia is already this good at judging men, we shouldn't be surprised when she literally turns into a judge of men. Her graceful acceptance of her destiny is not simply resignation, but an acknowledgement of her identity and her past which the men themselves ought to study.

The casket scene, of course, ritually epitomizes the traditional helplessness and passivity of a woman, who has no "will" (with both assertive and sexual overtones) of her own, who must wait for the right man to come along, whose identity is concealed in a riddle, whose sexuality, displaced here in the caskets, is the central question. But Portia bears up under all of it quite well, and in fact is eventually delighted as one "blinking idiot" (II.ix.53) after another is dismissed in failure. She begins to discover how constraint can also be freedom. When Bassanio chooses among the caskets, the stakes for Portia suddenly go considerably higher, for she has fallen in love with him, the 'right' man, and she invokes a particularly melodramatic image of feminine helplessness at this point:

> Now he goes,
> With no less presence, but with much more love,
> Than young Alcides, when he did redeem
> The virgin tribute paid by howling Troy
> To the sea monster. I stand for sacrifice;

The rest aloof are the Dardanian wives,
With bleared visages come forth to view
The issue of th'exploit. Go, Hercules!
Live thou, I live.
                (III.ii.53-61)

Here is the historical and psychological condition, to an extreme, of most women, ready for sacrifice, their virgin tribute not in their own control, their lives dependent on their men. At one stage in his career, Hercules had suffered the ignominy, under Omphale's rule, of cross-dressing—the specific case Sidney quoted to indicate the power of love:

> so in *Hercules*, painted with his great beard and furious countenance, in woman's attire, spinning at *Omphales* commaundement, it breedeth both delight and laughter. For the representing of so strange a power in love procureth delight; and the scornefulnes of the action stirreth laughter.[9]

But Portia herself will play Hercules rather than the sacrifice, as all Shakespeare's comic heroines are inclined to do, when *she* cross-dresses, appearing in man's attire and defeating the judicial equivalent of the sea monster.

Portia's generosity, her willingness to give and receive, to risk and hazard, have all been commented on, beginning with John Russell Brown's study.[10] Such qualities actuate her to assist Bassanio in helping his friend Antonio; the method of aid is by now familiar:

> PORTIA. I'll hold thee any wager,
>   When we are both accoutered like young men,
>   I'll prove the prettier fellow of the two,
>   And wear my dagger with the braver grace,
>   And speak between the change of man and boy
>   With a reed voice, and turn two mincing steps
>   Into a manly stride, and speak of frays
>   Like a fine bragging youth; and tell quaint lies,
>   How honorable ladies sought my love,

Which I denying, they fell sick and died—
I could not do withal! Then I'll repent,
And wish, for all that, that I had not killed them.
And twenty of these puny lies I'll tell,
That men shall swear I have discontinued school
Above a twelvemonth. I have within my mind
A thousand raw tricks of these bragging Jacks,
Which I will practice.

NERISSA.　　　　　　Why, shall we turn to men?
PORTIA. Fie, what a question's that,
　　If thou wert near a lewd interpreter!
　　　　　　　　　　(III.iv.62-80)

Their imitation will double the one we're watching even now.
The hallmark of playing a young man, "between the change
of man and boy" (the role itself is on a boundary), is the
ability to lie—in other words, to feign; a young man is easy
to imitate because the pose is all talk, the transformation as
much of *vox* as anything. Moreover, turning to men, as the
final joke has it, is both transformative and sexual—that is,
the same.

Portia and Nerissa are not the only women to become men
in this play, for Jessica also disguises herself when fleeing her
father Shylock:

I am glad 'tis night, you do not look on me,
For I am much ashamed of my exchange.
But love is blind, and lovers cannot see
The pretty follies that themselves commit;
For if they could, Cupid himself would blush
To see me thus transformed to a boy.
　　　　　　　　　　(II.vi.34-9)

Jessica's shame, supposedly for the "exchange" itself, may be
generated as much by the shame of what she is doing, in
betraying and stealing from her father. For both Jessica and
Portia, however, the power of love has generated the transformation. Cupid is more than willing to see his victims swap

clothes and gender. Yet Shakespeare implies a real distinction between these two sexual exchanges: Jessica merely dons a costume so she will not be noticed, and her change is thus accidental and passive rather than essential; but Portia changes in order that she might be noticed, with full self-consciousness, in order to act in a man's world, so her transformation is willed, beneficent, and potentially redemptive.

In the trial scene, the second of the tests, the Duke expects that Shylock will experience a willed transformation and that, "touched with human gentleness and love" (IV.i.25), he'll forgive Antonio's debt; but Shylock is one of those rigid anti-comic characters unable to change, and conversion on all levels must be forced upon him. Portia's intervention in the trial as Balthasar ("I never knew so young a body with so old a head"—IV.i.162-3) is opportune but inauspicious, for her first question—"Which is the merchant here? And which the Jew?" (l. 173)—suggests in part that she can't tell the difference between them, in part that there may be less difference between them than either would admit.[11] Still, Portia quickly indicates that she knows how to play the men's game, and bears the same relation to them as did her father's will to her earlier. She now embodies the law, finding, as Sigurd Burckhardt has demonstrated, that the most rigid and literal enforcement of it will paradoxically lead to its transcendence, and so save Antonio and defeat Shylock. Portia has changed from a helpless and passive woman to her own antithesis— male, active, judging rather than judged, the power to give life or death in her hands. Her exquisite tact and judgment in this scene raise her above everyone else including the audience (even if the folklorists do know what's coming for Shylock). Her famous argument for mercy, moreover, is not only explicitly Christian but conventionally feminine, and when it fails, she knows she can also play the men's game with power.[12]

As the second ritual test ends, the third begins when Portia and Nerissa are given the rings they had entrusted to their husbands. Each test has epitomized a given stage in Portia's transformation, and this third case reveals her as once again a woman (though of course still *not* a woman also), but no longer so passively, so conventionally feminine. Something of the magisterial Balthasar lingers in her manner, and her formal position in relation to Bassanio—as the judge exacting the rigid penalty from a transgressor—recalls that of the judge, or even Shylock, earlier. In other words, Portia has imaginatively become all the chief male characters, while transcending their limitations. At the end, she has become herself again, but both she and her relation to Bassanio have subtly changed. The iconography of the ring, as Sigurd Burckhardt has argued, suggests perfection, return, marriage, the closing of the law upon itself, even, in Gratiano's final pun, the organs of generation.[13] To that list I would add the circular metamorphic system Portia inhabits here. The women in Ovid generally experience metamorphosis as an escape or a punishment, but for Portia, and others to follow, it is a liberation in itself which can lead to yet other desirable changes: from one kind of woman to man to another kind of woman.

The final act of *The Merchant of Venice* has been defended in a number of ways, but chiefly through an account of the "touches of sweet harmony" (V.i.57) which sound through Belmont.[14] It is also worth noting, from the view I have been following here, that the final act overflows with images of metamorphosis as well. It takes place under the goddess of mutability, the moon; as Portia says when she has returned, "How the moon sleeps with Endymion, / And would not be awaked" (ll. 109-10). Lorenzo has already noted "How sweet the moonlight sleeps upon this bank!" (l. 54), but Portia's personification reminds us, perhaps from Lyly's well-known version, of Endymion's transformations through Cynthia's power. The final act has begun, moreover, with what I take to be ambivalent allusions to love and metamorphosis, though Lorenzo and Jessica seem unaware of the implications of their allusions. As they proceed through their famous mythological duet—

In such a night as this,
When the sweet wind did gently kiss the trees
And they did make no noise, in such a night
Troilus methinks mounted the Troyan walls,
And sighed his soul toward the Grecian tents
Where Cressid lay that night—
(ll. 1-6)

we become aware that all these lovers have failed; and all have suffered change. Not all the stories come from Ovid, but they might as well have. Troilus sighs after Cressida, whose affections have suddenly changed. Thisby, whose blood will transform a flower, flees the lion at the tomb. Dido waves after Aeneas, who has abandoned her, just before she mounts a funeral pyre. And we once again encounter the legend of Medea:

In such a night
Medea gathered the enchanted herbs
That did renew old Aeson.
(ll. 12-14)

This transformation is like Endymion's, one of age to youth, but in Ovid's version the psychological transformation of Medea by the power of love is equally great, and she is performing this magic out of love for Jason. But like all the others here, that love collapses when Jason abandons her.

Whether Lorenzo and Jessica will be subsumed by this pattern of loss, or triumph over it, is impossible to say; it is strongly suggested by the ring test and its symbolism that Portia and Bassanio, and presumably also Nerissa and Gratiano, have already gone through a ritualized failure and recovered from it. They act out the lovers' failure adumbrated in the mythological allusions:

PORTIA. What ring gave you, my lord?
Not that, I hope, which you received of me.
BASSANIO. If I could add a lie unto a fault,

124

I would deny it; but you see my finger
Hath not the ring upon it—it is gone.
PORTIA. Even so void is your false heart of truth.
By heaven, I will ne'er come in your bed
Until I see the ring!
(ll. 184-91)

But they go beyond the failure when the men beg forgiveness
and Antonio offers to "be bound again, / My soul upon the
forfeit, that your lord / Will never more break faith advisedly"
(ll. 251-3). And now Portia, in a kind of fusion of Balthasar
and the Portia of the first three acts, judges *and* forgives, gives
and receives, accepting the men's promised conversion rather
than forcing it upon them. She has learned even more than
they have.[15]

In the midst of this remarkable ending, this mixture of
music and metamorphosis, it is not at all surprising that we
encounter Orpheus. Lorenzo is explaining to Jessica the power
of music to change man's nature:

For do but note a wild and wanton herd
Or race of youthful and unhandled colts
Fetching mad bounds, bellowing and neighing loud,
Which is the hot condition of their blood:
If they but hear perchance a trumpet sound,
Or any air of music touch their ears,
You shall perceive them make a mutual stand,
Their savage eyes turned to a modest gaze
By the sweet power of music. Therefore the poet
Did feign that Orpheus drew trees, stones, and floods;
Since naught so stockish, hard, and full of rage
But music for the time doth change his nature.
(ll. 71-82)

The "poet" is undoubtedly honest Ovid, but the real point
here is the equally ritualistic invocation of Orpheus, with his
powers to animate and metamorphose nature, and most importantly, the invocation of the poet's power to "feign." Sev-

eral modes of transformation are thus visible here. Yet lest it all sound too harmoniously in our ear, we are reminded as well of that stubborn element in human nature which will not or cannot change, the Caliban and the Malvolio in us that would rather curse than sing:

> The man that hath no music in himself,
> Nor is not moved with concord of sweet sounds,
> Is fit for treasons, stratagems, and spoils;
> The motions of his spirit are dull as night,
> And his affections dark as Erebus.
> Let no such man be trusted.
> (ll. 83-8)

Shylock is not named here not only to help 'distance' him from us, to place him at the remove of myth, as many readers have noted, but also to emphasize that the power to "change [a man's] nature" is at best only "for the time," and that some may be "not moved" at all. Orpheus would have been the first to acknowledge this, for even his power failed to change the nature of the mad Ciconian women, Ovid tells us, as

> backe ageine to Orphy ward they went,
> And (wicked wights) they murthred him, who never till
> that howre
> Did utter woordes in vaine, nor sing without effectuall
> powre.
>
> (*Met*, XI.40-2)

Orpheus' fate suggests that metamorphosis, like feigning, has its limits. *The Merchant of Venice* ends with a number of puns recalling the play's various transformations—Portia ironically says to Bassanio, "I'll die for't but some woman had the ring!" (l. 208) and Nerissa says the "clerk" who has taken Gratiano's ring will wear hair on his face only "if a woman live to be a man" (l. 160). Well, we have seen a woman live to be a man in this play, and we have also been reminded that a man, crossing a theatrical boundary, lives to be a woman.

ROSALIND

"Do you not know I am a woman?" (III.ii.250) Rosalind asks Celia. It is a difficult question to answer, given the complex levels of her disguise and role-playing, not to mention the negative phrasing of the question, by which either yes or no may mean the same thing. In no other play by Shakespeare does a woman stand so centrally as Rosalind does in *As You Like It*; and her sexual disguise as Ganymede, "Jove's own page" (I.iii.123; cf. *Met*, X.161-7) represents the transformed otherness of the lover even as it liberates her to be more truly herself.[16]

Shakespeare creates a circle of real and apparent transformations around Rosalind, from Celia's comic oath, "when I break that oath, let me turn monster" (I.ii.20-1), through Duke Senior's complaint about the absent Jaques, "I think he be transformed into a beast, / For I can nowhere find him like a man" (II.vii.1-2), to Rosalind's mockery of Silvius, "Well, go your way to her, for I see love hath made thee a tame snake" (IV.iii.68-9). The pastoral forest of Shakespeare's romance sources was just such a place where one might turn monster, be transformed into a beast, or be made a tame snake. It was the natural locus of transformation, the place, like the woods in *A Midsummer Night's Dream*, where the boundary between man and beast might disappear. But in *As You Like It* the forest of Arden is something else again, more "reflecting mirror" (in David Young's phrase) than anything else, a *selva oscura* with the accent on the last term. The beastly transformations in Arden are figurative or hypothetical, yet more instances of the virtue of "if."

Shakespeare seems both skeptical and credulous about transformation in *As You Like It*, making it by turns "real" and "feigned." The miraculous conversions of Duke Frederick and Oliver at the end of the play seem deliberately contrived and unconvincing; other transformations, through the power of love for example, are enacted quite seriously. One mythological model for the action is that of Jove's adventures in

Arcady in Book II of the *Metamorphoses*, and the story of Baucis and Philemon in Book VIII. But this background is clearly viewed in the play as extravagant and comical. Phebe's letter to Rosalind invokes transformation simply as a poetic cliché: "Art thou god, to shepherd turned, / That a maiden's heart hath burned?" (IV.iii.41-2). In the play's famous passage about "feigning," Ovid (in exile) appears once again:

TOUCHSTONE. I am here with thee and thy goats, as the most capricious poet, honest Ovid, was among the Goths.

JAQUES. [*Aside*] O knowledge ill-inhabited, worse than Jove in a thatched house!

TOUCHSTONE. When a man's verses cannot be understood, nor a man's good wit seconded with the forward child, understanding, it strikes a man more dead than a great reckoning in a little room. Truly, I would the gods had made thee poetical.

AUDREY. I do not know what poetical is. Is it honest in deed and word? Is it a true thing?

TOUCHSTONE. No, truly; for the truest poetry is the most feigning, and lovers are given to poetry, and what they swear in poetry may be said as lovers they do feign.

(III.iii.6-21)

From the thatched house through the little room to the great stage, from Ovid through Marlowe to Shakespeare, we can trace the history of an attitude toward feigning as something by turns magical and preposterous, true and false. The ability to "feign," as we will see, allows Rosalind freely to transform herself as she likes it.

Like Jove and Mercury among the rustics, or Ovid among the goats, Celia and Rosalind ("Aliena" and "Ganymede") walk transformed in Arcadia. But even before they depart for Arden, they have undergone the psychological transformation of fusion, as Celia testifies:

> We still have slept together,
> Rose at an instant, learned, played, eat together;

And wheresoe'er we went, like Juno's swans,
Still we went coupled and inseparable.
. . . .

. . . thou and I am one.
Shall we be sund'red, shall we part, sweet girl?
(I.iii.72-5, 96-7)

This friendship will reach even to a joint wedding with brothers, when they will be made two in one, coupled and inseparable, in quite another way. There is a hint of this further
change to come in the allusion to Juno's swans; the Arden
editor believes that this is a transposition of the legend of
Venus' swans, which traditionally drew her chariot (as in *Met*,
X.831, the story of Venus and Adonis), though they might
also be the men whom Venus angrily transformed into swans
(*Met*, XIV.564ff). In either case, Venus, or love, engineers the
transformation. Yet Rosalind and Celia will discover that even
the love which makes them one will dissolve and reform in
another direction.

Just as the forest of Arden is a real mirage—a bare stage
but also a verbal and imaginative forest—so Touchstone shows
us how to see it both ways, offering us a "natural perspective"
of the shepherd's life that wholly depends on the viewer's
transforming eye:

Truly, shepherd, in respect of itself, it is a good life; but
in respect that it is a shepherd's life, it is naught. In respect
that it is solitary, I like it very well; but in respect that
it is private, it is a very vile life. Now in respect it is in
the fields, it pleaseth me well; but in respect it is not in
the court, it is tedious. As it is a spare life, look you, it
fits my humor well; but as there is no more plenty in it,
it goes much against my stomach. (III.ii.13-21)

But the fact is that everyone from the court, not just Touchstone, sees things double, with "parted eye." The Duke has
been able to "translate the stubbornness of fortune / Into so
quiet and so sweet a style" (II.i.19-20), Jaques can be counted
on to "moralize this spectacle" (l. 44), and Jaques admires

Touchstone precisely because he can "moral on the time" (II.vii.29).[17]

We find that only Rosalind, whose way is to conjure us, can "translate," "moralize," or transform herself without deception, however; she best exemplifies the pleasures of transformation in the forest. She is not only Celia's double but, as one of Orlando's poems asserts, always seems more than one person:

> Therefore heaven Nature charged
> That one body should be filled
> With all graces wide-enlarged.
> Nature presently distilled
> Helen's cheek, but not her heart,
> Cleopatra's majesty,
> Atalanta's better part,
> Sad Lucretia's modesty.
> Thus Rosalind of many parts
> By heavenly synod was devised,
> Of many faces, eyes, and hearts,
> To have the touches dearest prized.
> (III.ii.141-52)

For us as well as for Orlando, she is a quintessence, an epitome of many qualities squeezed into one body, a kind of metaphysical conceit. The several layers of her actual physical disguising repeat the effect.

Rosalind's transformation into Ganymede is considerably more complex, and developed further, than similar sex-changes in the earlier comedies. All possible permutations of crossdressing are at work now, and it is more important than ever before that Rosalind be changed into a male. The change begins like all the others, with the obliteration of the boundaries of the feminine:

> Were it not better,
> Because that I am more than common tall,
> That I did suit me all points like a man?

A gallant curtle-ax upon my thigh,
A boar-spear in my hand; and, in my heart
Lie there what hidden woman's fear there will,
We'll have a swashing and a martial outside,
As many other mannish cowards have
That do outface it with their semblances.
(I.iii.113-21)

Again manliness is just a matter of props, and once again the
woman assumes the most stereotypically masculine qualities.
The urge to forget she is a woman drives Rosalind to adopt
the kind of clichés she will mock elsewhere, as in Orlando's
marks (or lack of them) as a lover (III.ii.371-81). Yet her
transformation will not be so complete as to annihilate all
trace of her former self; Ganymede is still both Rosalind and
not Rosalind. At the end of the play Orlando tells Rosalind's
father, "the first time that I ever saw him / Methought he was
a brother to your daughter" (V.iv.28-9), and the description
of her given to Oliver declares that "the boy is fair, / Of female
favor, and bestows himself / Like a ripe sister" (IV.iii.84-6).
Rosalind is thus both her own brother and her brother's sister.
Shakespeare does not develop Ganymede's androgynous nature as he will Cesario's in *Twelfth Night,* where both male
and female fall in love with the pliant hermaphrodite, but
Ganymede's ambivalent nature—"I thank God I am not a
woman, to be so touched with so many giddy offenses as he
hath generally taxed their whole sex withal" (III.ii.346-9)—
forms the heart of the wooing scenes.

It is in the forest scenes with Orlando that Rosalind/Gan-
ymede best reveals her ability to transform herself suitably for
a ripe occasion. Within six lines of one scene, she says both
"And I am your Rosalind" and "What would you say to me
now, an I were your very very Rosalind?" (IV.i.62, 66-8). The
space between asserting and feigning, in which the assertion
is (doubly) feigned and the feigning is actually true, is once
again the natural locus of transformation. The play's well-
known "if" clauses serve as a rough index to the amount of

transformation required of Rosalind, reaching a crescendo in the fifth act when she begins to promise everyone a fulfillment as he likes it. This ability to feign all takes on an emergency quality when Ganymede faints upon hearing Oliver's story of the lion, and Rosalind employs one of Falstaff's favorite words, "counterfeit," to explain how she had only feigned. In her relief at recovering her presence of mind, she responds to Oliver's "take a good heart and counterfeit to be a man" with a duplicitous self-assertion, "So I do; but, i'faith, I should have been a woman by right" (IV.iii.1/1-4).

Rosalind's role frequently requires her to remind Orlando of the essential natural mutability of things, which we cannot evade or prevent, even as she exemplifies willed and redemptive change for us in her role-playing. Against Orlando's absurdly rigid lover's vows ("for ever and a day"), somewhat reminiscent of Proteus's, Rosalind opposes a quite different image of change in life:

> Say "a day," without the "ever." No, no, Orlando. Men are April when they woo, December when they wed. Maids are May when they are maids, but the sky changes when they are wives.

And she describes her future actions, half-seriously, as a series of antithetical reactions:

> I will be more jealous of thee than a Barbary cock-pigeon over his hen, more clamorous than a parrot against rain, more newfangled than an ape, more giddy in my desires than a monkey. I will weep for nothing, like Diana in the fountain, and I will do that when you are disposed to be merry; I will laugh like a hyen, and that when thou art inclined to sleep. (IV.i.142-52)

Although each emblematic simile depicts her in a constant attitude, always weeping or always laughing, the sum total of the images implies a constant inconstancy, "more giddy" than all of them put together in fact. Earlier, she had told Orlando

132

how she had been able to cure one other lover, who had
imagined Ganymede his mistress:

> I set him every day to woo me. At which time would I,
> being but a moonish youth, grieve, be effeminate,
> changeable, longing and liking, proud, fantastical, apish,
> shallow, inconstant, full of tears, full of smiles; for every
> passion something and for no passion truly anything, as
> boys and women are for the most part cattle of this color;
> would now like him, now loathe him; then entertain him,
> then forswear him; now weep for him, then spit at him;
> that I drave my suitor from his mad humor of love to a
> living humor of madness. (III.ii.403-13)

Here is totally protean life. Having described masculine stereotypes when taking on her disguise, Rosalind now, as a
putative male, invokes feminine clichés of fickleness and un-
predictability. Shakespeare is making comically explicit what
has been implicit in most of these comedies, that transformation and mutability are powers somehow linked to feminine energies, and that these powers are finally healthier and
more realistic than the masculine rigidities of, say, Shylock or
the *senex* fathers, or even the harmless but sterile melancholy
of Jaques. Spenser had identified Mutability as a goddess, to
be sure, but Shakespeare goes beyond the allegory to locate
this power of self-transformation in individualized, mysterious, believable young women.[18]

As You Like It concludes in a flood of transformations,
with the tide of "if" clauses demonstrating the complete virtuosity of Rosalind's powers: "Believe then, if you please, that
I can do strange things. I have, since I was three year old,
conversed with a magician, most profound in his art and yet
not damnable" (V.ii.58-61). In a *commedia* pastoral, this would
be literally true, and Rosalind would herself have actual magical powers. But Shakespeare has redefined and transformed
transformation, so that here it is an expression of the fictive
self, the virtue of "if," and it requires a complicity of imagi-

native belief on the audience's part. The audience within the play must approach our own faith in Ganymede:

> [To Silvius] I will help you if I can. [To Phebe] I would love you if I could. Tomorrow meet me all together. [To Phebe] I will marry you if ever I marry woman, and I'll be married tomorrow. [To Orlando] I will satisfy you if ever I satisfied man, and you shall be married tomorrow. [To Silvius] I will content you if what pleases you contents you, and you shall be married tomorrow. (V.ii. 110-17)

Rosalind's round of hypothetical promises, and the play's deepest movement, runs towards the transformations of marriage. The earlier comedies have moved under the same impulse, but none has had so many and such appropriate marriages, as Jaques notes: "There is, sure, another flood toward, and these couples are coming to the ark" (V.iv. 35-6). *Twelfth Night* reveals most spectacularly how marriage becomes the deepest transformation of two into one, in which the energies of desire, the very origins of transformation, are harnessed but not suppressed by this ritualized institution. In *As You Like It,* Rosalind and Celia will undergo division of their "coupled and inseparable" state to form new and more lasting (though not for "ever") relations with Orlando and Oliver, and become if not sisters then sisters-in-law.

The appropriate but unexpected figure presiding over these ceremonies—and it should be noted that he enters just after Touchstone's virtuoso rendition of the degrees of lying (more feigning) and "much virtue in *if*"—is Hymen, god of marriage.[19] His presence is almost inevitable here because his function is to preside over, to embody, the metamorphic process of marriage:

> Then is there mirth in heaven
> When earthly things made even
> Atone together.
>
> (V.iv.108-10)

The verb "atone" has a New Testament echo in it, and also bears its literal meaning, "to set at one"—to make two into one. Marriage is a strange thing, a "blessed bond" (l. 142) which both binds and liberates.

Like Julia, Portia, and Viola, Rosalind has been destined for this encounter with marriage, but only after her love has transformed her into someone else, only after she has become the embodiment of masculine *and* feminine love. She disguises herself initially for reasons of safety, but she soon realizes the potential of play-acting. Before Hymen has even made an appearance, Rosalind/Ganymede engineers a feigned, "if" marriage with Orlando as the natural culmination of their wooing scenes:

> ROSALIND. Come, sister, you shall be the priest and marry us. Give me your hand, Orlando. What do you say, sister?
> ORLANDO. Pray thee marry us.
> CELIA. I cannot say the words.
> ROSALIND. You must begin, "Will you, Orlando—"
> CELIA. Go to. Will you, Orlando, have to wife this Rosalind?
> ORLANDO. I will.
> ROSALIND. Ay, but when?
> ORLANDO. Why now, as fast as she can marry us.
> ROSALIND. Then you must say, "I take thee, Rosalind, for wife."
> ORLANDO. I take thee, Rosalind, for wife.
> ROSALIND. I might ask you for your commission; but I do take thee, Orlando, for my husband. There's a girl goes before the priest, and certainly a woman's thought runs before her actions.   (IV.i.120-37)

Rosalind plays all the parts here, bride, bridegroom, priest; *she* is Hymen. This scene seems even more tantalizing when we realize that this mock marriage has the legal authority of a valid marriage, as marriage *per verba de praesenti*[20]; thus Rosalind's insistence on Orlando's precise present-tense acceptance of her. This is her true marriage as Ganymede, presided over by herself as Hymen; as the play ends, and Rosalind (unlike Viola) has returned to her own shape, she will be married as herself, her own magical powers now embodied in Hymen. Among the couples "coming to the ark" in the final scene are Touchstone and Audrey, whose mock marriage in III.iii, under the auspices of Sir Oliver Mar-text, had failed of completion. For Touchstone, "wedlock would be nibbling" (III.iii.80-1), and Rosalind would certainly agree (in the first act, Orlando, she says, is already "my child's father" I.iii.11). Yet marriage is also something more mysterious and transcending than mere nibbling. Even Touchstone, "amongst the rest of the country copulatives," presses in "to swear and to forswear, according as marriage binds and blood breaks" (V.iv.57-9). These "rites" will end, like all true marriages, "in true delights" (l. 198).

Shakespeare's disguised women have been hermaphroditic, the boundaries of their femininity and masculinity increasingly an issue in the plays, culminating in Viola's Cesario, who attracts both male and female devotion. These young women have always been at least two beings by the sheer fact of their disguises, and frequently more, as they have learned to control their transformative powers. Shakespeare seems to have seen yet more potential in each succeeding play, ending in the specially triumphant mysteries of Rosalind and Viola. The disease is catching, for even the melodramatically bad brother Oliver is reformed at the end of *As You Like It*:

> 'Twas I. But 'tis not I. I do not shame
> To tell you what I was, since my conversion
> So sweetly tastes, being the thing I am.
> (IV.iii.134-6)

He doesn't yet realize that his "conversion" hasn't ended, that only the end of the play will place limits on it. And in fact the experience of conversion may leap across the boundary of the stage to engulf the audience. The most fundamental transformation, the most important taking on of disguise, occurs among the actors, before the audience sits down. But in *As You Like It,* Shakespeare is confident enough to disenchant us, as he had once before with the fairies in *A Midsummer Night's Dream,* to undo the one mimetic transformation we never saw begin but placed a complicit belief in. The epilogue begins with Rosalind speaking but ends with the actor's words: another case of " 'Twas I. But 'tis not I." The speaker's initial difficulty is to overcome the limitations of disguise:

> What a case am I in then, that am neither a good epilogue, nor cannot insinuate with you in the behalf of a good play! I am not furnished like a beggar; therefore to beg will not become me.

But the solution is by now a familiar one: "My way is to conjure you" (ll. 7-11). She has been a combination of entreatment and magic (as the pun has it) all along, and the final demystification occurs when *she* metamorphoses into *he,* as a kind of theatrical Iphis or Gallathea, with the play's final hypothetical:

> If I were a woman, I would kiss as many of you as had beards that pleased me, complexions that liked me, and breaths that I defied not; and I am sure, as many as have good beards, or good faces, or sweet breaths, will, for my kind offer, when I make curtsy, bid me farewell. (ll. 16 22)

Rosalind's last transformation thus occurs before our eyes, though as usual we don't know it has happened until its cessation is asserted. We had forgotten she was not a woman.

Part Three ❧ Comic Monsters

"And behold neither feathers did burgeon out nor appearance of wings, but verily my hair did turn into ruggedness and my tender skin wore tough and hard; my fingers and toes leaving the number of five grew together into hooves, and from the end of my back grew a great tail, and now my face became monstrous and my mouth long and my nostrils wide, my lips hanging down, and mine ears exceedingly increased with bristles; neither could I see any comfort of my transformation, save that the nature of my members was increasing likewise to the great discomfiture of Fotis, and so without all help (viewing every part of my poor body) I perceived that I was no bird, but a plain ass. Then I thought to blame Fotis, but being deprived as well of language as human gesture, I did all that I could, and looked upon her with hanging lips and watery eyes, as though to reproach her."

LUCIUS APULEIUS
The Golden Ass, trans. William Adlington (1566)

Chapter Five ❧ A Midsummer Night's Dream: Monsters and Marriage

"Monsters are not shocking, if they are seen at a proper distance." So said Hazlitt after his more famous comment about *A Midsummer Night's Dream:* "Fairies are not incredible, but fairies six feet high are so."[1] By definition, however, monsters are always shocking, even when they are comic, and even when they are seen at a "proper" distance. In the most explicitly metamorphic of Shakespeare's comedies—*A Midsummer Night's Dream*—the boundaries between the human and the monstrous continually dissolve and reform. Shakespeare continued his comic exploration of marriage, monsters, and metamorphosis with Falstaff in *The Merry Wives of Windsor*, as we will see in the next chapter.

In *Something of Great Constancy*, David Young first commented extensively on the question of metamorphosis in *A Midsummer Night's Dream*. He argued that there are two kinds of change in the play:

> The first is the alteration of characteristics, physical and otherwise, at the bidding of some powerful force: Puck becomes a stool; the pansy becomes a sacred and powerful herb; Bottom is changed to an ass. The second involves a character, object, or concept, through asso-

141

ciation or actual merging, with some opposite or unlike character or quality: love is turned to hate; nature becomes art; tragedy turns to comedy; Bottom is made the paramour of the fairy queen.

Young goes on to note that the second kind of transformation is actually more remarkable than the first:

> Bottom changed to an ass is but a short step, a revelation of inner qualities already familiar to us, while Bottom as the consort of Titania is a huge leap, so great that we feel he never truly makes it: just as the "marriage" is probably never consummated, so is the transformation incomplete.[2]

Though I disagree with Young's conclusion about the marriage, the descriptive framework he provides offers an enlightening perspective on the play. Certainly the metaphor of "marriage" as the merging of opposites suggests a way of uniting the very different kinds of change in this play, as it has in the other comedies we have examined, and it dramatizes once again the generation of metamorphosis from love. The amor in metamorphosis is nowhere so clearly revealed as in this play. More recently, in *Dream in Shakespeare,* Marjorie Garber analyzes the "dream" elements and their connection with the play's changes, and goes on immediately to link transformation with the imagination's powers: "this transforming creative process becomes the subject as well as the technique of the play."[3] This aspect of *A Midsummer Night's Dream* has received close attention from Young, C. L. Barber, and R. W. Dent as well.[4] Yet these estimates of the play's transformations need to be supplemented, in my view, by a stronger emphasis on another feature of metamorphosis, the play's embodied fear of the monstrous, and its corollary, the attempted suppression of the erotic, and then by an examination of the various representations of metamorphosis within the play. Before making the leap from mimetic transformation to the complete self-referentiality of the play, we should examine more closely their subjects, the monsters and marriages which dominate the action.

🐾

The human characters of *A Midsummer Night's Dream* frequently confront the boundaries of the human and the infringements by the "monstrous" or non-human. Theseus is glibly confident in the boundaries that allegedly exist: " 'tis almost fairy time" (V.i.363) is purely a figure of speech for him. But the young lovers and the mechanicals experience a startling initiation under cover of darkness and confusion, and the play suggests that love cannot be completed, in marriage, until the lovers have gone through a metamorphosis and become something other. Transformation will become the necessary detour to marriage and prove to be not a detour at all but the true journey.

In *The Forest of Symbols,* Victor Turner has speculated on the frequency with which monsters are associated with "liminal" or threshold stages of initiation rituals. Arguing against the more traditional view that bizarre and monstrous masks in this stage are the result of dreams or hallucinations, Turner suggests to the contrary

> that monsters are manufactured precisely to teach neophytes to distinguish clearly between the different factors of reality, as it is conceived in their culture . . . Monsters startle neophytes into thinking about objects, persons, relationships, and features of their environment they have hitherto taken for granted.

For example, whatever was once unthinkingly associated, then, like man and animal, becomes in such rituals dissociated, to define boundaries and clarify by contrast. *A Midsummer Night's Dream* places its characters in its own forest of symbols, the world of a liminal period, which Turner describes as in part "a stage of reflection . . . the realm of primitive hypothesis, where there is a certain freedom to juggle with the factors of existence."[5] Such shadowy places are of course the natural habitat of metamorphosis, whether one begins with anthropological analysis or traces back the generic associations of romance. Shakespeare's audience, no less than his characters, will experience the startling though comic dissociations of the monstrous.

Once implicated in the maze of the forest, all the lovers experience persistent encroachments of the animalistic upon the human. As the connections between the lovers dissolve, so do the once-clear demarcations of human, and even fairy, identity. Oberon's revenge against Titania, for example, is that she will see "lion, bear, or wolf, or bull, / . . . meddling monkey, or . . . busy ape" (II.i.180-1), and fall in love, but what follows in the next stage direction seems, though only at first, rather different: "Enter Demetrius, Helena following him." Helena too is already recognizing her figurative identity with the animal world:

> I am your spaniel; and, Demetrius,
> The more you beat me, I will fawn on you.
> Use me but as your spaniel, spurn me, strike me,
> Neglect me, lose me; only give me leave,
> Unworthy as I am, to follow you.
> (II.i.203-7)

This traditional love-engendered metamorphosis is bad enough, but she soon begins to speak of more explicit kinds of Ovidian metamorphosis, and promises, in a further transformation, to change even that:

> Run when you will, the story shall be changed:
> Apollo flies, and Daphne holds the chase;
> The dove pursues the griffin; the mild hind
> Makes speed to catch the tiger.
> (ll. 230-3)

From nymph (into tree) to dove to mild hind, Helena links herself with the vegetative and animal rather than the human, and Demetrius might argue that his persistent pursuer is far more the tiger than the hind. The ferocity of desire turns things

144

into their opposites, and even turns the myths around. Soon Helena appreciates the transformation that has worked in her:

> No, no, I am as ugly as a bear,
> For beasts that meet me run away for fear.
> Therefore no marvel though Demetrius
> Do, as a monster, fly my presence thus.
>
> (II.ii.94-7)

Desire, even its transformation, prompts transformation; the ambiguous double grammar of "as a monster" implies an alteration in Demetrius as well.

Lysander has similarly fallen into these inexplicable changes: "Not Hermia but Helena I love: / Who will not change a raven for a dove?" (II.ii.113-14). The end of this scene finds Hermia awakening from the dream of the "crawling serpent" eating "my heart away" (ll. 146-9). In the next act, Hermia will accuse Demetrius of being a "dog ... cur ... serpent" (III.ii.65,73) in the same kind of progression seen earlier. Lysander in turn accuses his former beloved in similar terms:

> LYSANDER. Hang off, thou cat, thou burr! Vile thing, let loose,
> Or I will shake thee from me like a serpent!
> HERMIA. Why are you grown so rude! What change is this,
> Sweet love? (III.ii.260-3)

The "change" is universal and occurs on several levels. But the changes noted by the audience, as the lovers shift partners, are only partly matched by the characters' awareness of them; the lovers find changes only in each other, not in themselves, and so never truly *experience* metamorphosis. In fact, what was previously "normal" for them now becomes less than human. Thus Hermia's lack of height becomes an attribute of monstrosity in Lysander's curse: "Get you gone, you dwarf; / You minimus, of hind'ring knotgrass made; / You bead, you acorn!" (III.ii.328-30). When Puck brings the four lovers together at the end of the "weary night" of confusion, the neophytes fall asleep longing for daylight and an end to the ambiguities associated with their liminal state. When the hunting party awakens them, they find their previous errors "melted as the snow" (IV.i.167), as Demetrius says of his love for Hermia, their long night's experiences fading quickly. But the return from transformation must still be described in the terms of transformation. As love melts and memory fades, only a glimmer remains:

DEMETRIUS. These things seem small and undistinguishable,
   Like far-off mountains turned into clouds.
HERMIA. Methinks I see these things with parted eye,
   When everything seems double.
                    (ll. 188-91)

Mountains to clouds, snow to water, nymphs to trees: the metamorphic vision consists precisely in seeing everything "double," with "parted eye." But the dream of erotic confusion cannot be so easily dismissed as the lovers would have it; the audience at least will remember the freakish allusions to curs and serpents, apes and dwarfs, and perhaps see the play's suggestive link between desire and the monstrous.

The goal of desire is of course physical union, so the sanctified resolution of the lovers' "double" vision of eros and chastity, darkness and daylight, forest and court, is marriage. Theseus assumes that the four sleeping lovers had risen "up early to observe / The rite of May," with the usual implications of grass-stained smocks and drowsy fulfillment, and he gently mocks them, "Saint Valentine is past" (IV.i.140). Love has been shown to be unruly indeed, so that the only acceptable channel for it, the institution which harmonizes and transforms the opposites of eros and chastity, is marriage. The lovers cannot be married, however, until they pass through this liminal stage in the forest. Lysander has prematurely proposed a natural but unsanctified "marriage," where the natural turf and civilized pillow are identical:

One turf shall serve as pillow for us both,
One heart, one bed, two bosoms, and one troth.
                    (II.ii.41-2)

Their chastity, however, is technically preserved—Hermia and Lysander lie apart "in *human* modesty" (my italics, II.ii.57), preserving a discreet separation of the "virtuous bachelor and a maid" (II.ii.59) until the proper time.

Shakespeare seems to be suggesting here that young love can only, should only, be consummated (in all senses) after some trial of the monstrous has been survived, some transformational stage passed through. The way to marriage, to achieved eros, is thus through the monstrous, or through encounters with it; in *The Taming of the Shrew,* the consummation of the marriage was deferred until that comic monster, the shrew, had been transformed. Whereas Demetrius repulses Helena with the threat to abandon her in the dark forest "to the mercy of wild beasts" (II.i.228), Hermia's dream within this *Dream* as Lysander abandons her provides the most frightening of erotic nightmares, in which "this crawling serpent" at her breast, both devouring and devoured by her, "eat[s] my heart away."

The experience of the lovers in the forest outside Athens, as has frequently been shown, reveals that, in Bottom's words, "reason and love keep little company together nowadays" (III.i.142-3), that love is the greatest and most magnificent of irrationalities, and that it engenders nearly uncontrollable metamorphosis if not channeled in some way. Love is worse than blind; its capricious and arbitrary nature—"therefore is Love said to be a child, / Because in choice he is so oft beguiled" (I.i.238-9)—leads the lovers to exchange love partners in the forest with metronomic regularity. Everything has gone to show that love engenders metamorphosis even as it is itself subject to metamorphosis. The course of true love, as Hermia and Lysander tell us, never did run smooth:

> momentany as a sound,
> Swift as a shadow, short as any dream,
> Brief as the lightning in the collied night,
> That, in a spleen, unfolds both heaven and earth,
> And ere a man hath power to say "Behold!"

The jaws of darkness do devour it up:
So quick bright things come to confusion.

(I.i.143-9)

This sounds so apocalyptic in its "Ecce," so much like a description of human life, so much like Bede's famous description of the bird's brief flight through the lighted hall and back into darkness, that it might stand for all human experience in the play. The "jaws of darkness" threaten everything, but the metaphor of the jaws reminds us specifically of the monstrous which lurks nearby and within, however comic it might seem. The reach of Lysander's description seems even larger when we begin to hear the code words which link it to the rest of the play—"shadow," "dream," "heaven and earth," "darkness," "quick bright things," and "confusion." This is the vocabulary of metamorphosis as well.

BOTTOM

The erotic implications of the long night are suppressed during the lovers' experience, but are far more open and highly comic for Bottom. The lovers' encounters with the monstrous generally are dreamlike or figurative, and are finally suppressed in daylight, whereas Bottom's experience is direct. Moreover it is the only onstage physical man-to-beast transformation in all of Shakespeare's plays. That alone justifies the closest attention to it.

It is no doubt true in *A Midsummer Night's Dream* that "the creatures of the dream world enact literally what is undergone figuratively or metaphorically by the citizens of the court,"[6] but applying this formula to Bottom's experience is difficult. We can readily see that "Bottom is an ass" and that "this metaphor is latent in his characterization from the start."[7] Therefore his literal metamorphosis *into an ass* is not surprising. But surely the metamorphosis itself is what is unexpected and comically shocking; Dogberry and Malvolio are equally asinine and deserving of metamorphosis, but escape

148

it. If Bottom is to experience metamorphosis, then clearly an ass is appropriate. The question is, why must he experience metamorphosis to begin with, and why must the change be physically rendered?

Bottom's metamorphosis occurs, in part, for the reason Turner has suggested: to startle neophytes (like the audience) "into thinking about objects, persons, relationships, and features of their environment they have hitherto taken for granted." Bottom's change is essentially for the audience's sake, since none of the courtly characters, except his immediate colleagues, ever sees him as an ass. He becomes for us the visible, indeed the great comic instance, of boundaries transgressed. His literal transformation will also suggest, as we will see, how comic as well as threatening the animalistic erotic can be. His metamorphosis is greeted with an hysteria that contrasts with the audience's laughter:

> QUINCE. O monstrous! O strange! We are haunted.
> . . . .
> SNOUT. O Bottom, thou art changed! What do I see on thee?
> . . . .
> QUINCE. Bless thee, Bottom! Bless thee! Thou art trans-
> lated.   (III.i.103-18)

Bottom is "translated" as one meaning can be conveyed in two different languages, so he is an ass in both human and animal form. Bottom's obtuseness to all this ("this is to make an ass of me"—l. 119) has been much remarked, but his is exactly the same reaction that the young lovers experience in their transformations. The metamorphs in this play notice nothing; since they are unaware of these changes when they occur, no anxiety or fear distresses them.

Because of the mechanicals' ludicrously horrified reactions, every audience laughs at Bottom's asinine appearance, for the boundary between the human and the animal seems, in his case at least, to be located precisely at the neck; his transformation is far from total. Here, as elsewhere in the play, Shakespeare reminds us of the double nature of metamorphosis, for Bottom is and is not an ass, his identity never clearer than when it has been lost in another shape. He can be recognized by his friends as Bottom even as they deny his former identity.

Titania's enraptured approval of Bottom's appearance—

What angel wakes me from my flow'ry bed?
. . . .
I pray thee, gentle mortal, sing again:
Mine ear is much enamored of thy note;
So is mine eye enthralled to thy shape;
And thy fair virtue's force perforce doth move me
On the first view to say, to swear, I love thee.
(III.i.127, 136-40)

—reflects her own internal transformation, and her perceptual power now to transform Bottom yet again, from silly ass to "angel"; by this point, the audience changes him back in *its* mind, insisting that he's an ass. Doesn't she see him? If neither horror nor idolatry will do, what then are we supposed to say to a monster, even a likable one? Evidently there is no established protocol concerning griffins or satyrs.

Still other human boundaries are transgressed in Bottom's discussions with the fairies Peaseblossom, Cobweb, Moth, and Mustardseed. Each character is a reification. Bottom talks to them as people (and of course they are played by children), yet comically reverses their transformations, reducing them back to objects at the same time; to "Master Cobweb," he says, "if I cut my finger, I shall make bold with you," referring to the cobweb's supposed healing properties. By the fourth act, Bottom is bossing them around quite comfortably:

Scratch my head, Peaseblossom. . . . Mounsier Cobweb, good mounsieur, get you your weapons in your hand, and kill me a red-hipped humblebee on the top of a thistle; and, good mounsieur, bring me the honey bag.
(IV.i.7, 10-13)

What makes Bottom's reactions so inappropriate and so comic is that he is completely unconscious of all the boundaries observed by the audience. For him, the metamorphosis did not take place. To cross from the human to the animal or, in the other direction, to mate with the Fairy Queen, is all one. Fairies and monsters coexist happily within his spacious, not to say vacant, mind. Bottom's imagination is, if any thing, *too* inclusive and encompassing. It recognizes no distinctions. It glances from heaven to earth, from earth to heaven. It stands in complete opposition to Theseus' imagination, which the play shows to be limited and delimiting. Such an oblivion makes Bottom comic in all the usual ways. It enables him to ask, not for a drink of ale but for a "bottle of hay. Good hay, sweet hay, hath no fellow" (IV.i.34-5), and to admit ruefully, "I am marvail's hairy about the face; and I am such a tender ass, if my hair do but tickle me, I must scratch" (IV.i.25-7). It's not a bad life at all, once you get used to it.

Puck explains to Oberon that "My mistress with a monster is in love," that "An ass's nole I fixed on his head," that the frightened mechanicals scattered like "russet-pated choughs, many in sort, / Rising and cawing at the gun's report" (III.ii.6, 17, 21-2). This lively description proceeds through its own comparative transformations to an account of how the fleeing mechanicals could transform a bush into a bear:

> Their sense thus weak, lost with their fears thus strong,
> Made senseless things begin to do them wrong;
> For briers and thorns at their apparel snatch;
> Some sleeves, some hats, from yielders all things catch.
> (III.ii.27-30)

Puck concludes that he "left sweet Pyramus translated there" (l. 32). It is interesting that Puck refers to Bottom throughout this description only as "Pyramus," and at one point as "my mimic" (III.ii.19), as if the mimetic transformation had indeed succeeded. Clearly two kinds of comparable impersonation are linked together. (I will return to the "mimic" implications later.)

151

Puck's description of Pyramus—"A lover that kills himself, most gallant, for love" (I.ii.24-5)—reemphasizes how "A paramour is," as Flute says, "God bless us, a thing of nought." Bottom's love story shows us how a lover may be, as the pun has it, either nothing ("nought") or sexually powerful ("naught"). If love is accompanied by, and in some cases inhibited by, a sense of loss, a crossing over into nothing, then "A lover that kills himself . . . for love" is the perfect tautological emblem of this ambivalent power; in a sense *every* lover kills himself for love. Such is the role Bottom plays for us, both as Pyramus and as himself, the transformed lover of the Fairy Queen. The hints of erotic encounter surrounding the young lovers in the forest become comic effusions in the play-within-the-play ("My cherry lips have often kissed thy stones"—V.i.190), but we need only recall *Romeo and Juliet*'s darkly rich eroticism to remember how compulsive a theme sexual death was for Shakespeare at this time.

At the exact moment that Pyramus and Thisby, in the rehearsal, are to meet in the tomb for their assignation, Shakespeare has Puck transform Bottom into an ass. The timing is impeccable. The lovers' consummation in the rehearsal of the play-within, which is interrupted by one animal, the Lion, is itself interrupted by another animal, the ass. Meanwhile, Bottom and Titania apparently consummate *their* "marriage" off-stage, comically grotesque though it sounds, in contrast to Pyramus and Thisby, but also in anticipation of the various human marriages which are to occur in the play, and after its end in the real audience. Titania's language, bidding the fairies take Bottom to her bower, is most suggestive:

> The moon methinks looks with a wat'ry eye;
> And when she weeps, weeps every little flower,
> Lamenting some enforced chastity.
> Tie up my lover's tongue, bring him silently.
> (III.i.198-201)

I find this last line explicit: Titania is tired of Bottom's voice, and wants him now to perform. The personification of the moon here seems to work in two directions. If "enforced" means "violated," then the moon mourns the loss of chastity, but I cannot see how mourning such a loss is appropriate to Titania's situation. If "enforced" means chastity "forced upon" someone, then the moon laments that sexual completion has not occurred; this reading fits the eager Titania's desires more closely. Moreover, it reminds us that marriage *does* mean sexual completion (otherwise the marriage is not legally enforced). The rigidity of the law in Act One, as Theseus articulates it to Hermia, is anti-natural, even inhuman; he asks her

> Whether, if you yield not to your father's choice,
> You can endure the livery of a nun,
> For aye to be in shady cloister mewed,
> To live a barren sister all your life,
> Chanting faint hymns to the cold fruitless moon.
>
> (I.i.69-73)

To be "mewed" up, to be "barren" or "fruitless," is obviously life-denying. The moon here, as in Titania's speech, is "fruitless" if chastity is *not* "enforced." To live forever only as a "sister" is a denial of the process of nature, and an impossible attempt to render stasis permanent, when all the energies of life press for transformation.

Theseus continues the threat to Hermia in a contradictory and somewhat self-serving manner:

> Thrice-blessed they that master so their blood,
> To undergo such maiden pilgrimage;
> But earthlier happy is the rose distilled,
> Than that which, withering on the virgin thorn,
> Grows, lives, and dies in single blessedness.
>
> (I.i.74-8)

In describing sexual completion in marriage, Theseus must resort to a metaphor of transformation: the "rose distilled," a flower deflowered into a perfume. Theseus tries to have it both ways throughout, separating heaven and earth and the kinds of happiness each offers, but suggesting how truly happy each state is. Enforced chastity is "thrice-blessed" on the one

153

hand, but "withering on the virgin thorn" on the other hand, though even here it is, paradoxically, a "single blessedness." This may be Theseus' view, but it is not Shakespeare's. Everything in the play, human and non-human alike, moves toward "marriage" in every sense.

As we saw in *The Taming of the Shrew* and *Twelfth Night*, marriage is a metamorphosis, signifying both a loss and a gain. In *Twelfth Night*, the prospect was enthralling, once the stunning "natural perspective" was properly viewed. In *A Midsummer Night's Dream*, however, Shakespeare makes marriage seem more threatening, more loss than gain, attended now by a grotesquely comic animal monstrosity. For both man and woman, the loss of self, of human shape, becomes a primary though temporary fear; for women, the loss is a double one, for the physical boundary between the virgin and the wife will also be broken. *A Midsummer Night's Dream* confronts the audience with "human" characters led to the edge of such boundaries, and with "mythical" or fantastical characters who have already crossed over (who are themselves a crossing over). Bottom experiences literal transformation because it is in part a correlative to, in part the cause of, the sexual metamorphosis he enjoys.

A Midsummer Night's Dream must be seen in part as a play about, and celebrating, marriage, as we all know, but I think also as simultaneously an *exorcism* of the fears attendant on marriage.[8] Bottom's sexual encounter with Titania figures the extremity of carnal attraction, even as it burlesques the elevated language of Petrarchan eros. But what might seem solemn or even frightening turns out to be hugely comic. Beauty and the Beast take to one another quite easily. The morning after finds Titania and Bottom replete: he orders a bottle of hay, she wreathes roses in his hair and kisses his "fair large ears." As they fall asleep once more, she sends the fairies away and winds him in her arms, employing metaphors of embraces between species:

> So doth the woodbine the sweet honeysuckle
> Gently entwist; the female ivy so

Enrings the barky fingers of the elm.
O, how I love thee! How I dote on thee!
(IV.i.43-6)

This is about as explicit as a Fairy Queen can get, and the "dote" is an iterated verbal link to the rest of the lovers in the play. In the next moment Oberon says, "Her dotage now I do begin to pity" (l. 48), and he orders Puck to "take this transformed scalp / From off the head of this Athenian swain" (ll. 65-6).

When Bottom awakens from his "dream," he is still in the rehearsal of the play-within and in mid-dalliance: "When my cue comes, call me, and I will answer. My next is, 'Most fair Pyramus' " (l. 201-2). He soon recalls what he has been and whom he has been with, though he finds himself unable to articulate the mysteries he has experienced; even an approach to the ineffable triggers a comically confused synesthesia, itself a transmutation of a Biblical passage (I Corinthians II.9):

> I have had a most rare vision. I have had a dream, past the wit of man to say what dream it was. Man is but an ass, if he go about to expound this dream. . . . The eye of man hath not heard, the ear of man hath not seen, man's hand is not able to taste, his tongue to conceive, nor his heart to report, what my dream was. I will get Peter Quince to write a ballet of this dream. It shall be called "Bottom's Dream," because it hath no bottom; and I will sing it in the latter end of a play, before the Duke. Peradventure to make it the more gracious, I shall sing it at her death. (IV.i.205-19)

His ballad accounting for his "vision" will find a place in the play-within, sung at Thisby's death. It is curious how frequently Bottom's experiences are made to coincide with those of Pyramus.

Bottom's transformation, though shocking, is not frightening—exactly the point for the lovers, and the audience, to recognize. To change is strange, but not to be feared. Jan Kott has argued this point in a more extreme way:

The slender, tender, and lyrical Titania longs for animal love. Puck and Oberon call the transformed Bottom a monster. The frail and sweet Titania drags the monster to bed, almost by force. This is the lover she wanted and dreamed of; only she never wanted to admit it, even to herself. The sleep frees her from inhibitions. The monstrous ass is being raped by the poetic Titania, while she still keeps on chattering about flowers. . . . Of all the characters in the play Titania enters to the fullest extent the dark sphere of sex where there is no more beauty and ugliness; there is only infatuation and liberation.[9]

Though it might be argued that this darker view reflects some subconscious fear in the audience's psyche, the evidence of the play, and of most reactions to it, suggests something much less than "ugliness" and more like "shocking," "amusing," or even "arousing." Kott argues that "the love scenes between Titania and the ass must seem at the same time real and unreal, fascinating and repulsive. They are to rouse rapture and disgust, terror and abhorrence. They should seem at once strange and fearful"; but this represents the *idea* of animal union rather than what Shakespeare actually gives us, which is fascinating indeed but not, given that it is still bully Bottom (and only his head is changed), repulsive or disgusting. On the contrary, Bottom's unwitting sexual luck is refreshing; if there is a victim, it is Titania, who has found her innocent and inexperienced male changeling swapped for something entirely contrary—in effect, an older, far more potent kind of changeling.

The undoing of metamorphosis, the return to the waking world, requires the countervailing force of "Dian's bud o'er Cupid's flower" (IV.i.74). One does not simply cancel out the other. Instead, an equilibrium, as in marriage itself, is established. The metamorphic return coincides with the incipient marriages of the humans and the restored marriage of Oberon and Titania, but it is more than just concord from discord. If

156

love causes metamorphosis, then marriage completes it. With Titania returned and Bottom changed back, Oberon's speech to his Fairy Queen marks more than a perfunctory wrap-up, since marriage has been the focus throughout:

> Now thou and I are new in amity,
> And will tomorrow midnight solemnly
> Dance in Duke Theseus' house triumphantly,
> And bless it to all fair prosperity.
> There shall the pairs of faithful lovers be
> Wedded, with Theseus, all in jollity.
>   (IV.i.88-93)

When Bottom returns to his fellow mechanicals, he declines (after some confusion) to speak of his vision, though he alone, of all the human beings in the woods, recalls that he has had a "vision" (as opposed to a mere "dream," as Garber and Kermode point out[10]), and that it was beyond explanation. Only Bottom experiences metamorphosis, finally, by *remembering* it, though he was unaware of it at the time; the four lovers shrug it off like a hangover.

PYRAMUS AND THISBY

The theme of the monstrous comes to the surface in the mechanicals' play immediately. To begin with, the alternative plays mentioned by Philostrate have titles suggestive of the monstrous though they are also comic: "The battle with the Centaurs, to be sung / By an Athenian eunuch to the harp" (V.i.44-5). The virile centaurs, half-men, half-horses, are balanced by the eunuch, half-man half-no-man. To have the impotent relate a story of brute licentiousness makes a telling and ironic emblem of the poet's narrative powers. The second offering, "The riot of the tipsy Bacchanals, / Tearing the Thracian singer in their rage" (ll. 48-9), would give us the killing of the father of poets, Orpheus, by the drunken Bacchanals—in effect, what the mechanicals do in *their* play. The third alternative is "The thrice three Muses mourning for the death / Of Learning, late deceased in beggary" (ll. 52-3), which Theseus believes to be "some satire, keen and critical." What links these titles and topics together, among other things, is that each is about death: the centaurs are slaughtered, Orpheus is murdered, and "Learning" dies of malnutrition and poverty. Small wonder, incidentally, that Theseus doesn't want to hear the battle with the centaurs ("We'll none of that"), for (in Ovid) Theseus figures prominently in the drunken riot that occurs—where else?—at a wedding feast for Pirithous and Hippodame. The description of the battle runs on for hundreds of lines—shattered teeth, gaping wounds, bloody vomit, gouged eyeballs, hardly the sort of thing appropriate for Theseus' wedding, but then it wasn't exactly right for Pirithous' either. In the battle, Theseus saves the bride from rape by the centaurs: "he thrust way such as preast / About the bryde, and tooke her from them freating sore thereat" (*Met*, XII.259-60).

The coincidence of marriage, sex, and violence with the characters in this play has become routine. These elements are not in the foreground of the play, I hasten to add, and certainly not Jan Kott's foreground, but they contribute to the ominous backdrop behind this otherwise genial comedy. The impressive figures of Theseus and Hippolyta, for another example, who speak so calmly of reason and imagination, are revealed to have rather shady pasts. Even Titania and Oberon have been romantically linked with their human counterparts: Titania accuses Oberon of past encounters with "the bouncing Amazon, / Your buskined mistress and your warrior love," while Oberon rebukes her for her past dalliance with Theseus:

> Didst not thou lead him through the glimmering night
> From Perigenia, whom he ravished?
> And make him with Aegles break his faith,
> With Ariadne and Antiopa?
>> (II.i.70-1, 77-80)

158

Titania dismisses this accusation as "the forgeries of jealousy," but they are, of course, the forgeries of Plutarch. Neither virginity nor chastity is to be found among the "adults" of the play; but as the one couple's marriage is restored and the other's anticipated, the various sexual transgressions are being regulated and harnessed. As the glimmering night of the play continues, the forces of erotic desire are being recognized, released, and civilized.

Which brings us to "A tedious brief scene of young Pyramus / And his love Thisby; very tragical mirth" (V.i.56-7). Theseus is struck by the obvious oxymoron, but what strikes me is the ironic, unexpected appropriateness of this play to a *marriage* ceremony: violence, sexual conflict, death. The mechanicals' play is to be performed in a special time: *after* the wedding but *before* the consummation, a moment poised between spiritual achievement and physical completion. The anxieties of such a time—"the anguish of a torturing hour" (l. 37) as Theseus jokingly calls it—mark the perfect locus for a play. The space between desire and fulfillment, becoming and being, the spiritual and the physical, provides the natural location for metamorphosis as well.

This space in between also provides a local habitation for the monstrous, and "Pyramus and Thisby" will offer us something comparable to the play of the centaurs. The mechanicals' play is, to state the obvious, about sex and death—that is to say, two aspects of the same phenomenon, the loss of identity. The physical loss of virginity heralds the much greater loss of an innocent self, but also the gain of a fuller and richer self through marriage. The mechanicals' play adumbrates what is about to occur for all the newly wedded couples, in the play that surrounds them and in the real audience that watches. Done lightly and paradoxically, of course. It provokes a reaction in its onstage audience exactly the opposite of what its subject might portend. As Philostrate tells Theseus:

> And tragical, my noble lord, it is,
> For Pyramus therein doth kill himself.

Which, when I saw rehearsed, I must confess,
Made mine eyes water; but more merry tears
The passion of loud laughter never shed.
(ll. 66-70)

Laughing at death offers a good way "to ease the anguish of a torturing hour," however ironically that antidote is meant. It can remain comic just because the actual boundary is not breached.

The inner play itself begins with a verbal transformation— a dislocation of punctuation and therefore of meaning. The Prologue doth not stand upon points:

If we offend, it is with our good will,
    That you should think, we come not to offend,
But with good will. To show our simple skill,
    That is the true beginning of our end.
(ll. 108-11)

Verbally, the Prologue transgresses the periodic boundaries of the sentence. "Like a tangled chain; nothing impaired, but all disordered," it anticipates the other transformations yet to come, while the reference to disorder in normality suggests also a typical dream logic; under the pressure of metamorphosis, even words begin to lose their shapes and shift identity.

As presented, the story of Pyramus and Thisby is reduced entirely to the lovers' rendezvous and death in the tomb: the bare essentials. The prominent features of the play-within are the murderous Lion "with bloody mouth" and the double suicide with "bloody blameful blade." Here again the monstrous intervenes to thwart sexual completion. Throughout the scene, comic eroticism seasons the mechanicals' malapropisms and mimetic failures, as in Thisby's unfortunate address:

O wall, full often hast thou heard my moans,
For parting my fair Pyramus and me!
My cherry lips have often kissed thy stones,
Thy stones with lime and hair knit up in thee.

. . . .
I kiss the wall's hole, not your lips at all.
(ll. 188-91, 201)

As the lovers head for the tomb, we find that their goal—to avoid the barrier which keeps them separate, or different—on the contrary leads directly to violence and death as well as (or instead of) sex. We are close here to the analysis of culture suggested by Rene Girard: the collapse of difference leads to violence.[11] The collapse of boundaries generally signifies transformation, as we have seen; when lovers try to become one rather than two, strange energies are unleashed. Girard would probably argue that these energies are inevitably violent in result, since they eliminate difference, but in *A Midsummer Night's Dream* the violence is itself deflected and transformed.

As the consummation in the play-within nears, Lion appears on stage, announcing his real identity as Snug, telling the ladies not to be afraid. This is the second time a character in *A Midsummer Night's Dream* has donned an animal's head, but this time Shakespeare makes much of the disguise's non-mimetic qualities. In one sense, this theme is a commentary on how Shakespeare himself has gone about creating the fairies, or any character, and how the audience should apprehend them. But in another sense Snug's subversion of the "reality" of the role, his fear that its verisimilitude may be too great, serves in fact to call greater attention to the centrality of Lion's part. Bottom had earlier seen the dramatic potential of the role: "I will aggravate my voice so that I will roar you as gently as any sucking dove; I will roar you an 'twere any nightingale" (I.ii.81-3). Lion might become anything, then, even a bird. But the key to Snug's performance is that the monster is clearly and explicitly also a man: "Then know that I, as Snug the joiner, am / A lion fell" (V.i.222-3). Victor Turner's work again provides a useful commentary:

Put a man's head on a lion's body and you think about the human head in the abstract. Perhaps it becomes for you, as a member of a given culture and with the appropriate guidance, an emblem of chieftainship; or it may be explained as representing the soul as against the body; or intellect as contrasted with brute force, or innumerable other things . . . the relation between man and lion, empirical and metaphorical, may be speculated upon. . . .[12]

Shakespeare seems less interested in "heads and headship" than he is in the relation between man and any beast. Snug-Lion shows us the impossibility of a man becoming a beast; Bottom-ass shows us the apparent fact of a man becoming a beast. For Bottom, the transformation is deceptively simple, since he was always an ass; for Snug the leap to the king of beasts is much greater, and he fails spectacularly.

As Turner suggests, these two men-beasts enfranchise speculation: they suggest, for one thing, the extremes of transformation. The greater effectiveness in metamorphosis seems achieved by the less conscious, more obtuse Bottom, whereas the cautious Snug achieves little in his too-elaborate self-consciousness. The distinction between the two provokes other questions about acting, for Snug's self-consciousness about roles and realism, contrary to the usual formula, produces nothing in the way of mimetic transformation, yet Bottom, an equally poor actor, is suddenly taken up and altered, mostly by chance—that is, by Puck, the spirit of metamorphosis.

Robin Starveling similarly reassures us, with the same good-natured but complete ineffectualness, that "Myself the man i'th' moon do seem to be" (l. 243), as if even he can't believe it. If he *did* seem it, he wouldn't have to identify his role. Snout, however, senses that the audience might have to do some of the imaginative work themselves:

> In this same interlude it doth befall
> That I, one Snout by name, present a wall;
> And such a wall, as I would have you think,
> That had in it a crannied hole or chink.
>
> (ll. 155-8)

The mechanicals, ironically, violate the boundary between pretended role and self because they fear that the audience will not be able to see difference, but this transgression brings about no transformation at all. No greater comic emblem of boundaries could exist than their representation of a wall, "that vile Wall which did these lovers sunder" (l. 132), as if Shakespeare found even the idea of a real boundary laughable.

Lion's action is the turning point of the play-within, and, as Pyramus remarkably describes it, a comic emblem of human/animal sexual ferocity:

> O wherefore, Nature, didst thou lions frame?
> Since lion vile hath here deflow'red my dear.
> (ll. 289-90)

Defloration is, as I have been suggesting, one of the play's main subjects, from the impending marriages, through Puck's plucking of the "love-in-idleness" or pansy, to Pyramus' astonishing malapropism here (presumably for "devoured," which is almost as suggestive). The flower Puck is to pick has already received a suggestive blow: struck by "young Cupid's fiery shaft" (II.i.161) which missed its original virginal target, the pansy itself is already a deflowered flower.

Desire, attempted union, defloration, death: the suggestions are ominous in the extreme, but they are also there to be exorcized, to be transformed and rendered harmless. A final example of this comic detoxification can be seen in the lovers' oaths to one another:

> PYRAMUS. . . . I am thy lover's grace;
>   And, like Limander, am I trusty still.
> THISBY. And I like Helen, till the Fates me kill.
> PYRAMUS. Not Shafalus to Procrus was so true.
> THISBY. As Shafalus to Procrus, I to you.
> (V.i.195-9)

All these allusions, indeed the story of Pyramus and Thisby itself, are spectacularly violent and presumably inappropriate for a pre-consummation play. Each lover mentioned (except

Cephalus) dies, by accident or suicide. Each pair of lovers, moreover, represents a different stage of sexual completion: Pyramus and Thisby never sexually unite, but "die" together; Hero and Leander, if that is who "Helen" and "Limander" are, die after their union; and Cephalus and Procris were married, but jealousy destroyed them. Thus the three pairs of lovers represent courtship, seduction, marriage, and jealousy. The only thing left is death, and they find that as well.

Beyond death, though, these legendary lovers, whatever their stage of sexual love, also experience metamorphosis. The point is worth lingering over. Marlowe's poem, for example, ends with Hero and Leander awakening after a night of pleasure, long before the drowning, but Chapman's continuation completes the full myth through their death and transfiguration. Taking pity on the dead lovers, according to Chapman, Neptune

> for pity in his arms did take them,
> Flung them into the air, and did awake them
> Like two sweet birds, surnamed th'Acanthides,
> Which we call thistle-warps, that near no seas
> Dare ever come, but still in couples fly,
> And feed on thistle-tops, to testify
> The hardness of their first life in their last:
> The first in thorns of love, and sorrows past.[13]

Ovid's story of Cephalus and Procris includes metamorphosis in the beginning, when the long-absent Cephalus tries to test the honor of his wife:

The Morning fooding this my feare, to further my device,
My shape (which thing me thought I felt) had altered with a
    trice.
By meanes whereof anon unknowne to Pallas towne I came,
And entred so my house.
    (*Met*, VII.932-5)

He thus manages the paradox of seducing his own wife, in words at least, but the two come back together and live happily for many years. Finally Procris, now jealous of Cephalus, spies on him and is unwittingly killed by her husband with the hunting javelin she had given him: Procris in fact died as the result of a pun, thinking Cephalus had called a lover when he beckoned "Aura," the wind.

And what of our chief examples, Pyramus and Thisby? It is rarely if ever observed that the mechanicals, and Shakespeare, halt the story long before Ovid does—before another metamorphosis occurs—and even suppress part of it. Thus when Pyramus kills himself in Ovid, his heart pumps blood in the air, which falls on the white mulberry tree (it marks their meeting place):

The leaves that were upon the tree besprinckled with his blood
Were died blacke. The roote also bestained as it stoode,
A deepe darke purple colour straight upon the Berries cast.
(*Met,* IV.150-2)

When Thisby finds the stained tree and her lover's corpse, she prays that after her suicide the tree might "of this same slaughter holde the sicker signes for ay" and they might lie in a common tomb:

Hir prayer with the Gods and with their Parentes tooke effect.
For when the frute is throughly ripe, the Berrie is bespect
With colour tending to a blacke. And that which after fire
Remained, rested in one Tumbe as Thisbe did desire.
(*Met,* IV.193, 198-201)

So the story of Pyramus and Thisby in Ovid ends with yet another symbolic deflowering, their moment of death achieving a transformation even while they were denied the death they preferred. That the mechanicals' play should end before this moment, that the three lovers' stories invoked should include death and transformation, suggests that Shakespeare has carefully crafted an incompleteness. Something like the mulberry-bush transformation, in fact, is described much earlier in the play, when Oberon relates the fall of "young Cupid's fiery shaft":

It fell upon a little western flower,
Before milk-white, now purple with love's wound,
And maidens call it love-in-idleness.
(II.i.166-8)

Why not include the transformational powers of Pyramus and
Thisby in the play-within, since the entire play is otherwise
filled with examples of such powers? And why invoke these
other lovers in particular? Perhaps one answer is that the
wedding party that constitutes the onstage, and perhaps offstage, audience is also suspended in incompletion. Indeed, they
leave the stage to perform their own "death," to turn crimson
the white sheets of the wedding beds, to open love's wound
themselves. As the audience completes Ovid's story in their
memories, the lovers complete it, and transform it, in their
offstage rites.

Shakespeare's resistance to completing the Ovidian metamorphoses, especially in "Pyramus and Thisby," may be linked
with the recurrent unawareness of the metamorphosed characters in this play. The more self-conscious the human beings,
the less believable their changes—Snug is typical. The corollary is that the more obvious the change, the less aware of
it—so Bottom and the four lovers. Since these court characters
are unaware of their own transformations, they are not allowed to have metamorphosis presented to them in such a
clear and explicit manner as Ovid's story would indicate.
Whatever the cause, the result is a play which frequently investigates the representation of metamorphosis on the stage.
Shakespeare has always had available the Italian-Lylyan mode
of representation: metamorphosis may be "actually" shown
by means of trick properties—magic trees, exploding fountains, ass's ears that fall off at a touch.[14] Shakespeare says, in
effect, if you want *that* kind of metamorphosis, here it is:
Bottom becomes an ass. Yet the joke is that this change makes
no essential difference at all to Bottom, though the play which
contains Bottom contains any number of more powerful alternative transformations. In his most openly Ovidian play,
then, Shakespeare halts his equally Ovidian play-within-the-

play just before representing a second Ovidian metamorphosis. The point is that that kind of representation will no longer succeed *on the stage*. It pretends to a kind of verisimilitude which Lion and Moonshine have already comically discredited.

The threat of sexuality and violence in the play is also left incomplete; it is present only to be transcended, or transformed, as an example to those in the audience, particularly those risking themselves in love and marriage. Between desire and completion lies a shadow; but even death ought to be welcomed, for it is only a metamorphosis.

THE FAIRIES

Puck's final benediction, on the house of Theseus, on the offstage lovers consummating their marriages, and implicitly on the appropriate members of the audience, gathers together all the play's fears and hopes. His broom will sweep away more than the dust behind the door; Lion and Moonshine are transformed by art into the memory of a ballad:

> Now the hungry lion roars,
>   And the wolf behowls the moon;
> Whilst the heavy plowman snores,
>   All with weary task fordone.
> Now the wasted brands do glow,
>   Whilst the screech owl, screeching loud,
> Puts the wretch that lies in woe
>   In remembrance of a shroud.
> Now it is the time of night,
>   That the graves, all gaping wide,
> Every one lets forth his sprite,
>   In the churchway paths to glide:
> And we fairies, that do run
>   By the triple Hecate's team,
> From the presence of the sun,
>   Following darkness like a dream,

Now are frolic. Not a mouse
Shall disturb this hallowed house:
I am sent, with broom, before,
To sweep the dust behind the door.
(V.i.370-89)

Whatever wretches lie in woe offstage, presumably the three
newly married couples are not at the moment in remembrance
of a shroud but in the sheets of another kind of death. "Now
it is the time of night" when not only spirits, but lions, wolves,
owls, and mice run free. The graves gape wide, but lovers
meet. The wasted brands glow dimly here, but stronger fires
kindle elsewhere. Included in the fairies' blessing of the human
lovers are the results of this night's procreation on each "bride-
bed." No monsters will result:

And the issue there create
Ever shall be fortunate.
So shall all the couples three
Ever true in loving be;
And the blots of Nature's hand
Shall not in their issue stand.
Never mole, harelip, nor scar,
Nor mark prodigious, such as are
Despised in nativity,
Shall upon their children be.
(ll. 404-13)

No disfigurement, no failure or recriminations or punishment,
and therefore no guilt. All the lovers will "in safety rest" with
"sweet peace." The monstrous will be banished, or at least
be tamed and domesticated; asses and lions will be only men.
Eunuchs will not be allowed in to speak of centaurs. Defloration, we see, leads not only to death but to new life.

The blessing by the fairies may come as a surprise to some
members of the audience, for there has been something ambiguous, if not quite sinister, about them.[15] Their condescen-
sion towards humans, finding mortals to be fools or worse,

is fully justified but occasionally unsettling. But this play eventually transforms everything threatening into something good, every bear back into a bush. The fairies are the chief agents of transformation in this play, just as they were considered masters of shape-shifting in folklore. Skeptics existed, of course. Reginald Scot specifically rejected one fairy by name:

> And know you this by the waie, that heretofore Robin goodfellow, and Hob gobblin were as terrible, and also as credible to the people, as hags and witches be now: and in time to come, a witch will be as much derided and contemned, and as plainlie perceived, as the illusion and knaverie of Robin goodfellow.[16]

Some Elizabethans argued that fairies were really demons; others defended them against this charge. Disputes existed over how many of the four elements they were composed of. But their metamorphic powers are stressed everywhere.

Our introduction to the fairies in *A Midsummer Night's Dream* stresses their shape-shifting powers. The unnamed fairy answers Puck's "Whither wander you" with a catalogue of the four elements in which he may appear:

> Over hill, over dale,
>   Thorough bush, thorough brier,
> Over park, over pale,
>   Thorough flood, thorough fire,
> I do wander everywhere,
> Swifter than the moon's sphere.
>   (II.i.2-7)

One famous exchange mentions little else but Puck's sportive and whimsical powers of metamorphosis, his ability to "Skim milk, and sometimes labor in the quern, / And bootless make the breathless housewife churn, / And sometime make the drink to bear no barm, / Mislead night wanderers, laughing at their harm." Puck *may* "do their work, and they shall have good luck," but his metamorphic powers are usually more mischievous:

I jest to Oberon, and make him smile,
When I a fat and bean-fed horse beguile,
Neighing in likeness of a filly foal:
And sometime lurk I in a gossip's bowl,
In very likeness of a roasted crab;
And when she drinks, against her lips I bob
And on her withered dewlap pour the ale.
The wisest aunt, telling the saddest tale,
Sometime for three-foot stool mistaketh me;
Then slip I from her bum, down topples she,
And "tailor" cries, and falls into a cough;
And then the whole quire hold their hips and laugh,
And waxen in their mirth, and neeze, and swear
A merrier hour was never wasted there.

(II.i.34-57)

It has often been noted that in this description the fairies are purely creations of the popular imagination, personified "causes" of minor natural disorders. Their metamorphic powers, however, remain considerable. Whether a filly foal, a roasted crab, or a three-foot stool, Puck can go anywhere, be anything, do what he pleases. The exercise of his powers makes merely for comedy, though, as we see even the misled "night wanderers" pass unharmed. The variety of Puck's names—Puck, Hobgoblin, Robin Goodfellow—also testifies to the number of his transformations.[17]

Oberon and Titania are more fixed in their shapes during the play, though Titania recalls Oberon's shifty past:

I know
When thou hast stolen away from fairy land
And in the shape of Corin sat all day,
Playing on pipes of corn, and versing love
To amorous Phillida.
(II.i.64-8)

Their quarrel has created major alterations in nature: the boundaries of the sea have vanished, the fold stands empty in the drowned field, mazes are undistinguishable. Nothing can be identified anymore because its shape has dissolved. The moon, chief emblem of mutability, oversees it all. "The seasons alter" and "the spring, the summer, / The childing autumn, angry winter, change / Their wonted liveries." The "mazed world," looking on at the changes, "now knows not which is which" (II.i.107-14), for everything is and is not. A world in universal and ungoverned flux is a frightening place: the dark side of metamorphosis is always chaos. But in a comedy, transformation will finally be positive, an equilibrium will be achieved, new boundaries erected.

The fairies may themselves become animals or monsters, but no such creatures shall afflict them in turn. When Titania sleeps, her attendants try to guard her:

> FIRST FAIRY. You spotted snakes with double tongue,
> Thorny hedgehogs, be not seen;
> Newts and blindworms, do no wrong,
> Come not near our Fairy Queen.
> CHORUS. Philomele, with melody
> Sing in our sweet lullaby;
> Lulla, lulla, lullaby, lulla, lulla, lullaby;
> Never harm
> Nor spell nor charm,
> Come our lovely lady nigh;
> So, good night, with lullaby.
> FIRST FAIRY. Weaving spiders, come not here;
> Hence, you long-legged spinners, hence!
> Beetles black, approach not near;
> Worm nor snail, do no offense.
> (II.ii.9-23)

The *scale* of the threats has been reduced to the same size as the fairies here—newts, not lions; beetles, not asses—though one wonders how appropriate a voice is that of Philomela, the victim of Tereus's uncontrollable lust (*Met*, VI.542ff). Titania is not sufficiently protected, in any event; after Oberon squeezes the flower on her eyes, she will at least be forced to *see* the monstrous and to fall in love with it. Her experience serves as a model (or a nightmare) for the other women in the play:

> Be it ounce, or cat, or bear,
> Pard, or boar with bristled hair,
> In thy eye that shall appear
> When thou wak'st, it is thy dear.
> Wake when some vile thing is near.
> (II.ll.30-4)

Some women might fear just the opposite on their wedding nights, of course, for their "dear" might, at the crucial moment, seem to be rather a "boar with bristled hair," a "vile thing." When Titania awakens, we recognize the extent of her psychological transformation—indeed, it seems more profound than Bottom's physical one. The mockery of love's transforming powers—"So is mine eye enthralled to thy shape" (III.i.138)—does not finally undermine our sense of its power, but the sheer foolishness and impotence of the metamorph have also been tellingly revealed.

Titania's edenic interlude—or her "dotage" as Oberon calls it—comes to an end once she has released "her changeling child" (IV.i.60) to Oberon. This unseen but suggestive changeling, the named vessel of the metamorphic, figures as one of the chief mysteries of the play. Whether the child represents some member of an actual audience or some esoteric metaphysical idea, he remains both an emblem of innocence and a disputed sexual object as well. Oberon wants him for his "henchman" (II.i.121) or page; Titania refuses because of her responsibility to the child's mother ("a vot'ress of my order"—l. 123). Since the dispute concerns possession, its terms parallel those of the other plots of the play, but the means of gaining the child—metamorphosis, animal sexuality—seem out of all proportion to the object desired, unless the changeling signifies something more than itself. This combination of innocence and desirability offers us a minor version of the young virgins about to marry, poised between two complex worlds, neither of which can exist without the other.

If Oberon and Titania are the fairies as lovers, comparable in their transformation to the humans, Puck exemplifies the spirit of metamorphosis for its own sake. Whether he is putting a girdle around the earth in forty minutes or turning into a three-foot stool, whether he is large or small, his function in the play is principally to move and to change. That he juices the wrong eyes is only to be expected. He is indifferent if "some true love turned, and not a false turned true" (III.ii.91) because "those things do best please me / That befall preposterously" (III.ii.120-1). Although it is not his intention, harm sometimes follows from his powers, and anyway "so far am I glad it so did sort, / As this their jangling I esteem a sport" (III.ii.352-3). The main thing is that *some* love has "turned."

Puck is most in his element when carrying out Oberon's explicit instructions in the third act:

> . . . [O]vercast the night.
> The starry welkin cover thou anon
> With drooping fog, as black as Acheron;
> And lead these testy rivals so astray,
> As one come not within another's way.
> Like to Lysander sometime frame thy tongue,
> Then stir Demetrius up with bitter wrong;
> And sometime rail thou like Demetrius.
>   (III.ii.355-62)

The rest of this scene shows the greatness of Puck's ventriloquism and his ability to "mislead night wanderers, laughing at their harm" as the will-o-the-wisp. His verbal transformations are as effective as his physical ones.

Oberon's instructions are interesting for what they specify. Puck is instructed to speak first "like to Lysander" and sometime "like Demetrius." The "like" sounds unnecessarily modest. Puck after all has the power actually to *become* anything. Yet even he has earlier described his powers as in part mimetic:

he deceives a horse by neighing "in likeness of a filly foal" or appears "in very likeness of a roasted crab" or is mistaken for a three-foot stool. His acting powers, as a species of metamorphosis, are thus indistinguishable from his other transformative capabilities.

The mimetic impulse underlies many of the changes in the play. The mime or mimic must attempt to "become" someone or something else, to speak in *vox*, even while the full achievement of mimesis would negate our being able to see it. The best mimesis is not the facsimile but the similitude which is so close but also, and always, different—not sameness but similarity. The edge of difference between object and mimic is critically important. Thus Snug naively feels the need to remind us that a man is a lion but also a man. The audience has no trouble bridging that gap, but also more importantly it *needs* that gap. The art is in the kind of gap, not the lack of measured distance. In *A Midsummer Night's Dream* the gaps are either naive, as in the mechanicals' play, or artful, as in Puck's ability to imitate. Bottom simply wishes to become everything—Pyramus, Thisby, lover, tyrant, wandering knight, Lion, even ass—and so remains only himself; no limits that *he* is aware of constrain him. Puck is by contrast more selective, or at least more responsive to Oberon's commands. Yet when Puck has seen a play, even a rehearsal, in progress, he cannot resist taking part: "What, a play toward! I'll be an auditor; / An actor too perhaps, if I see cause" (III.i.78-9). And in reporting his mischief to Oberon, Puck refers to Bottom as "my mimic": "Anon his Thisby must be answered, / And forth my mimic comes" (III.ii.18-19). Puck's term for Bottom is possessive, indicating his control of him, but it also seems reflexive, with Bottom as a mimic of Puck: a verbal doubling in a word that itself means a duplication. To think of these two characters in conjunction is to invoke hot ice and wondrous strange snow. But we might think of Bottom as playing a good-natured Caliban to Puck's Ariel (a comparison

which is often made); together they are the chief practitioners
of mimesis in the play.

Puck's famous epilogue, like Rosalind's and Feste's, exposes
the duplicity of metamorphosis a final time:

> If we shadows have offended,
> Think but this, and all is mended:
> That you have but slumb'red here,
> While these visions did appear.
> And this weak and idle theme,
> No more yielding but a dream,
> Gentles, do not reprehend:
> If you pardon, we will mend.
> And, as I am an honest Puck,
> If we have unearned luck
> Now to scape the serpent's tongue,
> We will make amends ere long;
> Else the Puck a liar call:
> So, good night unto you all.
> Give me your hands, if we be friends,
> And Robin shall restore amends.
>
> (V.i.422-37)

The speech offers us both the actor and Puck, indistinguishable
but different, two in one, their metamorphic and mimetic
powers perfectly expressed at once. The speech begins, moreover, with the hypothetical "if," invoking it three more times
later in the speech; but these last three depend on the audience's ability to change and adjust, and its complicity in the
fiction. The chief encounter with the monstrous now is but
with "the serpent's tongue," the hissing of a dissatisfied audience; we have met the enemy and he is us, as the play has
been suggesting all along. Anyone who dismisses all this as a
dream, of course, is inert, incapable of transformation himself.[18] But calling Puck a liar may not be far from the mark;
most poets are, and most theatrical transformation requires
feigning.

THESEUS

The place of Theseus' famous speech in this reading of the play should now be clear.[19] Theseus reinterprets metamorphosis as merely the transformative delusions of a deranged imagination; we can imagine him agreeing with Reginald Scot about the witches and other bugbears. In some ways the play has proven Theseus right: the lover *does* often see "Helen's beauty in a brow of Egypt"; a bush *is* often "supposed" a bear. The audience however has also seen how a "suppose" can truly become a comic monster. Despite this partial accuracy, Theseus's facile distinctions between apprehend and comprehend, and his condescending vision of simple deception, represent a myopic anti-metamorphic belief. The loss is his, not ours. His description of the poet's role, however, is even wiser than he knows in some ways, and does memorably emphasize the creative while employing the now familiar terminology of transformation:

> as imagination bodies forth
> The forms of things unknown, the poet's pen
> Turns them to shapes, and gives to airy nothing
> A local habitation and a name.
> (V.i.14-17)

The poet is creator and master of metamorphosis. Beyond the wonderful ironies in Theseus's own situation—a walking "antique fable" if ever there was one—we can easily see how this passage expands to encompass much of the play. The verb "to turn" has become increasingly important as a metamorphic signal. Theseus' statement even distinguishes the poet from his implement: it is the "poet's pen," like a magic wand perhaps, that achieves all this. Denigrating and limited as this is, Theseus is nevertheless the first to call for "masques . . . dances . . . revels. . . . Is there no play[?]" (ll. 32, 36), and he proves a fairly knowledgeable audience, even telling the others that the mimetic gap must be recognized, accepted, and bridged by the audience rather than the players: "The best in this kind are but shadows; and the worst are no worse, if imagination amend them" (ll. 211-2). Even this skeptic recognizes the audience's necessary complicity in making metamorphosis.

The central concerns of metamorphosis include almost everything in *A Midsummer Night's Dream*: lovers, mechanicals, fairies. The monstrous seems to be a stage, temporal and dramatic, that must be passed through; where Pyramus and Thisby fail, the lovers, both onstage and off, will succeed. But they will succeed, in part, because of the examples of failure they have seen, because of the specimens of the monstrous which were released into the world and then recaptured. The movement to deflower seems inevitably to lead to or proceed from metamorphosis; it verges on chaos, and invokes some of our greatest fears. But undergoing such risk—the jaws of darkness and confusion—is part of being human. In *A Midsummer Night's Dream* Shakespeare recognizes that the deepest metamorphic rhythms of human nature require man's yielding to a dream.

Chapter Six ❧ Falstaff and Ford: Forming and Reforming

The Henriad

Hal's transformation from madcap prince to the "mirror of all Christian kings" (*H5*, 2Prol.6) forms the official plot of the Henriad, and suggests the darker side of change as loss. (We will examine Falstaff's metamorphosis into a comic monster in a moment.) Most of the transformations in the Henriad and *The Merry Wives of Windsor* fall under the heading of "formation" and "reformation," terms suggesting not only the education of a prince but also the reforming self-inventiveness of Falstaff and the reversal of Ford's deformation. Hal's great transformation is of course quite self-conscious, contrived and staged for a variety of political and psychological reasons. The contrast to the prince's reformation in *The Famous Victories,* one of Shakespeare's sources, is striking, for there and in other versions of the story something magical, even religious, seems to happen, as in the simpler Morality-play pattern of Youth or Manhood suddenly repenting. In *Henry IV, Part I,* Hal speaks of his coming "reformation" (*I,* I.ii.210), but only the timing of it is in doubt, its religious overtones drained off by the cunning. And yet Hal's way of "becoming" a king works as well as Rosalind's way of becoming Ganymede: it entails the assumption of a role with its own rhetoric and costume. Taking a cue from his father's story ("My presence, like a robe pontifical, / Ne'er seen but wond'red at"—*I*, III.ii.56-7), Hal vows to become the worthy prince through magical masking: "I will wear a garment all of blood, / And stain my favors in a bloody mask" (*I*, III.ii.135-6). Even earlier, Hal had donned a vizard of buckram (*I*, I.ii.177) to deceive Falstaff at Gad's Hill. In *Part II*, Hal seems to be trapped in the guise he had earlier chosen freely. Now the madcap prince longs to break through into transformation but is aware that he would be thought, as Poins says, "a most princely hypocrite" (*II*, II.ii.52) if he wept. Thus his first transformation in *Part II*, mirroring the one in *Part I*, is downward rather than upward, not the bloody mask but "two leathern jerkins and aprons," to appear with Poins as a drawer in order to spy on Falstaff; Hal is now wryly aware that there are all kinds of transformations, not all of them ennobling:

> From a god to a bull? A heavy descension!
> It was Jove's case. From a prince to a prentice?
> A low transformation! That shall be mine, for
> in everything the purpose must weigh with the folly.
> (II, II.ii.172-5)

Still, Hal will finally achieve his own willed transformation, showing "th' incredulous world / The noble change that I have purposed" (*II*, IV.v.153-4), for the desired end, it may be necessary for god to turn bull, prince to turn prentice. Hal accounts for his self-shaping by means of a protean sea-change:

> The tide of blood in me
> Hath proudly flowed in vanity till now,
> Now doth it turn and ebb back to the sea,
> Where it shall mingle with the state of floods
> And flow henceforth in formal majesty.
> (II, V.ii.129-33)

The flow upstream is a dead end, he implies, and now the royal self will be reformed and finally revealed. When he turns away Falstaff, Hal claims to have awakened forever from a dream and warns,

> Presume not that I am the thing I was,
> For God doth know, so shall the world perceive,
> That I have turned away my former self.
> (II, V.v.56-8)

Hal's claim to have achieved a total transformation, in which his former self is annihilated and the "is not" triumphs, sounds chilling. As Alvin Kernan has put it, "In the process of becoming a ruler his personal self, some essential 'I,' is lost forever as the man disappears into the role his work demands." [1] Such completeness is impossible, however, judging by what we have seen in the other plays. But Hal must assert its possibility in order to mark his break with the past, even as he requires Falstaff—of all people—to "reform" himself (II, V.v.68), as if *that* shape could be annihilated as well.

Many other metamorphic themes ring through the Henriad, from the "beastly shameless transformation" (I, I.i.44) done by the Welshwomen on the soldiers' corpses to the Archbishop of York's linguistic ability to "translate [himself] / Out of the speech of peace that bears such grace, / Into the harsh and boisterous tongue of war" (II, IV.i.47-9), while the other rebels are "Turning the word to sword and life to death" (II, IV.ii.10). The inescapable energies of change are most strikingly acknowledged, however, in Henry IV's reflection in *Part II* on the "book of fate," with its echoes of Pythagoras' speech in Book XV of the *Metamorphoses*.[2] The world, Henry's world, melts and dissolves:

> O God, that one might read the book of fate,
> And see the revolution of the times
> Make mountains level, and the continent,
> Weary of solid firmness, melt itself
> Into the sea! And other times to see
> The beachy girdle of the ocean
> Too wide for Neptune's hips. How chances, mocks,

And changes fill the cup of alteration
With divers liquors! O, if this were seen,
The happiest youth, viewing his progress through,
What perils past, what crosses to ensue,
Would shut the book, and sit him down and die.

(II, III.i.45-56)

"Cormorant devouring Time" (*LLL,* I.i.4), Ovid's *tempus edax rerum,* suddenly opens like an abyss beneath the kings and clowns, and the chaotic energy of total flux threatens. Even as Hal transforms himself into a king, the King bleakly envisions the world as infinite transformation.

If that is the dark side of change, as an infinite "alteration" which brings everything into question, then the light side (figuratively speaking) belongs to Falstaff, who throughout the Henriad and even *The Merry Wives of Windsor* proves that age cannot wither him ("they hate us youth"—*I,* II.ii.86) nor custom stale his infinite variety ("I am not only witty in myself, but the cause that wit is in other men"—*II,* I.ii.9-10). His own appetite is rarely cloyed. He serves in part as both parallel and comic contrast to Hal's clear-sighted self-transformation. An agent of transformation himself, a master of self-invention, Falstaff will nevertheless resist and mock all attempts to reform him. He will finally succumb, like the dutiful male protagonist of any comedy, to the blandishments of desire and be transformed by love into a tumescent buck. Like Bottom, he will temporarily turn into a comic monster, embodying for others the grotesqueries of desire.

❦

Falstaff has always been a resilient character, bouncing back to life when we least expect it, surfacing from drink or debauchery to reaffirm his unquenchable spirit, evading capture by sheriff or charade, wriggling free of his friends' plots and his own. Inventive both in defending himself and in duping others, "as vigilant as a cat to steal cream" (*I,* IV.ii.58-9), and his identity almost endlessly mutable—"sweet Jack Falstaff, kind Jack Falstaff, true Jack Falstaff, valiant Jack Falstaff, and therefore more valiant being, as he is, old Jack Falstaff" (*I*, II.iv.480-3)—the knight seems to be invulnerable, almost immortal. Among all the things one could say about "JACK FALSTAFF with my familiars, JOHN with my brothers and sisters, and SIR JOHN with all Europe" (*II*, II.ii.131-3), I will single out the quality his signature exemplifies, his protean nature, his ability to mime, mock, parody, and take on new voices. Of course, Falstaff is absolutely, impossibly incorrigible, always himself finally, without the ghost of an inclination to "reform," as Hal well knows. He lives "out of all order, out of all compass" (*I*, III.iii.20-1), like a river flooded over its banks; indeed, he "lards the lean earth as he walks along" (*I*, II.ii.111-12), melting before our eyes. He is never more himself than when he is pretending to be someone else, when, like Feste, he speaks in *vox* to become another: "I must speak in passion, and I will do it in King Cambyses' vein" (*I*, II.iv.389-90), or in the voice of "Monsieur Remorse" (*I*, I.ii.113-14) or "Sir John Sack and Sugar" (*I*, I.ii.114). Even in *Part II*, he parodies the Lord Chief Justice. What else could we expect of one of the "squires of the night's body . . . Diana's foresters, gentlemen of the shade, minions of the moon" (*I*, I.ii.24-7), whose constancy is inconstancy? The fortunes of the "moon's men doth ebb and flow like the sea" (ll. 32-3), but Falstaff remains incurably himself even while melting.

Falstaff's disquisition on Diana's foresters also exemplifies his ability to create as well as to inspire constant verbal transformations. The flyting between him and Hal—how many ways can he abuse Hal's thinness?—is one index of his inventiveness (and he inspires Hal equally) and his ability to "counterfeit" (*I*, V.iv.111-22) a life or death includes the ability to create "incomprehensible lies" (*I*, I.ii.183-4) that will transform the mundane into the miraculous, failure into triumph. His friends expect it, look forward to it. His alleged assailants increase exponentially like the dragon's teeth sown by Cadmus, two men metamorphosing into dozens:

I know not what you call all, but if I fought not
with fifty of them, I am a bunch of radish! If there
were not two or three and fifty upon poor old Jack,
then am I no two-legged creature. (*I*, II.iv.186-9)

Ah yes, the familiar "if": there is much "if" in the old Vice.
Such enthymemic constructions are among Falstaff's greatest
gifts, as several commentators have shown, and they do not
entirely vanish in *Part II*. There, too, he remains capable of
comic metamorphosis, as the Prince remarks: "And the boy
that I gave Falstaff. 'A had him from me Christian, and look
if the fat villain have not transformed him ape" (*II*, II.ii.68-
70). Nor have his verbal transformations diminished, as we
see in the lengthy, fantastic description of Shallow, "like a
forked radish" (*II*, III.ii.314-35), and in the metamorphic
mythopoeia of the lecture on the twofold operation of good
sherris-sack, which transforms the entire "little kingdom, man"
(*II*, IV.iii.86-125).

Still, "time, that takes survey of all the world, / Must have
a stop" (*I*, V.iv.80-1), and "Death, as the Psalmist saith, is
certain to all, all shall die" (*II*, III.ii.39-40). Hotspur and
Shallow are not usually the most reliable commentators on
life, but in this case they are right. Falstaff's metamorphic
energies are slowly undermined by his own inescapable mutability, and not only does he break the audience's heart—"I
am old, I am old" (*II*, II.iv.277)—but his own heart is broken
by rejection, and he dies offstage, no "counterfeit" now. At
least we are spared the sight of it. This relentless progress of
time, and the ineluctable demands of politics and history,
make it clear that however comical Falstaff is, we are not
watching a comedy, since time, politics, and history are exactly
the things transformed by comedy.

The Merry Wives of Windsor

We should count ourselves fortunate that Shakespeare places
the same character in two quite different genres, in history

play and comedy, instead of bemoaning the fact that Falstaff does not forever remain what he was in the great tavern scene in *Part One*. Say a day without the ever. The comedies remake time by embracing metamorphosis, and, given that, Falstaff must eventually find himself in another land; in *The Merry Wives of Windsor,* in a relentlessly middle-class world, as we shall see, his metamorphic qualities continue in a different vein. On the whole, however, most modern readers have been disappointed in Falstaff's relocation to the suburbs. In a play which has been said to reveal Shakespeare's "bitter disillusionment,"[3] and which has been termed "Shakespeare's most heartless farce,"[4] Falstaff's share of the blame has been large. Indeed, in one formulation, Falstaff "has disqualified himself as a comic hero. He has let Shakespeare down."[5] Too many readers have occupied themselves with noting the differences between this Falstaff ("A new character with an old name"[6]) and the bulkier, more enchanting figure of the Henriad. The Falstaff of *Merry Wives* is frequently described as an outright impostor, some other fat man who has somehow taken over the "old name" and body, but not the soul, of the "true Jack Falstaff." I have argued elsewhere[7] that the play is a coherent work exploring the nature of the imagination, and that if it was overrated in the eighteenth century it has been underrated in the twentieth. The play represents a logical, perhaps inevitable, culmination of the question of metamorphosis, especially as it is revealed in Ford's curious relation to Falstaff in the play, and in Falstaff's sacrifice at the end.

❧

A shadow of his former self, the Falstaff we meet in *The Merry Wives of Windsor* does seem to be suffering from the effects of a spiritual and sexual diet that has been all too effective. Like the advertiser's "after" picture, he is now, as the Pages describe him, "Old, cold, withered" (V.v.156). The threat he supposedly offers to the honor of the merry wives is never convincing, and they easily overtake and outwit the once nimble knight. Never have the phallic implications of Falstaff's name seemed more appropriate, for his staff has apparently fallen beyond all hope of tumescence. When Mistress Quickly defends Mistress Ford by saying "that was not her fault. She does so take on with her men; they mistook their erection," the irony of her malapropism (presumably for "direction") cannot fail to strike even Falstaff, who replies with a new sense of his limitations, "So did I mine, to build upon a foolish woman's promise" (III.v.37-41). His elaborate plot against the merry wives is wishful thinking more than anything else. But at least he has sense enough to make his motivation ultimately financial rather than sexual: "I will use her [Mistress Ford] as the key of the cuckoldy rogue's coffer, and there's my harvest-home" (II.ii.267-9). Page's ultimate taunt at the end is not that Falstaff is impotent, but that he is "as poor as Job" (V.v.158). That is the sterility best understood in the relentlessly middle-class world of Windsor. And Ford's final triumph is to demand not sexual but financial vengeance upon Falstaff. "Over and above that you have suffered, I think to repay that money will be a biting affliction" (V.v.169-71). If these final insults seem to have relatively little effect, it is only because they seem to fall so wide of the more sensual Falstaff we have known in the Henry plays; the rules of the game seem to have been changed, as Shakespeare adopts a genre with quite different assumptions and associations.

It is made clear that Falstaff is a threat only to the extent that people think he is. Moreover, Ford is the only character in *Merry Wives* who considers him a threat, and thereby transforms him into one. Falstaff has retained his girth—he is still a "hodge-pudding . . . a bag of flax" (V.v.154)—but even Pistol and Nym are able to trick him now. Only Ford succumbs to him, and Ford's deception is self-induced. Falstaff becomes a grotesque incarnation of Ford's worst fears, a comic monster, a priapic bogeyman conjured up by a runaway imagination. Like Orgoglio in *The Faerie Queene*, Falstaff is a decrepit windbag pumped up by his victim's error—by Ford's mania, what Evans terms his "fery fantastical humours and jealousies" (III.iii.164) and what we might term his transformational mania. When Ford's "humour" is exorcised and he comes to his senses, Falstaff is suddenly deflated.

Recent critics of the play have stressed its ritual elements, and described Falstaff as a scapegoat figure, re-enacting a folk game Frazer called "Carrying Out Death."[8] Falstaff's general impotence, moreover, indicates that his final punishment is partly, as J. A. Bryant, Jr. has observed, "directed at the expulsion of evil which was not entirely of his own generating."[9] That is the very definition of the scapegoat's role—the embodiment of the sins or fears of the community, which will be purged once the scapegoat is driven off or sacrificed. Falstaff's role, as ever, leans toward allegory. The "reverend vice," "gray iniquity," and "father ruffian" of *Henry IV, Part I* (II.iv.458-9) attains the status of a full devil in Ford's mind, and the movement of *Merry Wives* indicates how it is Ford's mind that must be disenchanted, exorcized of a "devil" that represents an unsettling threat to the rest of society. Ford forms his suspicions and inclinations to arrive at Falstaphobia, then he must be re-formed to expunge the monster in his brain. At the end of the play, the entire community will transform Falstaff into an animal, exorcize his comic threat, and then invite him home to supper.

When we recall Falstaff's boast in *Part II*, "I am not only witty in myself, but the cause that wit is in other men," we recognize that his ability to ignite our imaginations, as he has incinerated Ford's, is exactly why we love Falstaff. But rather than a positive virtue in Windsor, "wit" is a potentially subversive power to be repressed and channeled.[10] "Wit" is one of the chief agents of transformation, internal and external, and the stolid middle-class folk of Windsor will have none of it. Falstaff poses a threat to their rigid and comfortable social order, and such a threat to safely established boundaries cannot be tolerated. At the end of *Merry Wives* the defeated Falstaff is made to utter a sententious maxim more characteristic of the inhabitants of Windsor: "See now how wit may be made a Jack-a-Lent, when 'tis upon ill employment!"

(V.v.129-31) The exhortation is directed to the Windsorites as much as it is to the audience.

Ford cannot get Falstaff out of his mind because Falstaff embodies everything that Ford has repressed and that threatens him most. At the first fruitless search of Ford's house, Page chides Ford: "Are you not ashamed? What spirit, what devil suggests this imagination?" (III.iii.207-9), and Evans theorizes that Ford suffers from a "pad conscience" (III.iii.212). After the second fruitless search of the house, Evans returns to the theme of demonic possession: "Master Ford, you must pray, and not follow the imaginations of your own heart. This is jealousies" (IV.ii.151-2) With this allusion to Jeremiah 13:10, Evans seeks to explain Ford's disturbance by the agency of external forces. But the play insists on internal turbulence instead:

> FORD. Well, he's not here I seek for.
> PAGE. No, nor nowhere else but in your brain.
> (IV.ii.153-4)

The wives agree with Page's analysis. When Mistress Ford asks of the just-cudgeled Falstaff, "Shall we tell our husbands how we have served him?" Mistress Page replies, "Yes, by all means—if it be but to scrape the figures out of your husband's brains" (IV.ii.207-10). This image equates an internal change with a physical one, as if Mistress Page was turning a pumpkin into a jack-a-lantern.

Ford has all along had an unhealthy predisposition to "figures" and "imaginings," for his jealous humor slides all too easily into paranoia, the rabid imagination transforming all outward signs into monsters and gargoyles. When Ford and Page first hear of Falstaff's intentions toward their wives, their very different reactions are set in apposition:

> PAGE. If he [Falstaff] should intend this voyage toward my wife, I would turn her loose to him; and what he gets more of her than sharp words, let it lie on my head.

FORD. I do not misdoubt my wife, but I would be loath
to turn them together. A man may be too confident.
I would have nothing lie on my head. I cannot be thus
satisfied.   (II.i.174-81)

Page's loose style indicates a mind at ease. The "if" clause
refers not even to his wife's infidelity, but to the issue of
whether Falstaff has such intentions at all; his hortatory conclusion shows the extent of his confidence. Ford's paratactic
nervousness, by contrast, jumps from assumption to assumption, as the hypothetical gives way to deluded declaratives,
and the feeble double negative "not misdoubt" emotionally
betrays the logically positive affirmation. Ford thus plays Iago
to his own Othello: he's divided against himself, fearing the
dread deforming horns upon his forehead which Page is confident of avoiding. When Ford, disguised as his watery name-
sake Brook, makes his self-cuckolding proposal to Falstaff,
all logic has been overturned.

Another index of Ford's susceptibility to delusional transformation is found in the references to the "witch" of Brainford. The name of the town almost too obviously suggests the
witch's origin in Ford's brain. Here we find the kind of imaginative complicity which helps create metamorphosis. To
commonsensical Mistress Ford, this unseen woman is merely
"My maid's aunt, the fat woman of Brainford." Significantly,
Falstaff, that other emanation of Ford's brain, is disguised in
her clothing. But of all the characters in the play, only Ford
believes her to be a witch, as his wife explains: "I would my
husband would meet him [Falstaff] in this shape. He cannot
abide the old woman of Brainford; he swears she's a witch,
forbade her my house, and hath threat'ned to beat her" (IV.ii.
80-3). When Ford does learn that "she" is in his house, he
becomes more hysterical (it is only a matter of degree by now):
"She comes of errands, does she? We are simple men; we do
not know what's brought to pass under the profession of
fortunetelling. She works by charms, by spells, by th' figure,
and such daubery as this is, beyond our element; we know

nothing. Come down, you witch, you hag, you; come down, I say!" (IV.ii.167-73). The transformation here is completely internal, for Falstaff has become the witch not through his own talent at mimickry but through the "figures" of Ford's brain. By beating Falstaff in the "witch's" clothing, Ford is cudgeling both phantoms of his brain at the same time, but his exorcism still has a further course to run.

Ford's encounter with the witch of Brainford marks an important turning point in *Merry Wives*. He rushes offstage in a frenzy, but when we next see him, just forty lines later, he is much changed. His mania has vanished: "Pardon me, wife. Henceforth do what thou wilt. / I rather will suspect the sun with cold / Than thee with wantonnese" (IV.iv.6-8). His sudden conversion, like Oliver's at the end of *As You Like It,* is only as arbitrary as the cause of his mania in the first place; Ford describes his former self (already in the third person) as "him that was of late an heretic," but now "as firm as faith" in the belief of his wife's honor. Yet his claim to an absolute change is suspect, and something of the old disease lingers, as Page warns: " 'Tis well, 'tis well; no more. / Be not as extreme in submission as in offense" (IV.iv.9-11). Whatever happened offstage (and the play offers no explanation), it is clear that the encounter with the "witch" represents the extremity of Ford's delusion. Middle-class Windsor may have been more susceptible to such superstition—we have already heard Evans suggesting possession as the cause of Ford's disease—but the play has everywhere stressed that Ford is alone, and without foundation, in his beliefs, a perfect study in uncontrollable transformational mania. The humor of it never fails, as audiences well know, but the same deranged imaginings will later be uttered more ominously by Othello and Leontes.

Ford's encounters with Falstaff become progressively more grotesque throughout the play, his delusions more absurd, and Falstaff's means of escape correspondingly more ludicrous. When Ford is about to break up the second attempted tryst, the "witch" Falstaff desperately seeks a hiding place:

"What shall I do? I'll creep up into the chimney." To which the wives reply, "There they always use to discharge their birding-pieces." "Creep into the kilnhole" (IV.ii.50-4). This exchange is a windfall for Freudian analysis. All of the hiding places which are suggested are dream-displaced images of female sexuality—"press, coffer, chest, trunk, well, vault." According to his wife, Ford "hath an abstract for the remembrance of such places and goes to them by his note." Of course: where else does one go in a dream? This passage also suggests that Ford knows these places by book or rote rather than experience. Mistress Ford concludes, "There is no hiding you [Falstaff] in the house" (IV.ii.50-60). Nor outside, either. The only way out for Falstaff is by sexual disguise, so that Ford's brain will not recognize its own creation; the female emanation temporarily displaces the male specter. Although succubus takes over for incubus, the implications are the same. Falstaff's "disguise" in woman's clothing, moreover, is completely ludicrous, a monstrous parody of women disguising as men so common in the other comedies; but here is no spunky Ganymede or light-toed Cesario. This disguise succeeds with Ford but doesn't deceive anyone else; at the end of the play, amid other discoveries and revelations, we will see, by contrast, how other disguises achieve mimetic transformation—how *we* were deceived.

Ford eventually gains control of himself, but Falstaff, like Frankenstein's monster, is still on the loose, a too-visible reminder of folly and sexual license. Ford's conversion precedes Falstaff's humiliation by a full act, and the rest of the play turns on how best to reform Falstaff (if such a thing is possible), an action on which the Anne-Fenton plot turns as well. Mistress Ford's suggestion that Falstaff crawl into the "kilnhole" takes us far in the direction of ritual, or at least fairytale. The play frequently reminds us, through Falstaff's links with ritual, of the animal nature of man—first Falstaff is a presumably tumescent buck, then a whimpering scapegoat—and it is precisely this animal-human boundary which the Windsorites want kept firm. It turns out that the Windsorites' way of dealing with Falstaff's "wit," his powers of transformation, is to turn the same energies against him, and in the second half of *Merry Wives* Falstaff is metamorphosed into a sacrificial animal himself. This fat Proteus suddenly turns into just another of Circe's victims, as his gigantic desires make him another victim of love's transforming powers. Falstaff's transformation is hugely comic, as Bottom's metamorphosis was, but it is edgy and uneasy, as if the ritual were to be real and Falstaff truly killed. Even in the Henriad, we recall, Falstaff was increasingly associated with animals, the "roasted Manningtree ox with the pudding in his belly" (*I*, II.iv. 457-8) served up for sacrifice in *Part I*, the "huge hill of flesh" (*I*, II.iv.245) ready to be quartered and roasted. By *Part II* he is explicitly a sacrificial beef, the "martlemas" (*II*, II.ii.100) [11] and, in Doll Tearsheet's phrase, a "whoreson little tidy Bartholomew boar-pig" (*II*, II.iv.234). On both Martinmas Day (November 11) and St. Bartholomew's Day (August 24), the young animal, specially fattened up, would be slaughtered. "Doth the old boar feed in the old frank?" asks Hal (*II*, II.ii.145-6); but more to the point is the question, who is going to feed on the old boar? To catalogue all the animal imagery associated with Falstaff would be to stand like Adam naming the beasts, and it is already clear that Falstaff—"this whale," as Mistress Ford says, thrown "with so many tuns of oil in his belly, ashore at Windsor" (II.i.63-4)—represents an aspect of man that Ford, and the others, would prefer to suppress. No wonder that the quelling of Falstaff has so many primitive, even savage, undertones.

As an emblem and agent of wit, Falstaff has embodied the possibilities, comic but often dangerous, of change and transformation. Circean energies represent the greatest threat, but more frequent is a simple fear of disruption and change in Windsor. Ford has fallen away from an implied better self and must be re-formed and brought back to it. Falstaff would overturn all sorts of social institutions, not the least of which is marriage, and must be re-formed. Above all, Falstaff is, in his own words, "a man of continual dissolution and thaw"

(III.v.111-12), continually renewing himself and reinventing his relation to those around him. Eventually he will maintain that he has "suffered more for their [the women's] sakes— more than the villainous inconstancy of man's disposition is able to bear" (IV.v.105-6). It is just this "inconstancy," Falstaff's natural condition, which is a threat to the rest of Windsor and which be harnessed. Shape-shifting is bad form.

After, but only after, Ford's great awakening, when Falstaff's dream-like power vaporizes, the fat knight begins to fear his own metamorphosis, and now turning passive victim, he loses control of this slippery energy. "I would all the world might be cozened," he says, "for I have been cozened and beaten too. If it should come to the ear of the court how I have been transformed, and how my transformation hath been washed and cudgeled, they would melt me out of my fat drop by drop, and liquor fishermen's boots with me" (IV.v.90-6). This punishment is both comic and scary. Surrounded in the forest, Falstaff cowers in fear of still another kind of "dissolution": "Heavens defend me from that Welsh fairy, lest he transform me to a piece of cheese" (V.v.83-4).

In one sense, such a transformation would be a desirable means of escape. Falstaff enters the final scene disguised as Herne the Hunter, *"with a buck's head upon him,"* and he invokes the Ovidian tradition of metamorphosis to justify his condition: "Remember, Jove, thou wast a bull for thy Europa; love set on thy horns. O powerful love, that in some respects makes a beast a man; in some other, a man a beast. You were also, Jupiter, a swan for the love of Leda. O omnipotent love, how near the god drew to the complexion of a goose!" (V.v. 3-8). This choric commentary reflects on much that has happened in the play, and looks back as well to such different comedies of metamorphosis as *Love's Labour's Lost* and *A Midsummer Night's Dream.* "Omnipotent" Love is the agent of change that has brought Falstaff to this ludicrous state as a comic monster, and love's darkest side—fanatic, hysterical jealousy—has induced Ford's mania and transformed Falstaff into a monstrous projection of fear. Ford dropped to the an-

imal when he temporarily lost his reason; when he was re-
formed, Falstaff, the "man of middle earth" (V.v.82), began
to sink more and more quickly down the chain of being himself. "You may know by my size," he says, "that I have a
kind of alacrity in sinking" (III.v.11-13). The two characters
complement each other, like buckets in a pulley-well: one up,
the other down. Falstaff embodies all the energy, vitality, and
imagination Ford has repressed and which therefore threatens
him. Ford represents all the security, wealth, and success Falstaff has never achieved.

Falstaff makes an ironic joke about Jove's rapes of Europa
and Leda: "A fault done first in the form of a beast. O Jove,
a beastly fault! And then another fault in the semblance of a
fowl; think on't, Jove; a foul fault! When gods have hot backs,
what shall poor men do?" (V.v.8-12). A question, as he tells
Hal in *Part I*, definitely "to be asked." The Windsorites seem
to have an answer, at any rate: ritual punishment. As Falstaff
stands there in the final scene, "a Windsor stag" hoping for
a "cool rut-time," we sense the inevitability of the approaching
sacrifice. It has been a long time coming, but everyone has
anticipated it—except Falstaff.

Pistol warned Ford to stop Falstaff, "or go thou, / Like Sir
Actaeon he, with Ringwood at thy heels" (II.i.115-16). Actaeon, of course, was pursued and killed by his own dogs,
and as a stag wore horns; hence he became a symbol of cuckoldry.[12] Even more to the point, Actaeon's story is an emblem
of self-destructive desire. The sacrificial overtones of the Actaeon myth—Ford goes on to call Page a "secure and willful
Actaeon" (III.ii.39)—are given their cruelest turn when Falstaff calls Ford, to his disguised face, a "jealous rotten bell-
wether" (III.v.105-6), a castrated male sheep ready for sacrifice,
which would seem to be the ultimate dream-punishment of a
cuckold. Indeed, in Ford's "dream," he himself is the neutered
scapegoat victim; but when he awakens from his nightmare,
the horns are on another head. Falstaff has become the impotent buck, afraid lest he piss his tallow, cheerfully willing
to be dismembered for the sake of a joke on cuckolds: "Divide

me like a bribed buck, each a haunch. I will keep my sides to myself, my shoulders for the fellow of this walk, and my horns I bequeath your husbands" (V.v.25-8). Somewhat pathetically, Falstaff tries to make the best of a bad disguise. Like Dionysius, the god whose power he most aspires to, Falstaff will scatter his remains among those who cannot accept his reign.

A similar ritual moment climaxes *Henry IV, Part I*. There, Falstaff has let his staff fall, and lies on the ground shamming death. Thinking he is dead, Hal says farewell:

> Death hath not struck so fat a deer to-day,
> Though many dearer, in this bloody fray.
> Emboweled will I see thee by-and-by;
> Till then in blood by noble Percy lie.
> *(I, V.iv.105-8)*

The lines anticipate Falstaff's fate in *The Merry Wives of Windsor*. In *Henry IV,* however, he is resourceful enough to elude his destiny—horrified at Hal's comment, Falstaff springs back to life: "Emboweled? If thou embowel me today, I'll give you leave to powder me and eat me too tomorrow" (I, V.iv.109-11). This robust variety of re-forming is quite beyond the suburban complacencies of Windsor. Shrewsbury is clearly a different world, and Falstaff brusquely rejects there the docile role imposed upon him in *Merry Wives. Part II* provides the closer analogy, for Hal's rejection of Falstaff is the political equivalent of the quasi-anthropological ritual being acted out in *Merry Wives.* When Falstaff admits, metaphorically, "I do begin to perceive that I am made an ass," Ford completes and extends the transformation by making it literal: "Ay, and an ox too: both the proofs are extant" (V.v.121-2).

❧

The final movement of *The Merry Wives of Windsor* climaxes in Falstaff's "reformation" in the woods, when he appears quoting Ovid and with the buck's head upon him. Earlier, Mistress Page relates the "old tale" of "Herne the Hunter," once a keeper in Windsor Forest. Like Puck in *A Midsummer Night's Dream*, he personifies natural disruption and embodies the darker powers of metamorphosis. Legend has it that Herne

> Doth all the wintertime, at still midnight,
> Walk round about an oak, with great ragg'd horns;
> And there he blasts the tree, and takes the cattle,
> And makes milch-kine yield blood, and shakes a chain
> In a most hideous and dreadful manner.
> (IV.iv.29-33)

The Windsorites claim not to believe this myth, but they recognize its immense influence on older, more gullible times.

> . . . well you know
> The superstitious idle-headed eld
> Received, and did deliver to our age,
> This tale of Herne the Hunter for a truth.
> (IV.iv.34-7)

Ford, of course, is another "superstitious idle-headed" elder mistaking a theory for a truth. Moreover, Mistress Page's description of Herne resembles the phantom of jealousy in Ford's brain—"hideous and dreadful," the horns an emblem of cuckoldry, possessing ("takes") others, turning milk to blood, thriving in darkness. Yet it is Falstaff who will appear on stage dressed as Herne the Hunter, the sexual hunter now hunted, aggressor become victim.

As preparations for re-enacting the myth proceed onstage. Quickly somehow persuades Falstaff offstage to approach the wives again for the obligatory third time. Mistress Ford describes the "device" to the schemers, while Mistress Page casts the parts to be played. The "plot" is simple—a ritual but comic exorcism of Falstaff by the children dressed as "urchins, ouphs, and fairies":

> . . . let them all encircle him about,
> And, fairy-like, to pinch the unclean knight,

195

And ask him why, that hour of fairy revel,
In their so sacred paths he dares to tread
In shape profane.
(IV.iv.56-60)

Agent and victim become one—Falstaff and Herne are both the buck. Certainly Falstaff does not plan on such a "shape profane," but the transformation, as usual, fails to take completely, and he remains both ludicrously Falstaff and mysteriously Herne/the buck.

Between the planning and the enactment of Falstaff's humiliation, a parallel sequence of intrigues and deceptions takes place, involving Evans and Caius (the trick of the stolen horses, in IV.v), and Fenton and the Host (to marry Anne, in IV.vi). Employing terms like "denote," "token," and "decipher," the simple though convoluted schemes assume more profound connotations; once again, something must be read, or deciphered. What has been going on throughout *Merry Wives* is more than just another exploration of the familiar appearance/reality problem. Shakespeare confronts us, again and again, with the question of *how* we know—how we shape our world in perceiving it, and how that shaping in turn transforms us. The power of love generates metamorphosis in Windsor as it does everywhere else, but we haven't seen all these twists and turns before. In contrast to the earlier comedies, this play seems to have kept the extremes figured by desire and dropped out the middle. No Rosalind or Viola is offered as an embodiment of life-giving redemptive transformation and love. The single marriage the play drives toward, of Fenton and Anne, doesn't have the accrued power to counter the grotesqueries at either extreme Ford and Falstaff have represented. Ford's final reformation was offstage, but Falstaff—the enemy of the stolid marriages in Windsor—must be reformed in public.

Falstaff's final entrance is both comic and eerie. What is this odd, touching man/beast? "For me, I am here a Windsor stag; and the fattest, I think, i' th' forest. Send me a cool rut-time, Jove, or who can blame me to piss my tallow? Who comes here? My doe?" (V.v.12-15). He welcomes the ladies to the woods in triumph: "Am I a woodman, ha? Speak I like Herne the Hunter? Why, now is Cupid a child of conscience; he makes restitution. As I am a true spirit, welcome!" (ll. 28-30). Cupid's restitution is all too quickly upon Falstaff, unfortunately. We have before us an almost perfect tableau illustrating the inevitable transformations prompted by unlimited desire, as the exorcising "fairy" song explains; Falstaff is "Corrupt, corrupt, and tainted in desire!":

> Fie on sinful fantasy!
> Fie on lust and luxury!
> Lust is but a bloody fire,
> Kindled with unchaste desire,
> Fed in heart, whose flames aspire,
> As thoughts do blow them, higher and higher.
>
> (ll. 95-100)

Is the "beastly fault" one of having desire in the first place, or of having an "unchaste" desire? The form of this play, and of most Shakespearean comedy, suggests that desire contained within marriage is the right goal, and that when it has gone uncontained, and become chaotic, as has happened with Falstaff (his ability to perform is another question altogether), something will be done about it. In fact, the disguises and confusions of the ritual provide the cover for a marriage taking place offstage at exactly the same time: the one ritual exorcizes the fears attendant on the other ritual, of marriage, though in a different way from the version seen in A Midsummer Night's Dream. There the lucky recipient of metamorphosis was granted the favor, and apparently the bed, of the equally deluded Fairy Queen; here the Fairy Queen (Mistress Quickly in Anne's place) turns out to be a sham, a crone, as if the "loathly lady" folktale had been reversed, and Falstaff's dream of a "cool rut-time" turns out to be something warmer: "I think the devil will not have me damned, lest the oil that's in me should set hell on fire. He would never else cross me thus" (ll. 36-8). Fighting one kind of fire with another, the fairies burn Falstaff-Herne-Actaeon with "trial-fire" (l. 86).

Falstaff is afraid to speak in the fairies' midst, with good reason, and as in *Henry IV, Part I,* he falls to the ground and counterfeits death when he sees them: "he that speaks to them shall die. / I'll wink and couch; no man their works must eye" (ll. 49-50). But the jig is finally up, and when Evans (dressed as a "satyr," half-man half-beast!) smells "a man of middle earth" (l. 82), the ritualistic sacrifice of Falstaff, the most striking scene in the play, begins in earnest. There is a strain of real cruelty in all the pinching and burning; referring to Falstaff as having "the flesh of a corrupted heart" (l. 89) seems the rhetorical overkill of a puritan. Yet the cruelty is mitigated by elements of ludicrous farce—it is Quickly, rather than Anne, who appears as a most unlikely Fairy Queen, a bit of inspired casting that ought to throw some doubt on the theory that this play was intended as a compliment to Queen Elizabeth. It is Quickly, moreover, in a superb moment of hypocrisy, who has described Falstaff's corrupted heart.

The audience's reactions to this remarkable scene must be complex. Falstaff has had it coming, but the process of exposure seems too drawn-out, too painfully vengeful: the Windsorites act as if a real animal were before them, but Falstaff's transformation into a buck is comically incomplete. The Fords and the Pages point out the moral and trumpet their own cleverness at perhaps excessive length. The initial mythic suggestiveness of this final scene—the legend of the tree and the hunter, the animal costume, the people coming out from town to a forest setting, the note of communal preservation—becomes unexpectedly explicit and harsh. The vindictiveness of their reaction suggests that the Windsorites might be expelling something they really need.

At the end, once the truth about the fairies is revealed, Falstaff is puzzled. He attributes his deception to the ability of the imagination to re-form reality and accept counterfeits:

> And these are not fairies? I was three or four times in
> the thought they were not fairies; and yet the guiltiness

of my mind, the sudden surprise of my powers, drove
the grossness of the foppery into a received belief, in
despite of the teeth of all rhyme and reason, that they
were fairies. See now how wit may be made a Jack-a-
Lent, when 'tis upon ill employment. (ll. 124-30)

Falstaff's admission provides the best commentary on Ford's
mania as well as his own. A "received belief" in the shape of
the outer world is a precarious thing, given the world's tendency to metamorphose at will. The grossness of foppery may
lie just beneath the surface of plausibility. Several more received beliefs are quickly shattered when Slender and Caius
return with boys rather than Anne, and the Pages are, for
once, tricked when Fenton returns with their daughter as his
wife. With the exorcism of Falstaff complete and desire harnessed, the marriage is announced: the necessary order of these
events is by now familiar. Each plot of intrigue ends with a
discovery, a literal revelation which strips away pretense and
unnecessary disguise—an un-transforming. Page will pronounce the comic benediction, a final choric commentary, on
this movement towards acceptance: "What cannot be es-
chewed must be embraced" (l. 236). Even the wary Falstaff,
his transformations ceased and the threat he represents detoxified, will be brought back to dinner with the sober Windsorites.

This final scene, as in most of Shakespeare's plays, begins
to distance us from too close an involvement with the action.
The patently mechanical resolution of the interlocking plots
is deliberate, I think; the revelations fall into place just as each
deceived person claims a victory for his point of view. But a
more important technique distances us in this final scene: a
sudden self-conscious reminder of theatricality, of the shifting
boundaries of apparent identity. As soon as Falstaff's exorcism
is completed, another transformation and exorcism is revealed. Slender was deceived by a costume; as Page tells him,
he "took the wrong":

SLENDER. What need you tell me that? I think so, when
I took a boy for a girl. If I had been married to him,

for all he was in woman's apparel, I would not have had him. (ll. 191-5)

Caius appears with a similar complaint:

By gar, I am cozened! I ha' married un garcon, a boy: un peasant, by gar, a boy; it is not Anne Page. By gar, I am cozened! (ll. 205-7)

But we have all been cozened in a similar way. Presumably we did not see through the initial substitution, and Caius and Slender abruptly remind us as well that Anne *is* a boy—a boy-actor—and the paradox strikes us anew as Anne and Fenton enter immediately after Caius and Slender's speeches. Both Anne and Fenton are boys, but the audience has been complicit in the illusion that one is not. If Falstaff can swallow for a "received belief" the premise that disguised children are fairies; if Ford can believe that Falstaff is a genuine sexual threat and that Falstaff's pathetic disguise as the Witch of Brainford is real; then the audience should not be surprised that we have succumbed to, even sought out, a comparable transformation. Although the willing suspension of disbelief is voluntary—dangerously self-induced in Ford's case—it is never complete, and Shakespeare's audience, well trained by now by other Shakespearean reversals, must have enjoyed still another "double excellency" (III.iii.169) in the knowledge that the "girl," like the Witch, was also a phantom, that fictions and illusions mingle cheek-by-jowl with putative realities as "positive as the earth is firm" (III.ii.44), as Ford said of his own delusion.

Falstaff makes the grandiose, and mistaken, claim that his "admirable dexterity of wit," his uncanny "counterfeiting the action of an old woman" (IV.v.114-15), had saved him from being set in the stocks for a witch (though it had also earned him a beating). The audience knows that Falstaff's wit was neither admirable nor particularly dexterous in that situation, and that the wives had suggested his disguise. No one would argue, either, that Falstaff's "counterfeiting" is convincing, for he remains hugely himself. Ford was the only gull. But the

character's failure is the author's triumph. Falstaff's counterfeiting reminds us, metadramatically, of Shakespeare's. It is a
special mark of the Falstaff of *Merry Wives,* in contrast to his
predecessor in *Henry IV, Part I,* that he is allowed to fail and
not really recover; his wit can still transform the world, but
the world shows more resistance to his force, and occasionally
even re-forms him in turn. Falstaff himself, in short, has changed
in the course of these plays, reflecting in part the shift in genre
from history play to citizen comedy, and in part the dramatist's awareness that this fat agent of transformation, this in-
comparable mimic and parodist, this great hogshead of desire
both carnal ("This is enough to be the decay of lust and late-
walking through the realm"—V.v.147-8) and gustatory ("'Tis
time I were choked with a piece of toasted cheese"—V.v.141-
2) could not, by either his own nature or that of desire, fail
to be transformed himself. Only a supremely confident artist
would risk re-forming his most successful character. If Shakespeare has not been granted full success in this effort, it may
be because his readers now prefer to freeze Falstaff in his
previous incarnation, having forgotten that he is "a man of
continual dissolution and thaw."

Though his deception went deep, Falstaff "three or four
times" doubted that fairies were pinching him, before he succumbed to the "received belief" that they were. If the production is a good one and if the actors are convincing, the
audience may in turn three or four times believe that Falstaff
and Ford are real, that they are alive to the point, not merely
of suspended disbelief, but across a theatrical boundary through
to that mysterious, exhilarating realm of received, and transforming, belief. No one can ask for more than that. "When
nightdogs run," as Falstaff says, "all sorts of deer are chased"
(V.v.237).

☙

The final change for this man of continual dissolution is his
own dissolution, an offstage death in *Henry V* as moving as
almost anything in Shakespeare. We are back in the histories

now, where no further onstage resurrections will be permitted, where time must have its stop. Falstaff's old gang point out that "the king has killed his heart" (*H5*, II.i.89), and as a result, "his heart is fracted and corroborate" (l. 125). Whatever the King's responsibility, though, we also recognize that Falstaff's time is up, that he is far better off in Arthur's bosom than in the cold new world of Hal's realpolitik. Quickly's eulogy notes that Falstaff passed from one world to the next "just between twelve and one, ev'n at the turning o' th' tide" (*H5*, II.iii.12-13), at two other moments of fallen boundaries and transformation. The Boy claims that Falstaff "cried out of" sack and women (here is a mighty change indeed), complaining of the latter that "they were devils incarnate" (ll. 31-2), as he himself was once accused of being by Hal. Quickly describes the actual moment of death as a chilling process of petrifaction, as the boundaries of life recede:

> So 'a bade me lay more clothes on his feet. I put my hand into the bed, and felt them, and they were as cold as any stone. Then I felt to his knees, and so upward, and upward, and all was as cold as any stone. (ll. 22-6)

As life drains out of him, as all change ceases, the great change that awaits us all transforms Falstaff for the last time.

Part Four ❧ Magic

. . . a girl of twenty-five years dreamt that she had cooked dinner for her family of five. She had just served it and she now called her parents and her brothers and sister to dinner. Nobody replied Only her voice returned as if it were an echo from a deep cave. She found the sudden emptiness of the house uncanny. She rushed upstairs to look for her family. In the first bedroom, she could see her two sisters sitting on two beds. In spite of her impatient calls they remained in an unnaturally rigid position and did not even answer her. She went up to her sisters and wanted to shake them. Suddenly she noticed that they were stone statues. She escaped in horror and rushed into her mother's room. Her mother too had turned into stone and was sitting inertly in her arm chair staring into the air with glazed eyes. The dreamer escaped into the room of her father. He stood in the middle of it. In her despair she rushed up to him and, desiring his protection, she threw her arms around his neck. But he too was made of stone and, to her utter horror, he turned into sand when she embraced him. She awoke in absolute terror, and was so stunned by the dream experience that she could not move for some minutes. This same horrible dream was dreamt by the patient on four successive occasions within a few days. At that time she was apparently the picture of mental and physical health. Her parents used to call her the sunshine of the whole family. Ten days after the fourth repetition of the dream, the patient was taken ill with an acute form of schizophrenia displaying severe catatonic symptoms. She fell into a state which was remarkably similar to the physical petrifaction of her family that she had dreamt about. She was now overpowered in waking life by behaviour patterns that in her dreams she had merely observed in other persons.

MEDARD BOSS
Analysis of Dreams, quoted in
R. D. Laing, *The Divided Self*

Chapter Seven ❧ The Changes of Romance

Although Shakespeare's romances also reveal his recurring interest in metamorphosis, particularly the Ovidian variety, much has changed since *Twelfth Night* and *The Merry Wives of Windsor*. The generic assumptions and conventions of the late romances are different enough from those of the romantic comedies to give us pause before affirming the obvious connections. Most readers have rightly found Shakespeare much changed in the late romances, though they have often disagreed on the exact nature of the change, from the world-weary boredom described by Lytton Strachey through G. Wilson Knight's vision of enraptured mysticism to more recent accounts of an experimental metadramatic self-consciousness.[1] Usually the romances have been seen at least as expressions of a deepened wisdom, the culmination of an enriched and complex life of experience. I would like to extend this understanding of the late plays by examining how they represent metamorphosis, and by meditating on what has changed for Shakespeare since *The Comedy of Errors*.

My task in this chapter will be lightened considerably because the romances have received illuminating critical readings in the past three decades, and because the topic of metamorphosis has been directly though briefly addressed by a few critics. For example, one reader finds that "the emphasis on the romances is directly upon metamorphosis and transfor-

mation as redemptive acts, and upon the created artifact as
it contains and crystallizes insights into the nature of man."[2]
This emphasis seems in part the result of generic causes, for
Shakespeare's turn to romance as a source and structure au-
tomatically lifts us into the realms of the marvelous and the
improbable. Coffins that float to shore, royal kidnapped children, statues that move, enchanted islands—almost anything
can and does happen now. If the plot should derive more from
pastoral romance than from the Greek romance, then the
possibilities of metamorphosis increase all the more. And yet,
even taking "Exit pursued by a bear" into account, Shakespeare never did anything quite like this:

> She wakes and escaping transforms herself first into
>   A bear after leaping and prowling she changes next into
>   A bull after the same performance into
>   A lion roaming to and fro to the astonishment of
> Fausto who will not leave her because of what Proteus
> has promised. At last the lion changes back into Filli's
> own shape. Fausto is amazed and begs her to accept his
> love.[3]

Nor did Shakespeare attempt to show this kind of transformation:

> Then out of the ayre a cloude descends, discovering six
> of the Knights alike, in strange and sumptuous atires,
> and withall on either side of the Cloud, on the two Pro-
> montories, the other sixe Maskers are sodainly trans-
> formed out of the pillars of golde; at which time, while
> they all come forward to the dancing-place, this Chorus
> is sung, and on the sodaine the whole Sceane is changed:
> for whereas before all seemed to be done at the sea and
> sea coast, now the Promontories are sodainly remooved,
> and London with the Thames is very arteficially pre-
> sented in their place.[4]

The dates of these transformation scenes—from the pre-
Shakespearean *commedia dell'arte* and Campion's masque for

the Earl of Somerset and the Lady Frances Howard (1614) respectively—demonstrate that the Renaissance stage always provided dramatic precedents for the most spectacular onstage metamorphosis imaginable. From the rough *commedia* through the popular stage to the sophisticated Stuart masque, the technical resources of the Renaissance stage could readily be mobilized for such elaborate displays. But the curious fact remains that Shakespeare, throughout his career, assiduously avoids such attempts at representation. The frequent onstage transformations wrought by his early rival, John Lyly, and by his later competitors, Ben Jonson, Inigo Jones, and other epigones in the Stuart court, seem to have had little or no effect on Shakespeare's own dramaturgy, except in the late romances, and even here they are quite different.

It may be that Shakespeare's resistance to such transformation scenes stems from a sense of his audience's varying levels of sophistication. On the one hand, such mechanical representations of metamorphosis might seem crude, no matter how fanciful the idea or how smooth the machinery involved; these scenes may strike us as the equivalent of bringing Moonshine or Lion into the play. On the other hand, the more spectacular the stage business, as Ben Jonson discovered in his uneasy collaboration with Inigo Jones, the less attention may be paid to the language. Shakespeare seems, in the late plays, to have struck a balance between the visual and the verbal, between stage and speech. Yet he also seems to tour these moldy old tales and whirling tempests with his own itinerary, impelled by the necessities of the theater, to be sure, but equally by the pressures of his own thought. In the romances, he rethinks, or has already reconsidered, the nature of metamorphosis and how it may be represented on a stage.

Reuben Brower has suggested that in contrast to the earlier plays, the romances take up metamorphosis more as their structure than merely as their subject; he contrasts the " 'sweet witty' Ovidianism of 'Venus and Adonis' and the metaphorical design of *The Tempest*."[5] Another way to consider the question of metamorphosis in the romances is to recall

G. Wilson Knight's classic description of them as myths of immortality; a specific form of metamorphosis—the change from mortal body to immortal spirit—dominates the last plays, he argues. There seems no end to the number of resurrection scenes in these plays, to be sure: Thaisa's resuscitation (*Per*, III.ii), Marina's "recovery" of Pericles's dumbness (*Per*, V.i), Thaisa's faint and second revival (*Per*, V.iii); and Imogen's false death and revival in IV.ii of *Cymbeline*, with her brother's astonishment ("Is not this boy revived from death?"—V.v.119) at the paradox of rebirth ("for I was dead"—V.v.259). These intimations of immortality reach a consummate perfection in the statue scene in *The Winter's Tale*, a play which twice lets us find that which was lost. In *The Tempest*, Prospero is so powerful that, he says, "graves at my command / Have waked their sleepers, oped, and let'em forth / By my so potent art" (V.i.48-50), and Ferdinand feels as if he has "received a second life" from Prospero (V.i.195). Indeed, the apparent deaths by drowning at the beginning of the play have turned out to be the illusions of a potent art. This strain of redemption and rebirth is not so great, however, as to include everyone in the romances, for corpses beyond revival and devouring bears may also be found.

Each of the romances thus includes some species of the greatest of all transformations; Shakespeare frequently links them to Ovidian analogues as well. Yet even the pyrotechnics of the statue scene avoid the stilting stagings of the transformation scenes I have quoted above. Just as in the earlier plays, where he found dramatic equivalents such as doubling or mimesis, so in the last plays Shakespeare finds structures of representation that reveal though they do not necessarily show metamorphosis. In one sense, the only thing that has changed from the earlier comedies is the *mode* of metamorphosis expressed, and even the mode is frequently familiar. In *Cymbeline*, for example, Imogen—the last of Shakespeare's heroines to become a man—receives instructions similar to, though more comical than Rosalind's:

PISANIO. You must forget to be a woman; change
    Command into obedience, fear and niceness—
    The handmaids of all women, or more truly
    Women it pretty self—into a waggish courage;
    Ready in gibes, quick-answered, saucy, and
    As quarrelous as the weasel. Nay, you must
    Forget that rarest treasure of your cheek,
    Exposing it—but O, the harder heart!
    Alack, no remedy—to the greedy touch
    Of common-kissing Titan, and forget
    Your laborsome and dainty trims, wherein
    You made great Juno angry.
IMOGEN.   Nay, be brief.
    I see into thy end and am almost
    A man already.
PISANIO. First, make yourself but like one.
                         (III.iv.155-68)

The changes worked by Imogen's disguise are, as usual, more
than external ones. She is especially prepared for this transformation, perhaps, by her reading of the *Metamorphoses,*
which Iachimo finds in her room: "She hath been reading late
/ The tale of Tereus. Here the leaf's turned down / Where
Philomel gave up" (II.ii.44-6). Again we find the habitual
connection between desire and transformation. The further
course of Imogen's plot fortunately follows the lines of those
of Julia, Portia, and Rosalind rather than of Philomel. Other
modes and conventions of metamorphosis already outlined in
earlier chapters recur frequently in the romances, so we are
in recognizable though often quite different territory most of
the time.

    A shift from the mode of extravagant doubling to staged
resurrection scenes implies other shifts in the dramatist's apprehension of the world and his craft. Now the family structure, especially in the father-daughter relation, becomes even
more the locus of transformation. The insistence on the wide
gap of time between one generation and the next insures,

moreover, that the structures of the romances will necessarily be cyclical and therefore implicitly redemptive. The insistence on patterns of generation and the cycles of the seasons leads inevitably to the perception that "great creating Nature" stands behind all the changes in these plays.[6] This sense of natural rebirth is enhanced in *The Winter's Tale* by the several references to 'flora' of all kinds, by the sheep-shearing scene and the great pastoral interlude in Act Four, and by the quite specific associations with vegetation myths:

> PERDITA.   O Proserpina,
> For the flow'rs now, that, frighted, thou let'st fall
> From Dis's wagon!
>   (IV.iv.116-18)

This allusion follows hard upon the famous debate between Polixenes and Perdita on Art and Nature. When she hands out flowers to those at the sheep-shearing feast, we begin to agree with Florizel that she *is* "Flora, / Peering in April's front" (IV.iv.2-3). Yet for all the emphasis on the "good goddess Nature" (II.iii.103), especially in the second half of the play, Shakespeare also makes it clear that the power which effects the deepest changes shown in this play is not simply mutability; the natural cycles of the seasons make Perdita possible, to be sure, but they do not account for Hermione's resurrection. Throughout the second half of the play, moreover, a design of allusion suggests that transformations more mysterious than those worked by great creating Nature are possible. I have already quoted, in Chapter One, Florizel's lengthy description of how the gods themselves "have taken / The shapes of beasts upon them" in the cause of love. Furthermore, we witness not only the usual pastoral conventions of disguise (Perdita herself is described as "some changeling"—III.iii.115), but an ironic reprise of it in Autolycus's clothes-switch with Florizel, and the triumph of the Shepherd and Clown when they appear in the clothes of a "gentleman born" (V.ii.136).

Another figure familiar from the earlier plays—the trickster-metamorph in the line of Puck—is seen in a new shape in *The*

Winter's Tale's Autolycus, a character right out of Ovid with a side trip through the cony-catching pamphlets. His generation by Mercury on Chyon identifies him as a thief, and something more:

Now when shee full her tyme had gone, shee bare by Mercurye
A sonne that hyght Awtolychus, who provde a wyly pye,
And such a fellow as in theft and filching had no peere.
He was his fathers owne sonne right: he could mennes eyes
   so bleere,
As for to make the black things whyght, and whyght things
   black appeere.
   (*Met*, XI 359-63)

Shakespeare's eye must have been drawn to Autolycus' power to make black things white, and white things black as much as to the idea of pure thievery, for it is just this power of "making" which comes to dominate the last half of the play. Before he enters the pastoral scene, Autolycus is described as a master of transformation and blearing men's eyes:

He hath songs for man or woman of all sizes; no milliner can so fit his customers with gloves. . . . Why, he sings 'em over, as they were gods or goddesses; you would think a smock were a she-angel, he so chants to the sleevehand, and the work about the square on't. (IV.iv. 191-2, 207-11)

Sly and ironic in his asides to the audience, Autolycus resembles no one so much as Proteus in his dealings with the people of Bohemia, shifting disguises constantly, taking on voices and roles along the whole social scale. He satisfies while he parodies the people's naive beliefs in metamorphosis in the ballads he sells; if they are "in print . . . then we are sure they are true" (IV.iv.260-1), but the actual audience may have its private doubts:

Here's another ballad, of a fish that appeared upon the coast on Wednesday the fourscore of April, forty thou-

211

sand fathom above water, and sung this ballad against
the hard hearts of maids; it was thought she was a woman,
and was turned into a cold fish for she would not exchange flesh with one that loved her. The ballad is very
pitiful, and as true. (IV.iv.275-81)

This ballad not only parodies the characters' desires for the
fanciful, and therefore anticipates our own wishes during the
final act of the play, but it also provides an exuberant mockery
of virtually all transformation, which is always a matter of
love and physical desire (the generation of Ovid's Autolycus
was itself a completely typical divine rape). Certainly the key
action is to "exchange flesh with one that loved her," in the
double sense of "exchange" as both sex and transformation,
which, as we have seen, amount to the same thing.

Many modes and instances of transformation in the romances reflect earlier examples, then. Yet in two preeminent
instances the ground shifts beneath us and something star-
tlingly new comes into sight: in the statue scene in *The Winter's Tale* and in the figure of the mage in *The Tempest*,
Shakespeare extends the representation and the very idea of
metamorphosis to a final stage. These two innovations—which
we will now examine in detail—have the greatest relevance
as well to a consideration of Shakespeare's attitudes toward
transformation and his own art.

The Winter's Tale

It was the most entrancing thing we ever remember to
have seen,—actually suspending the blood, and taking
the breath away. It was something supernatural almost;
and till the descent was fully accomplished, and the stone
turned to palpable woman again, something of a fine
fear sat upon us like a light chilliness.
. . . .
So complete was the illusion, so still the figure, so sight-
less the eyeballs, that you seemed insensibly to forget it

was a living being who stood before you; and when amidst the melody of music, she turned her head towards the king, the whole house started as if struck by an electric shock, or as if they had seen the dead arise.[7]

The great statue scene in *The Winter's Tale*—so transcendent, so mysterious, so beautiful—seems to turn its audiences into statues themselves, taking their breath away literally. As these nineteenth-century reviews of Helen Faucit's Hermione suggest, the audience turns to stone until Hermione's petrifaction ceases. "The spectator became an actor in the scene, and all 'Held their breath for a time,' " another reviewer of Faucit reported.[8] The statue scene has often seemed to involve its audience in that way, in part because, for the only time in Shakespeare, we have not been made privy to something as significant in the plot as the secret of Hermione's survival (to beg the question of the nature of her resurrection). Our own expectations, surprise, and wonder for a moment roughly coincide with that of the characters onstage. Part of the scene's mesmerizing power derives from all that it *means* in human terms—the power of forgiveness, the beauty and magnificence of love, the recovery of what seemed irretrievably lost, the momentary triumph over time even as its inescapable power is acknowledged in the fact of Hermione's wrinkles. I would suggest that the statue scene's peculiar and irresistible power is also the result of an audience's sense that it is watching something supernatural and utterly mysterious—metamorphosis.

It has often been noted that the statue scene derives from (among other sources) Ovid's story of Pygmalion and Galatea in Book Ten of the *Metamorphoses,* though Galatea had no existence before statuary, whereas Hermione's change is from life through stone to life again. Pygmalion's story is by no means the only account of petrifaction in Book Ten. Earlier, we hear of the foul Propoetides who, failing to acknowledge Venus's power, were turned into whores and then,

> when that shame was gone,
> And that they wexed brazen faast, shee turned them to stone,

In which betweene their former shape was diffrence small or
none.

(Met, X.258-60)

Most of Book Ten is narrated by Orpheus, who after losing
Eurydice was so stunned that he resembled the man who
"turned into stone" upon seeing Cerberus, or the unfortunate
couple, Olenus and Lethaea, "for whose pryde / They both
becomming stones, doo stand even yit on watry Ide" (X.77-
8). If the power of love can transform us, the loss of love can
produce the same effect, and Ovid frequently resorts in such
cases to the metaphor of petrifaction. Orpheus, the poet-singer,
can undo his own metaphorical petrifaction only through the
power of art, which is the route Shakespeare will take with
Hermione. As for Pygmalion, he has voluntarily fled the company of women, offended by "lyf in sin" of the "filthy Pro-
pets"; he believes that such vice is "packt within / The nature
of the womankynd." The analogy to Leontes is thus complex:
Leontes has also reached this life-denying conclusion about
women, at least his wife, and must live single ("without an
heir" as well, according to the oracle) until the prophecy of
Apollo is fulfilled. Here the exactness of the analogy fails
again, for Leontes is not the artist-figure that Pygmalion is,
though the terms of Pygmalion's art resonate with the entire
Art-Nature debate in *The Winter's Tale:*

> by wondrous Art an image he did grave
> Of such proportion, shape, and grace of nature never gave
> Nor can to any woman give . . .
> . . . .
> And such a one as that yee would beleeve had lyfe, and that
> Would moved bee, if womanhod and reverence letted not:
> So artificiall was the work. He woondreth at his Art. . . .

(Met, X.265-71)

Pygmalion's prayer to Venus is answered, and the image of
ivory comes alive under his loving hands. It is worth noting

that in his prayer Pygmalion refers to the statue as "my wife . . . (He durst not say bee yoon same wench of Ivory)," and that their love results in marriage—"the mariage that her selfe had made the Goddesse blessed so."

I do not wish to argue against those readings of the myth which find it a near-allegory of the power of Art, or part of a long-running debate about the relation between Art and Nature; these issues are crucial indeed both for Ovid and for *The Winter's Tale*.[9] The emphasis in Ovid's version, however, is on the metamorphic power of love, and it is an unusual story in the *Metamorphoses*, for the transformation of stone into woman not only reverses the usual direction of change for this mode (the soldiers turned to stone at the sight of the Gorgon's head, the petrifaction of Niobe over the loss of her loved ones), but for virtually all forms of change Ovid catalogues. The context of the story, moreover, is one of lost love and consequent deformation, and Pygmalion is the only character in Book Ten granted a happy ending. The recovery of love, like the initial experience of falling in love, generates metamorphosis—both in the loved one (the statue) and in the lover (Pygmalion leaves his life of singleness and calls the image "wife"). Leontes' awakening back into life parallels, or perhaps causes, Hermione's resurrection. The motif of resurrection in the romances seems partly explicable as the transformation resulting from the recovery of love.[10]

The loss of love in *The Winter's Tale*—Leontes' jealousy—releases a terrible power. It results in the most awful transformations of heart and mind, a dark counterpart to the positive transforming power of love. Jealousy's transformations are, appropriately, from flesh to stone. Stoniness suggests an extreme agony, a total deadness and stasis. We associate it with profound grief—"Theban Niobe, / Who for her sons' death wept out life and breath / And, dry with grief, was turned into a stone"[11]—or terror (Medusa). It is, more rarely, figuratively associated with the onset of love: "Thence flew Love's arrow with the golden head, / And thus Leander was enamoured. / Stone still he stood."[12] Hermione's transformation into a statue, however, signifies an absolute loss of self, occasioned by the loss of love; at the same time, her stoniness is a means to preserve the self until it can once again be safely acknowledged. The statue scene represents a second metamorphosis, something more than a reversal of the first. Yet neither metamorphosis is complete. Just as the first preserves life in death (the wrinkles in the stone), so the second retains death in life (the sadness of memory lives on). Hermione has become her "self" again by the end, though not exactly so, for the transformative powers unleashed by jealousy, by love gone mad, have taken their toll on everyone.

In the play's famous bear, by contrast, we are given a comical version, frightening but temporary, of the deranged metamorphic power of jealousy, located exactly on the boundary between two contrasted worlds, between "things dying" and "things new born." This boundary marks all kinds of transitions, some of them, as it turns out, only superficial. But "Exit, pursued by a bear" marks the change explicitly. What this infamous stage direction could mean and how the scene was to have been played have been controversial points for centuries. From my point of view, the bear is a comic incursion of the monstrous, both the symbolically destructive metamorphic result of Leontes' madness and a bizarre surrogate for him which, like a scapegoat, carries away the sin. If this "bear" was played by a man dressed in a bear's costume, as the preponderance of evidence now suggests,[13] then the audience would see a human-like bear, no matter how realistic the costume; and it might be useful to allow the actor's face to show through somehow. The bear already pulls us back in the direction of Snug the Joiner playing Lion, and there seems little point, in this of all plays, in straining for some kind of naturalism. If the bear, on the other hand, was a real bear, even a trained one, then the audience would have a sense that a metamorphic boundary has been completely crossed. Still, the action of metamorphosis itself signals a movement into comedy, into the possibilities of reversal and change; no matter how rigid Leontes' oath and Paulina's insistence, no matter

216

how impossible the recovery of love might seem, the very possibility of metamorphosis guarantees a change of tone. We are spared, for example, actually seeing Antigonus' death, and the clown's description of it transforms it into low comedy; no real horror attaches itself to the "things dying," certainly not in comparison with those of the tragedies. Geoffrey Bullough speaks for some readers when he argues that the bear scene is "not laughable but a sharp and frightening climax to a scene of pity and foreboding," but my experience is that only a reader, and not necessarily a member of an *audience*, experiences this.[14] The comedy or lightness of this scene may stem from our relief that the baby has been saved. The old man eaten is the price willingly tendered for the rescue of the child. The audience is not terrorized because it gets what it wants—salvation for Perdita. The thing found more than compensates for the thing lost. The same tilted bookkeeping gives us Hermione back at the price of the dead son. Everyone cannot be brought back, nor is everyone lost. Antigonus and Mamillius are the price regretfully but willingly paid.

The bear is only the first of a series of palpably true but untrue, credible but incredible transformations in the second half of the play. These other manifestations—the bear, the spirit-altering costume changes, the mercurial changes of Autolycus—each an example of the "exchange" of "flesh" in one sense or another, set the stage for the triumph of love in the final scene. The second scene of the fifth act, for example, with its excited reporting of offstage reunions and incredible news, prepares us for new possibilities of transformation— the gentlemen watching like frozen spectators, like witnesses to some staged scene, anticipate the court motionless as the statue moves. Here in V.ii, the boundaries between "joy and sorrow" are continually dissolved and confused, and those who saw Leontes' and Perdita's reunion were brought to life: "Who was most marble there changed color: some swooned, all sorrowed" (V.ii.92-3). Even the Shepherd and the Clown have been transformed into "gentlemen born" in the space of four hours. But nothing could really prepare us for the statue.

Leading Leontes and his court to the statue in its gallery, Paulina tells us to "prepare / To see the life as lively mocked, as ever / Still sleep mocked death" (V.iii.18-20); as David Young points out, the word "mock" throughout this scene has the double sense of "making fun" and "copying."[15] Thus the statue's effect, according to the characters in the play, is one of impossible mimesis—the most complete and naturalistic doubling imaginable, for "Julio Romano" could "beguile Nature" if he had "eternity and could put breath into his work" (V.ii.99 101). But this scene does not represent the triumph of art over nature, as Howard Felperin has pointed out; even Hermione's wrinkles, further examples of "our carver's excellence" (V.iii.30), are remarkable not so much for their verisimilitude as for their indication that some boundary is not being observed.[16] The effect on the immediate stage audience is like that on Helen Faucit's nineteenth-century audiences: Leontes wonders, "I am ashamed: does not the stone rebuke me, / For being more stone than it?" (ll. 37-8), and notes that it "From thy admiring daughter took the spirits, / Standing like stone with thee" (ll. 41-2). When Paulina bids the statue move and descend, the corollary petrifaction in the audience must take place: "then, all stand still," and Leontes assures her "No foot shall stir" (ll. 95, 98). Before long, Paulina notes, "My lord's almost so far transported that / He'll think anon it lives" (ll. 69-70). The statue's effect on us, the onstage and offstage audiences, is similarly profound. Again, we become like the gentlemen in the second scene, frozen witnesses to a miraculous theatrical experience.

What strikes Leontes and the others especially is the way in which the statue is and is not stone, the way in which it "mocks" their attempts to fix its boundaries. Leontes's first reaction is "silence" (l. 21), then he is able to address the "dear stone" (l. 24), and wonder at its wrinkles. Still, he can see only "warm life, / As now it coldly stands" (ll. 35-6). At this point, the statue is not much more than an iconological aid to his memory—"Oh, thus she stood, / Even with such life of majesty" (ll. 34-5)—yet with such evocative power as to seem uncanny: "O royal piece! / There's magic in thy majesty, which has / My evils conjured to remembrance" (ll. 38-40). Leontes has observed elaborate and rigorous rituals of memorialization for these sixteen years, yet even they, with Paulina's watchful insistence, have little power in comparison to the image before him. The vivid resurrection of Leontes' memory is the necessary prerequisite for the statue's resurrection; Hermione can only "live" again when Leontes' penance is completed by a certain power of memory. In the first scene of Act Five, Leontes responded to those wishing him to "forget your evil,"

> Whilst I remember
> Her and her virtues, I cannot forget
> My blemishes in them, and so still think of
> The wrong I did myself.
> (V.i.6-9)

Paulina is clearly associated with the virtue of "patience," but she is also, Leontes says, the one "Who hast the memory of Hermione, / I know, in honor" (V.i.50-1).

In the final scene, Leontes is coming to the memory not only of his own sins and Hermione's innocence, but of a much earlier and more innocent time. She now stands with such "life of majesty," he says, as "when first I wooed her" (V.iii.36). Paulina hearkens to this when the statue has descended and Leontes is unable to move himself: "Nay, present your hand. / When she was young, you wooed her; now, in age, / Is she become the suitor?" (ll. 107-9). This double sense of the statue's being and not being stone, of its symbolizing the past even as its wrinkles mimetically signify the passing of time, may recall for us those frequent moments in Ovid when the metamorph seems absolutely but yet not essentially changed. For Leontes, the statue is Hermione as she was before he sinned and as she would be after sixteen years and somehow also as she was *before* they had even married. The locus of transformation, to recall the terminology employed in our earlier discussions, is once again the space between the initiation and the *completion* of marriage—the completion in this case being not sexual intercourse but the issue from it. Three charged moments of time are collapsed together in this scene: the time when Leontes first wooed Hermione; the time when he sinned against her innocence; the time now when, "so far transported," Leontes becomes her husband again. These three moments mark various stages in the process of marriage, as it has been described earlier: courtship, sexual completion (Hermione nine months pregnant at the beginning of the play), and finally the acceptance of the results of sexual completion (Hermione's accused child becomes the means of reunion and resurrection; Hermione tells Perdita that she has "preserved / Myself to see the issue"—ll. 127-8) In *A Midsummer Night's Dream,* as we saw, various fears attendant on the idea of marriage had to be exorcised before the marriages could take place; the impingement of the monstrous represented part of the conflict. In *The Winter's Tale,* jealousy is the result of the greatest of such fears, and it must be not only exorcized, but atoned for. When Leontes rejects the oracle—that is, truth itself, the inevitable facts of existence—one child dies just after another has been born; Mamillius, Leontes's own image, ceases to exist and Perdita, Hermione's image, survives. The economy and suggestiveness of this symbolism is striking. It seems inevitable, at least in hindsight, that Leontes must first accept the daughter, the image, before the mother can be restored to him. The natural processes of mutability have brought Perdita back before her father "as is the spring to the earth," and made possible the far more mysterious changes known as metamorphoses. Paulina also sees how Perdita recalls Hermione when Leontes wooed her (V.i.225-7). Leontes' two references to "twenty years" (ll. 71, 84) in the latter part of this scene seem to refer not to the intervening period of his penance (the "sixteen winters" twice referred to by Paulina and Camillo, ll. 31, 50), but to that period before the play begins, before their marriage perhaps, "when first I wooed her." The transformations and dangers of marriage are both annulled and accepted at this mysterious moment; when Paulina notes that Leontes nearly believes that the statue lives, he replies:

> O sweet Paulina,
> Make me to think so twenty years together!
> No settled senses of the world can match
> The pleasure of this madness. Let't alone.
>
> (ll. 70-3)

But Paulina has just begun the pleasure of that madness. Why should all this slipping back and forth in time be represented by so much that is static, stony, and still? Some metamorphic power behind this apparently motionless scene allows motion through time.

The mere revelation of the statue, as a static iconological aid to the art of memory, is powerful enough. Its stillness has struck a corresponding stasis in its various audiences. The "carver's excellence" has seemingly triumphed to such an extent that the art itself is nature. But these intellectualized pleasures are quickly left behind. In every production I have seen, the audience has known that the "statue" was Hermione, somehow alive, long before anyone on stage has.[17] Part of our pleasure in the play from this point on diverges from that of the onstage audience: we know it's Hermione and wait for her sequel, but Leontes thinks it's a statue and is surprised to see it move. It's metamorphosis for him, and change for us in our awareness of the differences between his state of mind and ours. "Wonder" is common to both audiences, and we are certainly confounded in similar ways. But our wonder is as much that Shakespeare will dare to pull off this brilliant *coup de théâtre* as it is that Hermione "lives." Most of us, I think, *expect* her to move once we've seen her as the statue, and our profound gratitude and delight that she does move differs slightly from Leontes' relief and joy. The metamorphosis works for us on more than one level.

In the earlier comedies, stasis and rigidity were denials of life; and so here, the statue must move. If "still sleep mocked death" (l. 20), then we will prepare to "see the life as lively

mocked" (l. 19); the "lively" connotes motion, the stirring of
the artifact that now but "coldly stands" (l. 36). Leontes is
ready for a miracle, but still unprepared for the gradual dissolution of formal boundaries which Paulina leads him through
in this scene.[18] All attention is fixed on an ascending scale of
transcended boundaries. We have been told that the statue is
newly painted, "the color's / Not dry" (ll. 47-8), but that
merely prepares for Paulina's warning, "no longer shall you
gaze on 't, lest your fancy / May think anon it moves" (ll. 60-
1), the first stage of transformation. But Leontes already does
think this: "Would you not deem it breathed? And that those
veins / Did verily bear blood?" (ll. 64-5). Polixenes agrees,
finding even an illusion of heat: "the very life seems warm
upon her lip" (l. 66). Leontes is increasingly fascinated by the
statue's slow, subtle, unmistakable movement: "The fixure of
her eye has motion in't, / As we are mocked with art" (ll. 67-
8). He perceives that "Still, methinks, / There is an air comes
from her. What fine chisel / Could ever yet cut breath?"
(ll. 77-9). To this last question there is no answer, nor does
he wait for one; he attempts to kiss Hermione. These intimations of movement are enough for Leontes: they tell him
that a metamorphosis is occurring, that the statue is beginning
to be transformed in part by the power of his love. The equation works both directions: the statue moves as a result of
Leontes' awakened love, and his love awakens fully when the
statue moves. Paulina bids him

> resolve you
> For more amazement. If you can behold it,
> I'll make the statue move indeed, descend,
> And take you by the hand—but then you'll think,
> Which I protest against, I am assisted
> By wicked powers.
>   (ll. 86-91)

There is much power in that "if"—the capacity for metamorphosis here depends as much on the audience's complicity
as it does on any external magic. Not only our imaginative

concurrence is required, though, as Paulina goes on to make clear. The magic will work because only believers are present—a community of well-wishers hoping the best for Hermione, one of those closed complicit groups often necessary to the success of transformation. A Malvolio would have to be excluded:

> It is required
> You do awake your faith; then, all stand still.
> Or those that think it is unlawful business
> I am about, let them depart.
> (ll. 94-7)

These directions include Leontes and his "faith" in a deeply human way, and include the audience in even more complicated, metadramatic ways, for our "faith," our ability to "behold it," are also being invoked. Even as the human drama of Leontes' recovery and Hermione's resurrected love is being performed, Shakespeare offers us the supreme moment, in all his plays, of theatrical self-consciousness. It is difficult to imagine a scene which could be so emotionally gripping and so intellectually challenging at the same time. We are watching a myth, but we are not; we are watching a true transformation, but we are not. Shakespeare has perfectly fused here the metamorphoses of love and the metamorphoses of art.

The emphasis on movement throughout this scene is matched by the idea of descent (ll. 88, 99), suggesting the mythic possibilities of theophany, and perhaps reminding us of the myth of Proserpina referred to in Act Four. Leontes is already looking toward the next stage of transformation:

> What you can make her do,
> I am content to look on; what to speak,
> I am content to hear; for 'tis as easy
> To make her speak, as move.
> (ll. 91-4)

One thinks here of all those characters in Ovid, like Io, who lose the power of speech through metamorphosis, and how all the more emblematic this recovery seems. A metadramatic reading of this moment is almost inevitable—the power of the playwright to call static characters into a "living" dimension by giving them his words, giving local habitations and names to airy nothings. We recall that, besides eternity, the one thing "Julio Romano" lacked was the ability to "put breath into his work," but Shakespeare does not lack this ability: "it appears she lives, / Though yet she speak not" (ll. 117-8). In the next moments, Hermione will draw breath and speak, and the metamorphosis has ceased. The power of language both causes and ends this transformation.

The actual moment when the statue deliberately moves, steps down, and takes Leontes' hand is implied during Paulina's famous invocation. It has been described from almost every imaginable perspective—the fact that music "awakes" her; the theme of time; the religious intimations. It is important to note that this speech also resonates throughout with the language of metamorphosis:

> Music, awake her: strike.
> 'Tis time; descend; be stone no more; approach;
> Strike all that look upon with marvel; come;
> I'll fill your grave up. Stir; nay, come away;
> Bequeath to death your numbness, for from him
> Dear life redeems you. You perceive she stirs.
> [*Hermione comes down.*]
> Start not: her actions shall be holy as
> You hear my spell is lawful. Do not shun her
> Until you see her die again, for then
> You kill her double. Nay, present your hand.
> When she was young, you wooed her; now, in age,
> Is she become the suitor?
>   (ll. 98-109)

"If she pertains to life, let her speak too," the onlookers say; "make it manifest where she has lived, / Or how stol'n from the dead" (ll. 113-5). These secrets, these hints of resurrection, these "lawful" forms of magic, have been revealed to us under the guise of metamorphosis: an "old tale" (l. 117), but a true one.

The Tempest

"The isle is full of noises, / Sounds and sweet airs that give delight and hurt not" (III.ii.138-9), says Caliban. The commentators have agreed on the island's special qualities, from Reuben Brower,

> The island is a world of fluid, merging states of being and forms of life. This lack of dependable boundaries between states is also expressed by the many instances of confusion between natural and divine,

through David Young, for whom the island has a

> tendency to dissolve the normal barriers between the physical and the mental, exterior and interior events,

to Alvin Kernan, for whom the island is a place

> of joy and terror, of beauty and ugliness, where the "printless foot" flies across yellow sands bordering on flats of oozy mud; animal howls sound suddenly, wild fire flashes, and strange visions appear and disappear. Around its edges the deep ocean rises and subsides, revealing and covering again, like the stream of Nile, the muddy shallows; and beneath the dark blue waters the bones of drowned men slowly change to coral, and rich pearls glitter from the eye-sockets of the scattered sculls.
>   To this island every man must come, wrecked by great sea storms or helplessly adrift in the broad ocean.[19]

For us, this realm is evolutionary—a life-creating swamp and swill full of amphibious beings neither fish, flesh, nor fowl, where boundaries dissolve and reform continually. Shakespeare found in the island setting one of the richest and most evocative symbols in all of English Renaissance drama; and yet, the audience "sees" this fully realized island only in its own imagination, for it remains physically only the bare stage of the theater. Beyond all else, the stage seems to *be* that island, where the poet's dreams and the audience's visions are staged, where the analogies between magician and poet, between the metamorphoses of nature and those of art, have been collapsed into a single profound setting dominated by the figure of the mage.

The Tempest is an obvious and magnificent capstone to Shakespeare's long interest in metamorphosis. He has set this play in an almost purely metamorphic world—one that is fused with art, magic, and the theater throughout. As others, especially Brower, have shown in some detail, metamorphosis is simply the "key metaphor" in this play[20]—or, to put it more strongly, metamorphosis is the informing energy of *The Tempest*. The briefest examination of the play reveals the encompassing nature of this energy. Ariel's career alone—"he is at once the agent, the instrument, and the substance of transformation"[21]—suggests the mysterious powers we have by now found so frequently in Shakespearean comedy and romance, as he tells Prospero how he managed the illusionary "shipwreck":

> I boarded the King's ship. Now on the beak,
> Now in the waist, the deck, in every cabin,
> I flamed amazement. Sometime I'd divide
> And burn in many places; on the topmast,
> The yards, the boresprit would I flame distinctly,
> Then meet and join. . . .
> (I.ii.196-201)

Ariel's own appearances in the play make us think of Proteus: he appears "like a water nymph" (I.ii.319); he is "invisible" (I.ii.376); he enters "like a harpy" (III.iii.52); he may play the part of Ceres in the masque (IV.i.75; cf. l. 167); he joins in the hunt, setting the dogs on Caliban, Stephano, and Trinculo (IV.i.255); he serves as an efficient stage manager throughout; and he returns to himself, whatever that is, in the final act. Ariel has been imprisoned in a tree and released from it, like any number of Ovidian or romance characters; and his victims are transformed into lower states themselves—

> Then I beat my tabor;
> At which like unbacked colts they pricked their ears,
> Advanced their eyelids, lifted up their noses
> As they smelt music. So I charmed their ears
> That calflike they my lowing followed through
> Toothed briers, sharp furzes, pricking goss, and thorns,
> Which ent'red their frail shins.
>
> (IV.i.175-81)

Those who would defy this power of transformation end up in the "foul lake," smelling "all horse piss" (IV.i.199). Clearly not a power to be trifled with.

Along the way we hear of the magical powers of Sycorax and of the Orphic "miraculous harp" (II.i.89) of Amphion which raised the walls of Thebes and, according to Sandys, "brought the salvage people to civility." Moreover, we once again witness comic incursions of the monstrous, attendant on a planned marriage. Caliban sought "to violate / The honor" of Miranda (I.ii.349-50), as does Ferdinand in one sense, but Ferdinand will earn the privilege through his moral merit, and by the grace of the ritual of marriage. Prospero's insistence to Ferdinand that the lovers abstain before marriage—

> If thou dost break her virgin-knot before
> All sanctimonious ceremonies may
> With full and holy rite be minist'red,
> No sweet aspersion shall the heavens let fall
> To make this contract grow; but barren hate,
> Sour-eyed disdain, and discord shall bestrew
> The union of your bed with weeds so loathly
> That you shall hate it both. Therefore take heed,
> As Hymen's lamps shall light you—
>
> (IV.i.15-23)

—is not the crabby and neurotic restriction of an incestually repressed father, as the psychoanalytic critics have argued,[22] but a formalized statement of the necessary order of transformation wrought by marriage which has been implied in all the comedies before *The Tempest*. "Hymen's lamps" light the process of transformation known as marriage. The violation of this ordered process, like other violations of order and boundary, will result in the "discord" of a "union" (ll. 19-20). Caliban is the agent of the comic exorcism here, as the "translated" Bottom was in *A Midsummer Night's Dream*. Caliban is already a monster, a "thing of darkness," a "villain," a "poisonous slave." Stories of the cannibals and "salvage men" discovered in the new world seem sources in part,[23] but Caliban will turn into an even more grotesque monster when Stephano and Trinculo enter the play. Caliban complains that Prospero's spirits torment him in various changed shapes—

> Sometime like apes that mow and chatter at me,
> And after bite me; then like hedgehogs which
> Lie tumbling in my barefoot way and mount
> Their pricks at my footfall; sometime am I
> All wound with adders, who with cloven tongues
> Do hiss me into madness
>   (II.ii.9-14)

—when he tries to hide from the drunken Trinculo, who finds something like a "dead Indian," which "smells like a fish." "A man or a fish?" he asks (ll. 33, 26, 25). He is "legged like a man" and has "fins like arms"; he concludes it is no fish, "but an islander" (l.36). Hearing someone else approaching, Trinculo crawls under Caliban's cloak, and Stephano confronts "some monster of the isle, with four legs, who hath got, as I take it, an ague. Where the devil should he learn our language?" (ll. 65-7). This bizarre hybrid sounds like the kind of great fish Autolycus would sell a ballad about, and one mariner reported something like this in 1597, claiming to have seen a beast which had the "eares of a Dog, armes like a Man without haire, and at the elbows great Finnes like a fish."[24] The contemporary gullibility about metamorphosis is being parodied here, as it seems to be later when Gonzalo, whose head is full of romances, asks who would have believed that there were

> mountaineers
> Dewlapped like bulls, whose throats had hanging at 'em
> Wallets of flesh? Or that there were such men
> Whose heads stood in their breasts?
> (III.iii.44-7)

We might be ready to believe anything in *The Tempest,* and yet these grotesqueries, though "real" enough in the play's terms, nevertheless seem as if they can be harnessed. Stephano's final vision of the "monster" sounds like many an other "natural perspective" which we have seen in the comedies when two become one:

> Four legs and two voices—a most delicate monster! His forward voice now is to speak well of his friend; his backward voice is to utter foul speeches and to detract.
> (II.ii.91-4)

Pulling his friend from under the covering, Stephano wonders if "this mooncalf" has "vent[ed]" him (l.108). This wonderfully ludicrous parody of a birth reminds us of Caliban's own generation by Setebos upon Sycorax, who "litter[ed]" the island with this "freckled whelp" (I.ii.282-4), and looks forward to what will *not* happen with Ferdinand and Miranda, who have preserved the ceremonies and are assured of avoiding "barren hate" and "sour-eyed disdain." The monsters of marriage form a comic anti-masque, and they will be defeated by Prospero's magic, which presents a masque of marriage to counter these deformities.

The purpose of Prospero's wedding masque for Ferdinand and Miranda, Iris tells us, is

> A contract of true love to celebrate
> And some donation freely to estate
> On the blessed lovers.
> (IV.i.84-6)

Prospero has referred to it slightingly, as "some vanity of mine art" (l. 41), and asked Ariel to bring "thy meaner fellows . . . thy rabble" (ll. 35, 37) to perform it. But there is no doubt that he intends it seriously, and that it can be presented only after the "contract" has been sworn to, and Ferdinand promised never to allow temptation to melt

> Mine honor into lust, to take away
> The edge of the day's celebration
> When I shall think or Phoebus' steeds are foundered
> Or Night kept chained below.
>   (ll. 28-31)

The masque is a vision of marriage created by Prospero; if recent critics have focused on the latter half of this formulation ("This is Prospero's creation, the most palpable example we are shown of his art"[25]), we should not neglect its relevance to the idea of marriage. This vision clearly functions as an ideal, but reactions to its utopian quality vary enormously. Stephen Orgel has pointed out how the masque stands in contrast to the anti-masque of Caliban, how it suggests a wholly different scheme of time, how it nevertheless omits winter from its cycle of the seasons, and so elides the question of death: "So, when Prospero interrupts, it is to stress that what is missing from the masque is nevertheless very real. The vision of permanence is in danger of blinding us to the necessities of the moment."[26] Northrop Frye sees this masque as a supreme vision, presenting "the meeting of earth and heaven under the rainbow, the symbol of Noah's new-washed world, after the tempest and flood had receded, and when it was promised that springtime and harvest would not cease"; in the masque, he says, "the dialectic of Shakespearean romance is most fully and completely stated."[27] Harry Berger, on the other hand, sees it as a "brief withdrawal into the golden age, Gonzalo's dream as magical theater, yet the realities of life which it evades are woven into its texture, revealing those pressures which now distract Prospero and become ex-

plicit in the revels speech."[28] The current critical trend seems
to be to emphasize what Prospero has left out, to find his
"art" finally lacking, and thus to create some distance between
him and his creator.[29] Certainly Prospero's powers at the end
of the play seem limited, and the masque does take us only
from "spongy April" (l. 65) to August (l. 134), but, as in all
pastoral visions, the omission of certain facts of life is exactly
the point. The masque offers us a vision of a temperate, wholly
beneficent and natural harmony, in contrast to the comically
frightening representations of the monstrous we've already
seen; rather than withdrawing from these representations, as
Berger says, the masque transcends them, if only for a moment. For the masque is a place where the darkest Ovidian
forces of eros do *not* live, where Cupid's disorders cannot
cause harm. Ceres wants to know specifically

> If Venus or her son, as thou dost know,
> Do now attend the Queen? Since they did plot
> The means that dusky Dis my daughter got,
> Her and her blind boy's scandaled company
> I have forsworn.

She is assured by Iris that they have returned to Paphos, though
they thought

> to have done
> Some wanton charm upon this man and maid,
> Whose vows are, that no bed-right shall be paid
> Till Hymen's torch be lighted.

Now, "Mars' hot minion" and "her waspish-headed son"
have retreated; Cupid "has broke his arrows, / Swears he will
shoot no more, but play with sparrows / And be a boy right
out" (ll. 87-101). No Proserpinas will be seized here (nor in
The Winter's Tale, where Perdita invoked her—IV.iv.116),
and thus no generation of metamorphosis through violent
love; here is one explanation for the absence of winter. Instead, we are granted a vision of a far more beautiful and

natural series of transformations, culminating in the wish that "Spring come to you at the farthest / In the very end of harvest" (ll. 114-5). "Honor, riches, marriage blessing" (l. 106): this is the vision of fruitfulness resulting from the transformation of marriage.

The masque ends with the dance of the Naiades and the "sunburned sicklemen," a fusion of water and earth, sea and land. As they dance, Prospero "starts suddenly and speaks," as he recalls the conspiracy against him. Perhaps we can distinguish now between the vision of marriage and its blessings which has been granted us, and the aesthetic quality of the vision itself. It is undeniably folly to wish, as Ferdinand does at one point, to "live here ever"—say a day without the ever, we think; this place is only approximately "Paradise" (l. 124). Yet some readers speak as if they are glad that the masque is destroyed, preferring Caliban's "realism" to Prospero's "visionary" powers (Caliban seems destined to become our equivalent to the nineteenth century's elevation of Malvolio to tragic stature); this is doubly perverse, for the play is not asking us to *choose* between them, though surely the choice would be simple. Rather, we are shown both sides of the transformations that love can generate, figured in Caliban on the one hand and Ferdinand on the other. Neither of them can be denied, but the purpose of marriage is to transform the Caliban into a Ferdinand; the play's concern with the nature-versus-nurture question parallels this dialectic, and goes so far as to suggest that such a transformation may not always be possible, however desirable.[30] We have seen this obstinacy before, in Shylock, Malvolio, Jaques, and others.

Prospero's great "Our revels now are ended" speech serves as an interior epilogue, as it were, closing down the masque, and pronouncing the most profound vision of transformation imaginable.[31] The theatrical terminology in this speech ("revels," "actors," "great globe," "pageant," "rack") suggests, as every biographical critic has argued, that we are hearing something of Shakespeare's own farewell here; more concretely, we are hearing Prospero's growing awareness that even his own magical powers are limited, perhaps even worthless from one point of view. It is a vision of apocalypse, and so in some sense despairing; and it denigrates the theatrical experience. Yet we find the speech not entirely despairing: it marks an important stage of awareness for Prospero, for Shakespeare, and for the audience. We might place next to Prospero's speech the wonderful song Ariel sings to Ferdinand earlier in the play, with *its* metamorphic vision:

> Full fathom five thy father lies;
>   Of his bones are coral made;
> Those are pearls that were his eyes;
>   Nothing of him that doth fade
> But doth suffer a sea-change
> Into something rich and strange.
> Sea-nymphs hourly ring his knell.
>   (I.ii.399-405)

Here we have transformations which transcend death, which turn corpses into coral, eyes into pearls. Nothing is lost altogether, in this vision, for all suffers a sea-change (we need only think of the links between metamorphosis and water in the earlier plays); there is even a suggestion that whatever fades in death may actually be improved when it is transformed into something "rich and strange." This process seems slow and peaceful, without violence; coral and pearl take time to form, and are objects of rare beauty. Music rings a harmony which is more than a dirge.

In Prospero's "revels" speech, however, the sea-nymphs are not heard—the Naiades have vanished. Nor does the "ding-dong" bell sound; rather, with "a strange, hollow, and confused noise" (IV.i.138sd), the masque disappears. Though he has worked many a change himself, Prospero now realizes, as Henry IV did in his "book of fate" speech, that the world's metamorphic energies are larger even than his powers. It's not only Prospero's recollection of that "foul conspiracy / Of the beast Caliban and his confederates" that prompts this revelation, though they are the occasion of it. He also recalls the change beyond all change:

> Our revels now are ended. These our actors,
> As I foretold you, were all spirits and
> Are melted into air, into thin air;
> And, like the baseless fabric of this vision,
> The cloud-capped towers, the gorgeous palaces,
> The solemn temples, the great globe itself,
> Yea, all which it inherit, shall dissolve,
> And, like this insubstantial pageant faded,
> Leave not a rack behind. We are such stuff
> As dreams are made on, and our little life
> Is rounded with a sleep.
> (IV.i.148-58)

Prospero apologizes for this speech, saying he is "vexed," his "old brain . . . troubled" (ll. 158-9), but we are stunned by it. We have heard these metaphors of metamorphosis before—"melted," "dissolve," "faded," "dream"—but we have not witnessed such profundity, measured so vast a philosophical collapse, before. Brower describes the effect of this speech as an almost "Proustian merging of icon and subject," in which "we experience the blending of states of being, of substantial and unsubstantial, or real and unreal."[32] Taken abstractly, Prospero's speech says little that is not familiar; it breaks no new ground philosophically. And even its images are, in isolation, conventional. Yet there is something overwhelming about the speech which every audience has noted. Perhaps it is partly the result of its context, when we have been taken about as far in the direction of magic and omnipotent observation as we wish to go, though we don't know it yet. Perhaps too we are simply moved by the sight of a man painfully gaining the deepest wisdom that life has to offer. It is powerful enough, in the end, to allow Prospero's "nobler reason" to be engaged, and permit him to say what few of us in real life can ever accept: "The rarer action is / In virtue than in vengeance" (V.i.27-8).[33]

One of the models for *The Tempest*'s structure is that class of moldy old tales known as *commedia dell'arte* pastoral romance, or "shipwreck pastorals." The Arden editor, Frank Kermode, is skeptical that the *commedia* is the direct source which some, especially K. M. Lea, think it is, and says that "the transformations wrought by Prospero and Ariel are of the common stock of magic lore,"[34] though there is a huge difference between the onstage transformations of the sort quoted at the beginning of this chapter and what we actually see in *The Tempest*. Shakespeare has rather imbued the entire dramatic world of the play with a sense of metamorphosis, in which even the shifting relationships among the characters, and the characters' own changes of heart, seem part of an incomprehensible energy. What is especially noteworthy here is the way in which Shakespeare has remade the idea of the magician, making his transformative powers akin to those of a dramatist and, even more crucially, in revealing the limitations of those powers. As many recent readers have shown, Prospero does not succeed in maintaining the visionary masque, or in transforming the conscience of Antonio. The omnipotent magicians of the *commedia* pastorals never had an Antonio, much less a Caliban, to deal with. And it is part of this effort to transform the figure of the magician which leads Shakespeare to make so many analogies—so many identities—between the transformations of magic and those of art. The word "art" in fact doubles for both; as Young shows, "Prospero's 'art' consists mainly of shows and spectacles," and so the long-established link between the transformations of the magician and those of the dramatist is perfectly justified.[35] At the end of his career, Shakespeare employs the most mythically appropriate figure of metamorphosis available in his culture. As usual, Shakespeare himself transforms this character-type into something rich and strange we have never seen before.

※

Prospero's farewell to his art is a magnificent, elegiac moment in *The Tempest* and, as many instinctively feel, in Shakespeare's career; it is impossible not to be moved by it in ways beyond the play's context. When Prospero majestically invokes his powers, only to abjure them forever, he strikes a complex tone of celebration and loss:

> Ye elves of hills, brooks, standing lakes, and groves,
> And ye that on the sands with printless foot
> Do chase the ebbing Neptune, and do fly him
> When he comes back; you demi-puppets that
> By moonshine do the green sour ringlets make,
> Whereof the ewe not bites; and you whose pastime
> Is to make midnight mushrumps, that rejoice
> To hear the solemn curfew; by whose aid
> (Weak masters though ye be) I have bedimmed
> The noontide sun, called forth the mutinous winds,
> And 'twixt the green sea and the azured vault
> Set roaring war; to the dread rattling thunder
> Have I given fire and rifted Jove's stout oak
> With his own bolt; the strong-based promontory
> Have I made shake and by the spurs plucked up
> The pine and cedar; graves at my command
> Have waked their sleepers, oped, and let 'em forth
> By my so potent art. But this rough magic
> I here abjure; and when I have required
> Some heavenly music (which even now I do)
> To work mine end upon their senses that
> This airy charm is for, I'll break my staff,
> Bury it certain fathoms in the earth,
> And deeper than did ever plummet sound
> I'll drown my book.
>   (V.i.33-57)

Having seen this "rough magic" at work, *we* are reluctant to see it go, but Prospero's vow to return to the world prepares us for our own return from the theater. The moving quality of his farewell is deepened when we realize it is an allusion to, virtually a quotation from, Ovid.[36] What better muse to invoke at the end of a career than the one who has figured so prominently from the beginning? "Honest Ovid" is being heard one last time as well.

That Prospero's farewell is an adaptation of Ovid is most fitting, then, but that Shakespeare makes Prospero quote the speech of a witch, Medea, still requires some comment. The specific act for which the speech is invocation in Ovid is Medea's promise to restore Aeson, Jason's father, to his youth (a story also alluded to in *The Merchant of Venice*, V.i.12-14). Here is the transformation most truly against nature, and a peculiarly human one: mutability reversed by metamorphosis. Lyly had employed a similar magical reversal in *Endymion*, more than twenty years before *The Tempest*, but this kind of magical transformation will *not* be allowed here. Medea's story ends in betrayal, murder, and exile—rather as the story behind *The Tempest* began—whereas this story is turned around at the end of the play to avoid just these dangers.

Frank Kermode has noted that Shakespeare drains away the "black" magic of Medea in *The Tempest*: "Only those elements . . . consistent with "white" magic are taken over for Prospero, though some of the remnant is transferred to Sycorax."[37] But the question remains, why was Shakespeare attracted to this speech of Medea's in the first place? Rejecting Kermode's distinctions, Harry Berger sees the speech as a key part of the play's general qualification of "magical . . . modes of response to life's problems": unlike Medea, Berger argues, Prospero "is trying hard to give up his rough magic, forswear vengeance, and renew life for the next generation by less occult methods. The contrast is all in his favor, not because he is white and Medea black, but because she gives herself increasingly to her passion and art, while he fights against them."[38] This formulation takes us a long way toward understanding the speech's attractiveness, but its power derives from more than irony or contrast—Medea that way, Prospero this way.

The choice of Medea's speech is presumably quite deliberate, for it was widely quoted in the Renaissance as a notorious example of the power of witchcraft. The speech is quoted at length by believers and skeptics alike, including

Cornelius Agrippa and Bodin, among others. Medea's speech is referred to several times as one of the standard poetic "proofs" of the power of witchcraft in the encyclopedic rebuttal of Reginald Scot, who refers to Ovid contemptuously as "Bodin's poet" because Bodin "mainteineth for true the most part of *Ovids Metamorphosis,* and the greatest absurdities and impossibilities of all that book: marie he thinketh some one tale therein may be fained."[39] The speech is also quoted (by way of Bodin) in Thomas Middleton's *The Witch* (c. 1615). There, Hecate has been asked by the Duchess to kill Almachildes. When her powers are questioned, Hecate angrily replied, "Let scrupulous creatures know / *Cum volui, ripis ipsis mirantibus, amnes*" and so on, quoting Ovid in Latin for eight lines, and concluding,

> Can you doubt me then, daughter,
> That can make mountains tremble, miles of woods walk,
> Whole earth's foundations bellow, and the spirits
> Of the entomb'd to burst out from their marbles,
> Nay, draw yond moon to my involv'd designs?[40]

The answer is clearly no. It is likely, then, that the origins of Prospero's farewell would have been known and recognized by at least part of the audience, and that the associations were largely negative; Medea, George Sandys sums up in his commentary on the *Metamorphoses,* "invokes the Earth, Aire, Winds, Mountaines, Rivers, Lakes, and Wood-gods; as either producing or virtuating magicall ingredients: lastly the infernall powers."[41]

Medea's presence—in the form of Sycorax—is felt in *The Tempest* long before Prospero's quotation; the "infernal powers" have only recently departed the island, and it may be said that they live on in a different form in some of the human visitors. The demonic associations of Prospero's farewell remind us generally of the thin line (if it existed anywhere but in theory) between white and black magic, and more specifically of the uneasy parallels throughout the play between Prospero on the one hand, and Sycorax on the other. These parallels range from parallel banishments, both "with child," equal twelve-year exiles, and (in Caliban's view) parallel usurpations of the island, through similar imprisonings of Ariel, to close verbal echoes and parallel descriptions of their powers. Sycorax, Prospero says,

> was a witch, and one so strong
> That could control the moon, make flows and ebbs,
> And deal in her command without her power,
>   (V.i.269-71)

and Prospero himself has "put the wild water in [a] roar" (I.ii.2), "bedimmed / The noontide sun," and "called forth the mutinous winds" (V.i.41-2). The dark side of Prospero's magic, however "white" it may be technically, receives expression throughout the play. Prospero's recognition of Caliban, "This thing of darkness I / Acknowledge mine" (V.i.275-6), extends to his own instincts as well as to the offspring of Sycorax. Finally, just as Medea renewed Aeson's life by restoring his youth, so Ferdinand has "received a second life" from his "second father," Prospero (V.i.195).

The suggested link between Prospero and Sycorax culminates in his farewell to magic, where, by quoting Medea, Prospero temporarily *becomes* his dark other, a composite Medea/Sycorax figure, in his very leave-taking. At the most critical moment of the speech, when he quotes Medea's greatest and most notorious power—"graves at my command / Have waked their sleepers, oped, and let 'em forth / By my so potent art"—Prospero turns away from the parallel to become himself again, or rather, a new version of himself.[42] This moment occurs just when Medea's one power which Prospero has *not* employed or claimed in the play has been claimed—when becoming Medea means most fully ceasing to be Prospero. Furthermore, in becoming Medea temporarily, Prospero as it were voluntarily submits himself to metamorphosis for the first time. His magical implements will be returned to the elements which they once controlled, and with which the play began—the book, offering control of nature, will be drowned, the staff buried in the earth. Unlike some notorious practitioners of black magic, Prospero can exist separately from his powers of transformation. More to the point, Prospero will himself now begin a journey across water, back to Milan. This completion of the cycle of exile and return is also a setting forth into, a submission to, the world of flux he once controlled.

Yet metamorphosis continues to haunt even this renunciation of metamorphosis. Prospero no sooner abjures his art than he employs it again to summon "some heavenly music (which even now I do)" (V.i.52). The music sounds through the rest of the speech, as he looks forward to the further completion of "this airy charm" and the submission of his enemies. In offering to break his staff, furthermore, he will "bury" it certain "fathoms" in the earth, a metaphoric transformation of earth and water which leaves the staff and all it signifies within reach.

To drown the book, and bury the staff fathoms deep, reminds us inevitably as well of Ariel's great song, "full fathom five," heralding the metamorphosis of death into paradoxical life and proving that some sea-changes are worth having. Prospero's farewell, which begins with the quotation from Medea, ends with the rich suggestions of his own sea-change in progress, an immersion in the destructive element which is the only way of being human. Prospero is required to *become* Medea temporarily so that he can fully experience in her the extremity of his own desires and the dream she represents. The similarities between them, mentioned earlier, are equally matched as well by their differences—the composite Medea/Sycorax figure is female, her offspring male rather than female, her magic black rather than white, her powers marked more towards vengeance than forgiveness. But this otherness and difference are only the mirror reflection of a dark twin.

Prospero renounces here not only the black magic always inherently associated with transformation, but the artistic dream of controlling transformation at all.[43] The question of his own self-control, and thereby the control of his magical powers, is directly raised now. By Act Five, the very possibility of control has come to seem more and more dreamlike. Caliban's fundamental recalcitrance and Antonio's stony silence in the final scene are the most visible reminders that even the roughest magic has its limitations; the very elements that he controls—represented in Ariel and Caliban—resist Prospero tooth and nail. Even Medea's supernatural powers did not prevent her abandonment by Jason, or the transformation of her despair to vengeance. We have already heard how Sycorax was unable to control *her* metamorphic powers; as Prospero tells Ariel in Act One,

> Thou best know'st
> What torment I did find thee in; thy groans
> Did make wolves howl and penetrate the breasts
> Of ever-angry bears. It was a torment
> To lay upon the damned, which Sycorax
> Could not again undo. It was mine art,
> When I arrived and heard thee, that made gape
> The pine, and let thee out.
> (I.ii.286-93)

Whether it was through her death or her incapacity, Sycorax could not undo her metamorphosis of Ariel into the cloven pine; Ariel was imprisoned until Prospero had performed the Medea-like task of making "gape / The pine." When he claims later the Medean power to have made graves open, we can recognize the translation of his own powers into the more sinister terms of his demonic opposite. Prospero is not Medea or Sycorax, but he can confirm himself only by first becoming them willingly, by releasing his self in order to reclaim it.

After quoting from Ovid, Prospero moves quickly to become Prospero again—that is, the newly formed Prospero. He has not yet, it turns out, relinquished anything, though he soon will, for Alonso, Gonzalo, Sebastian, and Antonio, plus attendants, are in the next moment "charmed" in a magic circle, and after dispensing forgiveness and inward pinches by turn, Prospero tells Ariel,

Fetch me the hat and rapier in my cell.
I will discase me, and myself present
As I was sometime Milan.
(V.i.84-6)

Prospero can only now appear as Prospero as he "was sometime Milan" because he no longer *is* Prospero as he was sometime Milan. His self-conscious assumption of the clothing—
"I will discase me, and myself present"—marks the Prospero
who has already, in temporarily becoming Medea, submitted
himself to the powers of transformation, and who now, after
undergoing his own transformation, can "present" himself.

   This process of submission is extended further in the Epilogue where, as many have noted before me, Prospero appears
in the same position as Ariel or Caliban had earlier in the
play:

                    Now 'tis true
       I must be here confined by you,
       Or sent to Naples. Let me not,
       Since I have my dukedom got
       And pardoned the deceiver, dwell
       In this bare island by your spell;
       But release me from my bands
       With the help of your good hands.
       Gentle breath of yours my sails
       Must fill, or else my project fails,
       Which was to please. Now I want
       Spirits to enforce, art to enchant.

In moving from assuming Medea's *vox* and powers, through
the representation of *himself* as he was sometime Milan, to
the Epilogue where he claims the powers not of a Sycorax but
only of an Ariel, and finally reverting to the actor who has
played Prospero all along, Prospero has shown us the true
way of metamorphosis. His "rough magic" is surrendered for
an equally powerful but quite different energy. He abjures

control of the metamorphic elements in order to become a metamorph himself. In the final act of *The Tempest,* Prospero becomes if not Proteus, then the protean figure of the actor. To borrow an analogy from the gravedigger in *Hamlet,* Prospero now lets the water come to him, rather than going to it. Yet even the return voyage will enjoy some of Prospero's former powers, for he promises Alonso "calm seas, auspicious gales, / And sail so expeditious that shall catch / Your royal fleet far off. My Ariel, chick, / That is thy charge. Then to the elements / Be free, and fare thou well!" (V.i.315-19).

Prospero is made to quote Medea not to forswear Ovid, then, but to summon him once again. Shakespeare is not abjuring metamorphosis or magic, for he has long ago absorbed the lessons of experience which we see Prospero painfully learning; Shakespeare is rather showing that the dream of control must be surrendered if we are to be fully human. The trick is psychologically difficult and complex, but physically quite natural—it is to be protean, to embrace the energy, as the young lovers in the earlier comedies had done. As Prospero says, to the audience and himself as much as to Ariel, "to the elements / Be free, and fare thou well!"

Appendix

Appendix ❦ *Commedia dell'Arte* Transformations

Had Shakespeare and his audience never read Ovid in school, they would still have been saturated in metamorphosis through other sources. The Renaissance theater had itself been the site of innumerable plays in which metamorphosis played a central role: Shakespeare's predecessors and rivals frequently employed onstage transformations deriving as much from Italy as from Ovid. I would like here to take a very brief look at Italian Renaissance drama for its interest in metamorphosis.[1]

The chief location of metamorphosis in Italian drama is in *commedia dell'arte* pastoral. The *commedia erudita* seemed more interested in neo-realistic New Comedy plots; the rediscoveries of Plautus and Terence inspired a well-documented vogue of imitation. The major "serious" pastorals familiar in England in Shakespeare's time—such as Tasso's *Aminta* and Guarini's *Il Pastor Fido*—debate constancy and reveal some psychological transformations through the power of love, but are fairly restrained in what they attempt to represent on the stage. In *Aminta*, for example, Thyrsis receives a warning from the proverbial sage in the woods about going to an "enchanted abode": "perhaps you may stay there transformed into a willow-tree, into water or fire, water of tears, or fire of sighs" (I.ii)[2], but it never happens, in spite of all the other improbable

247

events in that play. In *Il Pastor Fido,* Dorinda has disguised
herself as a wolf, as Linco notes:

> Wondrous change!
> Thou a young Maid, so soft, so delicate,
> That wert (me thinks) an infant but of late
> . . . .
> Love shew'd his godhead here,
> From woman to a man transforming thee,
> Or rather to a wolf.
> (IV.i)[a]

The disguise is good enough that Silvio mistakenly shoots her
while hunting, but once again no full magical metamorphosis
takes place.

Nor are the magician plays of the *commedia erudita* more
fertile sources for onstage transformations. In Ariosto's *Il Ne-
gromante,* the magician is an outright fraud, spouting ma-
caronic gabble, and the ability to cause metamorphosis is
mocked throughout (esp. I.iii). Astrologo boasts of his power
to the foolish Camillo while the necromancer's servant Nibbio
offers cynical asides to the audience:

ASTROLOGO. If I want to, I can make you take the form
of a dog or a cat. Now, what would you say if you
found yourself transformed into something very small
like a mouse?

CAMILLO. Could you perhaps also change me into a flea
or a spider?

NIBBIO. (I'd better move away a bit so that I won't hear
this nonsense, for I couldn't listen to it without burst-
ing out laughing.) (III.iii)[4]

So too in Bibbiena's *Calandria,* the magician Ruffo promises
much but delivers nothing through magic. The cross-sexual
disguisings of Lidio and Santilla are one mode of metamorphosis, of course, and the end of the play reminds us of the
"natural perspective" of *Twelfth Night,* but onstage metamorphosis—of the sort we are about to see in the *commedia*

dell'arte— does not occur. In most of these plays, the "magicians" are fraudulent or ineffectual, and identity-confusion rather than transformation has resulted. The spirit of Ariosto's comedy reminds us in particular of Ben Jonson's *The Alchemist*. The victims of these magicians are only gullible simpletons, the society that allows such fraud to flourish is largely corrupt, and the tone of the plays is satiric. Metamorphosis is viewed skeptically, and the claims of the mage are undercut everywhere; the possibility of an actual transmutation through alchemy is dismissed as a fantasy of the ignorant.

The incidence of metamorphosis in drama seems to increase with the distance from the Plautine-Terentian tradition. (I take up the Shakespearean exception to this in Chapter Three.) When the scene shifts from city to island, from social decay to Arcadia, then the magicians gain real power, and the figures of speech congeal into unexpected phenomena, and personifications become persons. The richest trove of such enchanted isles is found in the pastoral scenari of the *commedia dell'arte*.[5] Here the magician's powers are wonderful indeed; frequently a kind of stage manager, he (and sometimes she) has at his command the full ingenuity of the property manager to produce such vehicles of metamorphosis as "suitable tree to accommodate Olivetta" (II, 637) or "Masks for an ass, a frog, and other transformations" (II, 638).

A glance through the scenari shows that, in *commedia* pastoral at least, metamorphosis was a perfectly commonplace occurrence, and in fact seems to have been especially relished for the exotic stage effects that were required. Metamorphosis meant spectacle above all. *The Enchantress* begins with disenchantment as "*Coradellino* emerges from the stone and does not know where he is" (II, 618), and "*Filli* emerges from a tree and is astonished to see Uranio" (II, 619). Later, the Enchantress "enchants the fountain giving it the power of turning love into hate and hate into love" (II, 619), which leads to many reversals and much confusion. Many of the scenari include such an external agent as the enchanted fountain or pool or garland which causes some transformation in all who come near; some trace of this external emblem of change may be seen in Oberon's "love-in-idleness" flower in *A Midsummer Night's Dream.*

In *Proteus,* Filli "declares that she could not live were it not for the art of metamorphosis taught her by her father, the magician Sabino" (II, 626), and to prove it is "turned into a flower" a moment later in order to avoid a rape. This power comes in handy again later when Fausto tries to embrace her:

> She wakes and escaping transforms herself first into
>   A bear after leaping and prowling she changes next
>   into
>   A bull after the same performance into
>   A lion roaming to and fro to the astonishment of
> Fausto who will not leave her because of what Proteus
> has promised. At last the lion changes back into Filli's
> own shape. Fausto is amazed and begs her to accept his
> love. She promises to be his if Diana will consent. (II,
> 629)

In *Pantaloonlet,* the metamorphoses are more comical. Pantalone has been turned into an ass and his wife Olivetta into a tree. The Magician says to bathe the ass "in the fountain and he will be restored to his proper likeness, and to water the tree from the same fountain for the like result. They do all this and Pantalone and Olivetta return to their own shapes and thank the Magician. . . . They are left delighted at their transformations" (II, 639). In *The Great Magician,* Zanni is struck dumb at one point (II, 651), and Pantalone eats near another of those tricky fountains "and turns into a mule" (II, 653) as a result. Burattino likewise "changes into a frog and as Filippa eats she becomes a tree" (II, 654). Finally they all bathe in the fountain and recover their original shapes. They decide to kill the Magician for causing all this, but as usually happens, "he unravels the story and puts an end to the play by making peace" (II, 657), as Prospero tries to do in *The Tempest* with somewhat less success. But in *The Ship,* the Magician is more sinister and does not escape so easily: "*Ma-*

gician is struck from the tower by a flash and is turned into a stone with the noise of fireworks" (II, 662). Here again we find magic garlands: the Magician "has enchanted them so that one when worn causes love and the other hatred" (II, 659). Earlier in this scenario Bacchus granted the shipwreck victims "that all that they touch as they call upon his name shall turn into bread, wine, and other provisions" (II, 659), and that ubiquitous fountain, sure enough, immediately "throws out wine, bread, and other provisions" (II, 659). In *The Three Satyrs,* the Magician appears sinister at first: "annoyed with Filli, [he] touches her with his enchanted rod; he makes a show of invoking Pluto and transforms her into a tree" (II, 664). Meanwhile, as Burattino "offers to make water against a rock," it explodes (what else?) and Zanni emerges. Eventually Filli is freed, but she is soon punished again. Annoyed by her love for Burattino, the Magician turns him into a woman (II, 667) and he is soon seen playing "tricks with Pantalone and Zanni who wish to enjoy [Burattino] against his will" (II, 668). But again, all drink at the fountain, recover their shapes, discover lost relatives, thank the Magician, and go off happily. And in *Arcadia Enchanted,* as a final example, we find again a garland enchanted by a Magician "so that whoever wears it shall resemble the beloved person" (II, 672), and as each lover comes in and sees, say, X wearing the garland, it seems as if it is really Y, the beloved. Thus this garland locates the power of transformation both in the enchanted external object and in the enchanted lover, and suggests how desire transforms a lover into his loved one, how two become one.

I take the scenari just summarized to be typical. Among the other suggestive titles in K. M. Lea's handlist are *L'Arbore Incantato* and several versions of *Arcadia Incantata; Argentina, or the Sorceress; Arlechino nell'Isola Incantata; L'Astrologo; Finto Astrologo; La Galatea;* various titles with *La Maga* in the name; *Le Metamorfosi d'Arlecchino; Le Metamorfosi di Pulcinella; La Tramutatione;* and so on (II, 506-554). The common denominator of these scenari is a straightforward belief in the possibility of magic, and an interest in representing magical transformations before the audience; metamorphoses are not just common, they are obligatory. The landscape of pastoral romance is alive: any tree might contain a transformed lover, any pissing-rock a clown; every fountain had metamorphic powers; male and female magicians had the run of the place. When Duke Senior in *As You Like It* finds "tongues in trees, books in the running brooks, / Sermons in stones" (II.i.16-17), he is speaking figuratively, but he might actually have found them on a *commedia Isola Incantata*.

We see in these *scenari* as well the recurring figures of metamorphosis, the topoi encountered again and again in the Renaissance: the mage with supernatural power; the process of sexual desire and frustration leading to some culminative change; the inevitable association with water—shipwreck, isolated island or enchanted place, enchanted fountain, repeated visions of Proteus and Circe; and the frequent association in which the achievement of a true shape parallels some emotional or sexual adjustment—not just the happy ending, but some deeper closing rhythm, some profound return.

It is also worth pondering for a moment what all this might have looked like on the stage. The property-lists for these *scenari* are wonderfully laconic: along with trick trees and exploding rocks, we find "chair and other necessities for the birth" (II, 637); "Painted wood for the transformation . . . Earthquake . . . Transformation for Arlecchino"[6]; or such items as "Chains, earthquakes, flames, and a hell to open for Pluto" (II, 636). The list for *The Three Satyrs* is a tour de force of the nonsequitur: "Tree, rock to explode, whale, fountain, temple, masks of a mule and an ox; a wood; macaroni; fire; eatables; a suitable book; cords; a woman's dress for Burattino; resin; stage sticks" (II, 663). These plays demanded a lot from their audiences, but they certainly gave a good deal as well. It becomes obvious that the audiences expected to *see* metamorphosis occur before them, along with all the other spectacle; coy offstage changes are the exception. The full resources of the theater were employed to gratify this taste.

We know what some of these properties looked like, but we can only wonder at some of the stage directions.

John Lyly seems to have known some of these plays, or similar ones; his plays offer many suggestive parallels which Violet Jeffrey, in *John Lyly and the Italian Renaissance* [7], has traced in considerable detail. But Italian influence or no, many of Lyly's plays—*Sapho and Phao, Gallathea, Endimion, Midas, The Woman in the Moone,* and *Love's Metamorphosis* (with its heroine, Protea)—feature central acts of transformation, and repeatedly sound the main themes of metamorphosis which will be taken up again, in another key, by Shakespeare.

Notes

Notes

All quotations from Shakespeare are from *The Complete Signet Classic Shakespeare*, ed. Sylvan Barnet (New York: Harcourt Brace Jovanovich, 1972). All quotations from Ovid are from *Ovid's Metamorphoses: The Arthur Golding Translation 1567*, ed. John Frederick Nims (New York: Macmillan, 1965), except the epigraph, which is from the Rolfe Humphries translation (Bloomington: Indiana Univ. Press, 1955). Quotations from other Renaissance plays, unless otherwise noted, are from *Drama of the English Renaissance*, ed. Russell A. Fraser and Norman Rabkin (New York: Macmillan, 1976). Quotations have been silently but conservatively modernized.

NOTES TO PREFACE

1. "Boundary" is a term frequently encountered in discourse about identity; for a famous example, see R. D. Laing's *The Divided Self* (Baltimore: Penguin, 1965), particularly his discussion of the three forms of anxiety encountered by the "ontologically insecure person: engulfment, implosion, petrifaction" (pp. 43ff). See also Leo C. Curran, "Transformation and Anti-Augustanism in Ovid's *Metamorphoses*," *Arethusa* 5(1972), 71-91. Curran's essay derives from the work of Laing and of Philip Slater, *The Glory of Hera: Greek Mythology and the Greek Family* (Boston: Beacon Press, 1968); see for example Slater's section, "The Serpent as Boundary Violator" (pp. 100-11). On metamorphosis in general see Irving Massey, *The Gaping Pig: Literature and Metamorphosis* (Berkeley: Univ. of California Press, 1976); Harold Skulsky, *Metamorphosis: The Mind in Exile* (Cambridge: Harvard Univ. Press, 1981); and Geza Roheim, "Meta-

257

morphosis," *AI* 5(1948), 167-72. For a catalogue of different types of metamorphosis, see Stith Thompson, *Motif-Index of Folk-Literature* (Bloomington, Ind.: Indiana Univ. Studies, 1933), II, 7-71, and for a survey of the concept of metamorphosis in science, see *Man and Transformation: The Eranos Lectures* ed. Joseph Campbell, Ralph Manheim, R.F.C. Hull (Princeton: Princeton Univ. Press, Bollingen Series, 1964). I have found many descriptions but few explanations of metamorphosis. Neither Massey nor Skulsky makes any particular reference to Shakespeare.

2. Tzvetan Todorov, *The Fantastic: A Structural Approach to a Literary Genre* (Cleveland: Case Western Reserve Univ. Press, 1973), p. 113. Skulsky is also largely concerned with questions of mind and body: "Among the crucial doubts that haunt the fantasy of transformation is not the non-issue of whether the human self resides primarily in physical or mental properties, but instead the hardily controversial issue of whether mental properties, under an unsentimental and unswerving gaze, dissolve without residue into physical. To a materialist, no doubt, this prospect holds no terrors. But with literature . . . the case is otherwise" (p. 92). See also the brief statement by Ernst Cassirer in *An Essay on Man* (Garden City, New York: Doubleday, 1953): for modern or scientific minds, "The boundaries between the kingdoms of plants, of animals, of man— the differences between species, families, genera—are fundamental and ineffaceable. But the primitive mind ignores and rejects them all. . . . There is no specific difference between the various realms of life. Nothing has a definite, invariable, static shape. By a sudden metamorphosis everything may be turned into everything" (p. 108). Cassirer does not pursue this notion in any detail, however.

3. Three recent works on Shakespearean comedy bear titles relevant to this study. In *Comic Transformations in Shakespeare* (New York: Methuen, 1980), however, Ruth Nevo focuses throughout on Shakespeare's transformation of earlier models of comedy, especially the Donatan formula for comic plots. And in "The Parted Vision: Metamorphosis as the Central Rite of Shakespearian Comedy" (Diss. Pennsylvania State Univ., 1976), Harry E. Curtis, Jr. means by "metamorphosis" primarily "a basic dramatic device that is analogous in some respects to the peripety or reversal of fortune that the protagonists in a comedy must undergo to achieve success at play's end" (p. vi). The peripety or metamorphosis of these protagonists is not "merely a turning in a direction opposite to that in which they began;

they undergo a marked change in character and condition in response to an environment that is in a state of transition too" (p. vii). Curtis confines his discussion throughout to this restricted sense of metamorphosis. In "Animals as Agents of Revelation: The Horizontalizing of the Chain of Being in Shakespeare's Comedies," in *Shakespearean Comedy*, ed. Maurice Charney (New York: New York Literary Forum, 1980), Jeanne Addison Roberts surveys several of the major comedies, tracing Shakespeare's changing attitudes toward the relation between men and animals; her central argument is conveniently summarized in her title. Anne Barton has argued (in " 'As You Like It' and 'Twelfth Night': Shakespeare's Sense of an Ending," *Shakespearian Comedy*, ed. Malcolm Bradbury and David Palmer [London: Edward Arnold, 1972]) that "It has become possible to agree that the comedies . . . are plays concerned primarily with transformation, with the clarification and renewal attained, paradoxically, through a submission to some kind of disorder, whether festive or not. We have learned to notice as typically Shakespearian the way characters move between two contrasted locales—one of them heightened and more spacious than the other—and we regard that 'new society' which makes its way back to the normal world at the end of the play as a subtler and more consequential achievement than older critics did" (p. 161). I fully agree with this assessment, but I believe that Barton's relation of transformation to the Barber/ Frye models of Shakespearean comedy unnecessarily restricts our sense of what transformation might be, or represent, in the comedies.

NOTES TO CHAPTER ONE

1. Whitney J. Oates, ed., *Basic Writings of Saint Augustine* (New York: Random House, 1948), *City of God, 18.18* (p. 421).

2. Thomas Aquinas, *Summa Theologica*, trans. Fathers of the English Dominican Province (Chicago: Encyclopedia Britannica, 1952), I, Q.114, Art.4.

3. Reginald Scot, *The Discoverie of Witchcraft* (London: Centaur Press, 1964), VII.xv (p. 139). Scot notes that even in the cases of metamorphosis which St. Augustine seemed to have affirmed, "he himselfe is no eiewitnesse to any of those his tales; but speaketh onelie by report . . . how much *Augustin* saith he hath seen with his eies, so much I am content to beleeve. Howbeit S. *Augustin* conclu-

deth against Bodin" (V.iii; p. 97). The same passage from *City of God* is cited again.

4. G. B. Harrison, ed., *King James the First: Daemonologie (*1597*)* (New York: Barnes and Noble, 1966), p. 4. Textual references are to this edition.

5. Whatever position on the reality of witches was taken, a similar essence-versus-accident distinction was usually made, from Ulric Molitor (*De lamiis et phitonicis mulieribus,* 1489), Gian-Francesco Pico (*La Strega;* published in Latin, 1523), and Nicolas Remy (*Daemonolatreiae libri tres,* 1595; translated into English, 1595), to Samuel Harsnett (*A Declaration of Egregious Popish Impostures,* 1603). Francesco Guazzo, *Compendium maleficarum* (1626) is typical: "No one must fall into the delusion that a man can really be changed into a beast, or a beast into a real man; for these are magic portents and illusions, which have the form but not the reality of those things which they appear to be."—quoted in Rossell Hope Robbins, *Encyclopedia of Witchcraft and Demonology* (New York: Crown, 1959), p. 345. The central texts on witchcraft were widely reprinted (often in English) in England. In addition to the ubiquitous ur-text, *Malleus Maleficarum* (1486), for example, Ben Jonson quotes, in his notes to *The Masque of Queens* (1609), from the central works by James I, Bodin, Remy, del Rio, Elich, Spina, Paracelsus, Agrippa, and Godelmann, among others.

6. Margaret A. Murray, *The Witch-Cult in Western Europe* (Oxford: Clarendon Press, 1962), p. 231. Textual references are to this edition. Murray's general theories are controversial; see C. L. Ewen, *Some Witchcraft Criticisms* (n.p., 1938); Keith Thomas, *Religion and the Decline of Magic* (Harmondsworth: Penguin, 1973), pp. 518n., 614-5; and Alan Macfarlane, *Witchcraft in Tudor and Stuart England* (London: Routledge & Kegan Paul, 1970), pp. 10-11. Still, Murray's emphasis on what people *believed* was happening seems valid. The primary and secondary literature on witchcraft in the Renaissance is enormous, repetitive, and difficult, and I will not succumb to its delusions and snares here. Very useful overviews of the subject from quite different viewpoints are available in Wayne Shumaker, *The Occult Sciences in the Renaissance* (Berkeley: Univ. of California Press, 1972), pp. 60-107, and H. R. Trevor-Roper, *The European Witch-Craze of the Sixteenth and Seventeenth Centuries and Other Essays* (New York: Harper & Row, 1969), pp. 90-192. Standard reference sources are Henry Charles Lea, *Materials Toward*

a History of Witchcraft, ed. Arthur C. Howland (Philadelphia, 1938), and Robbins, *Encyclopedia*. I have also found useful Robert H. West, *The Invisible World: A Study of Pneumatology in Elizabethan Drama* (New York: Octagon, 1969; rpt. 1939); Robert R. Reed, Jr., *The Occult on the Tudor and Stuart Stage* (Boston: Christopher, 1965); Alan C. Kors and Edward Peters, eds., *Witchcraft in Europe 1100-1700: A Documentary History* (Philadelphia: Univ. of Pennsylvania Press, 1972); Sydney Anglo, ed., *The Damned Art: Essays in the Literature of Witchcraft* (London: Routledge & Kegan Paul, 1977); and of course the magisterial work of Keith Thomas, *Religion and the Decline of Magic*.

7. Quoted in Wayne Shumaker, *The Occult Sciences in the Renaissance*, p. 93. In his *De la Lycanthropie, Transformation, et Extase des Sorciers* (1615), Jean de Nynauld makes a similar point, following Augustine's distinction and rejecting Bodin's position. See other points of view summarized by Shumaker, pp. 93-4. See also Scot's rejection of Bodin's position on lycanthropy, V.i (pp. 92-4); once again, the central quotations from Augustine are cited. See also the survey of Lycanthropy in Robbins, *Encyclopedia*, pp. 324-9, and the famous case-histories he cites. Robert Burton, somewhat surprisingly, did not attribute lycanthropy to melancholy: "I should rather refer it to *Madness*" (*The Anatomy of Melancholy*, ed. Floyd Dell and Paul Jordan-Smith [New York: Tudor Publishing, 1927], p. 122); Burton also refers the reader to the original passage in Augustine. The element of self-delusion is clear in the remarkable testimony of an accused werewolf, Jacques Roulet, in Angers, 1598:

Q. What are you accused of having done?

A. Of being a thief; of having offended God. My parents gave me an ointment; I do not know its composition.

Q. When rubbed with this ointment, do you become a wolf?

A. No. But for all that, I killed and ate the child Cornier. I was a wolf.

Q. Were you dressed as a wolf?

A. I am dressed as I am now. I had my hands and face bloody, because I had been eating the flesh of the said child.

Q. Do your hands and feet become paws of a wolf?

A. Yes, they do.

Q. Does your head become like that of a wolf—your mouth become larger?

A. I do not know how my head was at the time; I used my teeth. My head was as it is today. I have wounded and eaten many other little children. I have also been to the sabbat. (Quoted in Robbins, *Encyclopedia*, p. 324.)

8. John T. Shawcross, ed., *The Complete Poetry of John Donne* (Garden City, New York: Doubleday, 1967).

9. J. C. Smith, ed., *The Poetical Works of Edmund Spenser* (Oxford: Clarendon Press, 1909). Textual references are to this edition.

10. John Marston, *The Malcontent*, ed. M. L. Wine (Lincoln: Univ. of Nebraska Press, 1964), IV v 107-24 (p. 91).

11. *The Renaissance Philosophy of Man*, ed. Ernst Cassirer, Paul Oskar Kristeller, and John H. Randall (Chicago: Univ. of Chicago Press, 1948), pp. 224-5.

12. Ibid, p. 225.

13. Sir John Hayward, *David's Tears* (London, 1623), p. 251; quoted in Alvin Kernan, *Volpone* (New Haven: Yale Univ. Press, 1962), p. 18.

14. For useful studies of Ovid and metamorphosis, see William S. Anderson, "Multiple Change in the *Metamorphoses*," *TAPA* 94(1963), 1-27; Charles Segal, "Myth and Philosophy in the *Metamorphoses*: Ovid's Augustanism and the Augustan Conclusion of Book XV," *AJP* 90 (1969), 257-92; Leo C. Curran, "Transformation and Anti-Augustanism in Ovid's *Metamorphoses*," *Arethusa* 5(1972), 71-91; Brooks Otis, *Ovid as an Epic Poet* (Cambridge: Cambridge Univ. Press, 1966); Hermann Fraenkel, *Ovid: A Poet Between Two Worlds* (Berkeley: Univ. of California Press, 1969); L. P. Wilkinson, *Ovid Recalled* (Cambridge: Cambridge Univ. Press, 1955); and G. Karl Galinsky, *Ovid's Metamorphoses* (Berkeley: Univ. of California Press, 1975), esp. pp. 42-70. For useful general studies of Ovid in the Renaissance see T. W. Baldwin, *William Shakspere's Small Latine and Lesse Greeke* (Urbana, Ill.: Univ. of Illinois Press, 1944); Frederick S. Boas, *Ovid and the Elizabethans* (London: English Association, n.d.); Gordon Braden, *The Classics and English Renaissance Poetry* (New Haven: Yale Univ. Press, 1978), 1-54; Douglas Bush, *Mythology and the Renaissance Tradition in English Poetry*, New Revised Edition (New York: Norton, 1963); Clyde B. Cooper, *Some Elizabethan Opinions of the Poetry and Character of Ovid* (Menasha, Wisconsin: Collegiate Press, 1914); Davis P. Harding, *Milton and the Renaissance Ovid* (Urbana, Ill.: Univ. of Illinois Press, 1946);

Caroline Jameson, "Ovid in the Sixteenth Century," *Ovid*, ed. J. W. Binns (London: Routledge & Kegan Paul, 1973); Dietrich Klose, "Shakespeare und Ovid," *SJH* (1968), 72-93; Richard A. Lanham, *The Motives of Eloquence: Literary Rhetoric in the Renaissance* (New Haven: Yale Univ. Press, 1976); and J.A.K. Thomson, *Shakespeare and the Classics* (London: George Allen & Unwin, 1952). The most interesting work on Ovid in the Renaissance concerns his influence on amatory poetry, particularly the epyllion. See the classic studies by Hallett Smith, *Elizabethan Poetry* (Cambridge, Mass.: Harvard Univ. Press, 1952), pp. 64-130, and M. C. Bradbrook, *Shakespeare and Elizabethan Poetry* (Harmondsworth: Penguin, 1964; 1pt. 1951), pp. 51-70. Two recent, valuable studies are William Keach, *Elizabethan Erotic Narratives* (New Brunswick: Rutgers Univ. Press, 1977), especially Chapter One, and Clark Hulse, *Metamorphic Verse: The Elizabethan Minor Epic* (Princeton: Princeton Univ. Press, 1981), esp. pp. 3-15 and 242-51. Of the minor epic, Hulse argues, "Metamorphosis underlies the subject matter of the genre, its narrative principles, its mode of symbolism, its ability to combine and to remake other genres, and its power to transform the poet. Indeed, the study of metamorphosis within the poems leads one beyond them, so that Elizabethan literature as a whole can be seen, not just as an assortment of interesting texts, but as a literary system, dominated by the interplay of forms, changes of style, and the search for growth of the individual poet" (p. 4).

15. See Stephen Greenblatt, *Renaissance Self-Fashioning* (Chicago: Univ. of Chicago Press, 1980).

16. Hayward, *David's Tears*, p. 251 (Kernan, p. 18).

17. Heinz Lichtenstein, "The Dilemma of Human Identity: Notes on Self-Transformation, Self-Objectivation, and Metamorphosis," *JAPA* 11(1963), p. 214.

18. Heinz Lichtenstein, "Identity and Sexuality: A Study of Their Interrelationship in Man," *JAPA* 9(1961), p. 188.

19. Ben Jonson, *Works*, ed. C.H. Herford and Percy and Evelyn Simpson (Oxford: Clarendon Press, 1925-47), VIII, 597.

20. Mircea Eliade, "Masks," *Encyclopedia of World Art* IX, 524-5.

21. Northrop Frye, *Fables of Identity* (New York: Harcourt, Brace & World, 1963), p. 82; Brooks Otis, *Ovid as an Epic Poet*, p. 334.

22. Anna Freud, *Writings of Anna Freud IV* (New York: Inter-

national Universities Press, 1968), pp. 259, 258. See also Lichtenstein, "Dilemma," p. 215, and Leo A. Spiegel, "The Self, the Sense of Self, and Perception," *The Psychoanalytic Study of the Child* 14(1959), p. 103. Philip Slater, in *The Glory of Hera: Greek Mythology and the Greek Family* (Boston: Beacon Press, 1968), offers an even more explicit interpretation of this loss: "For individuals in whom narcissistic anxieties are severe, the sexual act shatters the body image of both male and female. The boundary between Me and Not-Me crumbles, since the female is penetrated and part of the male disappears inside of another . . . this may be experienced as a kind of death—as complete submersion in unconsciousness" (p. 101) Noting that "engulfment is felt as a risk . . . in being loved," R. D. Laing, *The Divided Self* (Baltimore: Penguin, 1965), following Sartre's analysis in *Being and Nothingness,* suggests that "relatedness as such" may be the deepest source of dread (p. 44).

23. Coppélia Kahn, *Man's Estate: Masculine Identity in Shakespeare* (Berkeley: Univ. of California Press, 1981), p. 127.

24. Charles Segal, "Myth and Philosophy in the *Metamorphoses,*" p. 273.

25. Francis Bacon, *Works,* ed. James Spedding, Robert Ellis, and Douglas Heath (London: Longmans, 1857-74), IV, 61. For a study of the mutability of language in the Renaissance, see my *The Great Feast of Language in Love's Labour's Lost* (Princeton: Princeton Univ. Press, 1976).

26. Kenneth Burke, *A Grammar of Motives* (New York: Prentice-Hall, 1952), p. 24.

27. Quoted in Edgar Wind, *Pagan Mysteries in the Renaissance* (New York: Barnes and Noble, 1967), p. 191.

28. Ibid, p. 196.

29. Ibid, p. 199.

30. Henri Bergson, "Laughter," *Comedy,* ed. Wylie Sypher (Garden City, New York: Doubleday, 1956), pp. 93, 97; italics removed.

31. Northrop Frye, *The Secular Scripture* (Cambridge, Mass.: Harvard Univ. Press, 1976), p. 54. Textual references are to this edition.

32. Northrop Frye, *A Natural Perspective* (New York: Harcourt, Brace & World, 1965), pp. 106-7.

33. The best study of Lyly, and of his relation to Shakespeare, remains G. K. Hunter, *John Lyly: The Humanist as Courtier* (Cambridge, Mass.: Harvard Univ. Press, 1962). See more recently Leah

Scragg, *The Metamorphosis of Gallathea: A Study in Creative Adaptation* (Washington, D.C.: Univ. Press of America, 1982), in which the extensive influence of Lyly's play is traced through several of Shakespeare's comedies.

NOTES TO CHAPTER TWO

1. See, for example, Maynard Mack, "Engagement and Detachment in Shakespeare's Plays," *Essays on Shakespeare and Elizabethan Drama*, ed. Richard Hosley (Columbia, Mo.: Univ. of Missouri Press, 1962), pp. 279-80, and Cecil C. Seronsy, " 'Supposes' as the Unifying Theme in *The Taming of the Shrew*," *SQ* 14(1963), pp. 25-8. For a more recent discussion, see Brian Morris in his Arden edition of the play (London: Methuen, 1981), pp. 115-19 and 137-8. Morris also briefly summarizes the whole theme of metamorphosis in the play (pp. 133-6), and notes with the others: "the whole game of shape-changing in the Induction is proleptic of the metamorphosis in the main play" (p. 134). For a recent, complementary study of metamorphosis in the play, see Jeanne Addison Roberts, "Horses and Hermaphrodites: Metamorphosis in *The Taming of the Shrew*," *SQ* 34(1983), 159-71. Roberts argues there, as in her other essays on the subject, that "although there are hints of Ovidian metamorphosis in the transformations of Bottom and Falstaff, these metamorphoses pose a basic threat to comedy since the changes are nearly always for the worse" (p. 160); I argue precisely the opposite throughout. Roberts' article on *Shrew* thoroughly demonstrates the ubiquity of the transformation theme in the play, with particular reference to Petruchio. The frequent invocation of bestial metaphors, she says, "facilitates their confrontation and rejection" (p. 171); I make a similar argument about *A Midsummer Night's Dream*.

2. The classic statement of metadramatic methodology remains James L. Calderwood's *Shakespearean Metadrama* (Minneapolis: Univ. Of Minnesota Press, 1971); his essays there on *Love's Labour's Lost* and *A Midsummer Night's Dream* are essential reading. See also his *Metadrama in Shakespeare's Henriad* (Berkeley: Univ. of California Press, 1979). See also the two useful volumes of essays edited by John W. Blanpied from MLA Special Sessions, both entitled *Shakespearean Metadrama* (published by Department of English, Univ. of Rochester, 1977, 1978).

3. The Arden editor concisely sums up the controversy (pp. 143-

9), from Shaw ("the last scene is altogether disgusting to modern sensibility") to Germaine Greer. Morris himself has no doubts: "Shakespeare cannot possibly have intended it to be spoken ironically. . . . The great final speech of *The Shrew* is a solemn affirmation of the great commonplace [of a wife's inferior degree]" (p. 146). Morris goes on to note the ironic context of the speech, and shows how Petruchio's various "commands" to Kate allow her to speak to the other women from her own position of authority. See also the fine article by John C. Bean, "Comic Structure and the Humanizing of Kate in *The Taming of the Shrew*," in *The Woman's Part: Feminist Criticism of Shakespeare*, ed. Carolyn Ruth Swift Lenz, Gayle Greene, and Carol Thomas Neely (Urbana, Ill.: Univ. of Illinois Press, 1980). Bean notes that Kate's final speech "in its use of political analogies and its emphasis on woman's warmth and beauty rather than on her abject sinfulness, is not a rehearsal of old, medieval ideas about wives but of relatively contemporary ideas growing out of humanist reforms" (p. 70). Bean emphasizes "the emergence of a humanized heroine against the background of depersonalizing farce unassimilated from the play's fabliau sources" (p. 66).

4. Alexander Leggatt, *Shakespeare's Comedy of Love* (London: Methuen, 1974), pp. 58, 61. Cf. J. Dennis Huston, *Shakespeare's Comedies of Play* (New York: Columbia Univ. Press, 1981): "She thus here answers his earlier play with an elaborate dramatic performance of her own, and this performance, in turning past failures to advantage, offers an example of play in a multitude of forms— as spontaneous joy, as ego-mastery, as true interpersonal exchange, as imaginative creation, and as assimilative vision" (p. 93). Marianne L. Novy offers a similar reading, turning on the concept of play, though she also relates play to questions of hierarchy and social structure ("Patriarchy and Play in *The Taming of the Shrew*," *ELR* 9(1979), 264-80).

5. The passage quoted is itself a quotation within Penelope's letter to Ulysses, a rather inappropriate recounting of how a safely returned veteran would relate the Trojan war.

6. Geoffrey Bullough, ed., *Narrative and Dramatic Sources of Shakespeare* (New York: Columbia Univ. Press, 1957-1975), I, 112; italics removed.

7. See the summary by Lawrence Stone in *The Family, Sex and Marriage in England 1500-1800* (New York: Harper & Row, 1977), which distinguishes five distinct stages: the written legal contract

between the parents; the spousals; the public proclamation of banns in church; the wedding in church; and the sexual consummation (pp. 31-7). In *Coming of Age in Shakespeare* (London: Methuen, 1981), Marjorie Garber, borrowing from Stone, examines "marriage" in its wide sense in several of the plays. She anticipates part of my argument here in her observation that "It is when the condition of virginity becomes a stasis rather than a stage that the plays invite us to regard it with a disapproving eye" (p. 131), but her emphasis on marriage as one of the ritual stages of human life diverges considerably from my own interest in marriage as a species of metamorphosis.

8. E. S. Donno, ed., *Elizabethan Minor Epics* (New York: Columbia Univ. Press, 1963), p. 304. George Sandys is somewhat skeptical about the literalness of this idea: "*Salmacis* clinges about the surprized youth like a serpent, till both become one body The reason why lovers so strictly imbrace; is to incorporate with the beloved, which sith they cannot, can never be satisfied." Sandys then quotes Lucretius' *De Rerum Natura* on lovers' embraces: "since nothing they can thence translate, / Nor wholy enter and incorporate. / For so sometimes they would; so strive to doe: / And cleave so close as if no longer two"—*Ovid's Metamorphosis* (Lincoln: Univ. of Nebraska Press, 1970), p. 207.

9. For copious examples, see the study by Laurens J. Mills, *One Soul in Bodies Twain: Friendship in Tudor Literature and Stuart Drama* (Bloomington, Indiana: Principia Press, 1937).

10. Cf. *KJ*, II.i.432-45; *H5*, V.ii.359-66; *Wiv*, IV.vi.50-1; *Ham*, III.ii.162-3; and *MND*, II.ii.47-52. Cf. also DuBartas' epithalamium of Adam and Eve (A. B. Grosart, ed., *The Complete Works of Joshua Sylvester*, I.81):

> Source of all joyes! sweet Hee-Shee-Coupled-One!
> Thy sacred Birth I never think upon,
> But (ravisht) I admire how God did them
> Make two of One, One of Two again.
> O blessed Bond! O happy marriage!
> Which dost the match 'twixt Christ and us presage!
> O chastest friendship, whose pure flames impart
> Two Soules in one, two Hearts into one Heart!
>
> (I.VI.1062-9)

11. Leone Ebreo, *The Philosophy of Love*, trans. F. Friedelberg-Seeley and Jean H. Barnes (1937), p. 31; quoted in Helen Gardner,

"The Argument About 'The Ecstasy'," *Elizabethan and Jacobean Studies Presented to F. P. Wilson,* eds. Herbert Davis and Helen Gardner (Oxford: Clarendon Press, 1959), p. 292.

12. Ibid, p. 260 (p. 293).

13. Castiglione, *The Book of the Courtier,* trans. Sir Thomas Hoby (London: J. M. Dent & Sons, 1966), p. 315.

14. D. J. Gordon, "*Hymenaei*: Ben Jonson's Masque of Union," *The Renaissance Imagination* (Berkeley: Univ. of California Press, 1975), p. 168. Cf. also Chapman's Fifth Sestiad to "Hero and Leander," with a parallel iconography of Hymen and the vision of "Love with Proteus and his pow'r . . . where Love's form is, Love is; Love is form" (Christopher Marlowe, *The Complete Poems and Translations,* ed. Stephen Orgel [Baltimore: Penguin, 1971], ll. 213, 227).

Notes to Chapter Three

1. See the very useful study by Leo Salingar, *Shakespeare and the Traditions of Comedy* (Cambridge: Cambridge Univ. Press, 1974), especially pp. 175-242.

2. Ben Jonson, *Works,* ed. C. H. Herford and Percy and Evelyn Simpson (Oxford: Clarendon Press, 1925-47), I, 144.

3. Quoted in S. Schoenbaum, *William Shakespeare: A Compact Documentary Life* (Oxford: Oxford Univ. Press, 1977), p. 185.

4. Geoffrey Bullough, ed., *Narrative and Dramatic Sources of Shakespeare* (New York: Columbia Univ. Press, 1957-1975), II, 269.

5. Deborah Baker Wyrick, in "The Ass Motif in *The Comedy of Errors* and *A Midsummer Night's Dream,*" *SQ* 33(1982), 432-48, explores the traditional symbolism of the ass—primarily as "licentious," "foolish," or "admirable"—and, perhaps overstating her argument, relates it to the references in this play: the ass motif "unifies the play . . . helps establish the comic perspective . . . aids in character delineation . . . acts as a paradigm of metamorphosis," and concludes, "The ass may be foolish and licentious, his mis-takings making him a target of laughter, but he has been chosen to carry the reconciling promise of wisdom" (p. 443). See also Beryl Rowland, *Animals with Human Faces: A Guide to Animal Symbolism* (Knoxville: Univ. of Tennessee Press, 1973), pp. 20-8.

6. See Harold Brooks, "Themes and Structure in 'The Comedy of Errors,' " in *Early Shakespeare,* ed. John Russell Brown and Bernard Harris (New York: Schocken, 1966); R. A. Foakes's introduc-

tion to his Arden edition of the play (London: Methuen, 1962), pp. xliii-xlix; A. C. Hamilton, *The Early Shakespeare* (San Marino, Calif.: Huntington Library, 1967), pp. 90-108; Ralph Berry, *Shakespeare's Comedies* (Princeton: Princeton Univ. Press, 1972), pp. 24-39; and Ruth Nevo, *Comic Transformations in Shakespeare* (London: Methuen, 1980), pp. 22-34. A fine recent essay of more general interest is Barbara Freedman's "Errors in Comedy: A Psychoanalytic Theory of Farce," in *Shakespearean Comedy*, ed. Maurice Charney (New York: New York Literary Forum, 1980), and her related essay, "Egeon's Debt: Self-Division and Self-Redemption in *The Comedy of Errors*," *ELR* 10(1980), 360-83.

7. Quoted in the Arden edition, p. xlii. In *A Natural Perspective* (New York: Harcourt, Brace & World, 1965), Northrop Frye makes a related point about the necessary dissimilarity of twins: "when they meet they are delivered, in comic fashion, from the fear of the loss of identity, the primitive horror of the doppelganger which is an element in nearly all forms of insanity, something of which they feel as long as they are being mistaken for each other" (p. 78).

8. See the account in the Arden edition, p. liv.

9. My point follows—somewhat distantly—the argument by René Girard in *Violence and the Sacred* (Baltimore: Johns Hopkins Univ. Press, 1977); I pursue his insight into the necessity for difference in more detail in Chapter Five, n.11.

10. My general comments on the play are obviously indebted to the solid critical tradition established by C. L. Barber's chapter on *Twelfth Night* in *Shakespeare's Festive Comedy* (Princeton: Princeton Univ. Press, 1959); and by Joseph H. Summers, "The Masks of *Twelfth Night*," *The University Review* 22(1955), 25-32; John Hollander, "*Twelfth Night* and the Morality of Indulgence," *SR* 67(1959); and the final chapter of Alexander Leggatt's *Shakespeare's Comedy of Love* (London: Methuen, 1974). See also M. E. Lamb's "Ovid's *Metamorphoses* and Shakespeare's *Twelfth Night*," *Shakespearean Comedy*, ed. Maurice Charney, for a useful discussion of the play's Ovidian background. In particular, Lamb explores the allusive significance of the characters' names—Orsino, Olivia, and Viola—as "implied metamorphosis" (p. 66).

11. In "Art and Nature in *Twelfth Night*," *CritQ* 9(1967), 201-12, D. J. Palmer discusses the theme of mutability in this play, and says of Cesario, "He is a figure of change by renewal, the complement to the theme of love's transitoriness and loss" (p. 211).

12. Barber, p. 256. Barber's theory of "festive release" encompasses my argument that the play dramatizes the necessity of taking on the risks of metamorphosis—of surrendering to its power—though transformation does seem possible outside of Barber's "festive" locations.

13. Barber, p. 255.

14. See Harry Levin's comprehensive survey of Renaissance attitudes toward the subject: "Jonson's Metempsychosis," *PQ* 22(1943), 231-9.

15. In *The Comic Matrix of Shakespeare's Tragedies* (Princeton: Princeton Univ. Press, 1979), Susan Snyder expands on the idea that comedy, in contrast to tragedy, is a mode which tends to reject all forms of singleness; the movement of comedy toward marriage, she notes, "implies that twoness is better than oneness" (p. 51).

16. Anne Barton, " 'As You Like It' and 'Twelfth Night': Shakespeare's Sense of an Ending," *Shakespearian Comedy*, ed. Malcolm Bradbury and David Palmer (London: Edward Arnold, 1972), p. 175.

17. Cf. Walter N. King, "Introduction," *Twentieth Century Interpretations of Twelfth Night*, ed. Walter N. King (Englewood Cliffs, New Jersey: Prentice-Hall, 1968), pp. 9-10; cf. S. Nagarajan, "What You Will: A Suggestion," *SQ* 10(1959), 61-7, who sees the subtitle as linked to the theme of unrequited love.

18. See, for example, Ernest B. Gilman, *The Curious Perspective* (New Haven: Yale Univ. Press, 1978), pp. 129-66, and Maurice Charney, "*Twelfth Night* and the 'Natural Perspective' of Comedy," in *De Shakespeare à T. S. Eliot: Mélanges offerts à Henri Fluchère* (Paris: Didier, 1976), pp. 43-51. For a history of the idea of "perspective," see Samuel Y. Edgerton, Jr., *The Renaissance Rediscovery of Linear Perspective* (New York: Harper & Row, 1975).

19. Gilman, p. 161.

20. Walter N. King, "Shakespeare and Parmenides: The Metaphysics of *Twelfth Night*," *SEL* 8(1968), 283-306, relates the "is and is not" and "that that is is" paradoxes to an earlier philosophical tradition.

21. The Folio shows the line "By the Lord, madam" in italics, without any stage direction, but it is clear from the context that Feste reads *like* a madman. I am indebted to my colleague Stuart H. Johnson in my discussion of this passage.

22. Northrop Frye, *A Natural Perspective* (New York: Harcourt, Brace, & World, 1965), p. 18.

23. For a psychoanalytic commentary on Shakespeare's general habit of doubling, and a quite different viewpoint from mine, see Joel Fineman, "Fratricide and Cuckoldry: Shakespeare's Doubles," *Representing Shakespeare,* ed. Murray M. Schwartz and Coppélia Kahn (Baltimore: The Johns Hopkins Univ. Press, 1980); rpt. *PsyR* 64(1977). Fineman's wide-ranging essay focuses on *As You Like It, Twelfth Night, Troilus and Cressida,* and *Hamlet.* His argument— "In the comedies Shakespeare's wit untangles the very webs of erotic homology that in the tragedies generate catastrophe" (p. 71)—offers a thorough psychoanalytic argument for the logical connection between doubling and sexuality: "the idea of androgyny goes with the idea of cuckoldry in the same strange, complex ratio that says we are, comically, what we are by virtue of reciprocal betrayal" (p. 83).

NOTES TO CHAPTER FOUR

1. For a recent general discussion of role-playing, see Thomas Van Laan, *Role-Playing in Shakespeare* (Toronto: Univ. of Toronto Press, 1978), especially pp. 102-116. Still useful studies of disguise include Victor O. Freeburg, *Disguise Plots in Elizabethan Drama* (1915; rpt. New York: Benjamin Blom, 1965), and M. C. Bradbrook, "Shakespeare and the Use of Disguise in Elizabethan Drama," *EIC* 2(1952), 159-68. Recent commentaries on sexual disguise in particular include F. H. Mares, "Viola and Other Transvestist Heroines in Shakespeare's Comedies," *Stratford Papers, 1965-1967,* ed. B.A.W. Jackson (McMaster Univ. Library Press, 1969); Juliet Dusinberre, *Shakespeare and the Nature of Women* (London: Macmillan, 1975), 231-71; Paula S. Berggren, "The Woman's Part: Female Sexuality as Power in Shakespeare's Plays," *The Woman's Part: Feminist Criticism of Shakespeare,* ed. Carolyn Ruth Swift Lenz, Gayle Greene, and Carol Thomas Neely (Urbana, Ill.: Univ. of Illinois Press, 1980); Nancy K. Hayles, "Sexual Disguise in *As You Like It* and *Twelfth Night,*" *ShS* 32(1979), 63-72; Nancy K. Hayles, "Sexual Disguise in *Cymbeline,*" *MLQ* 41(1980), 231-47; Peter Hyland, "Shakespeare's Heroines: Disguise in the Romantic Comedies," *Ariel* 9(1978), 23-39; and Peter B. Erickson, "Sexual Politics and the Social Structure in *As You Like It,*" *MR* 23(1982), 65-83. Hayles's argument ("Sexual Disguise in 'As You Like It' and 'Twelfth Night' ") reflects

the opinion of many critics today: "Shakespeare's use of sexual disguise shows a definite progression: whereas in the early plays he uses it to explore the implications of sexual role-playing, in the later plays he seems increasingly interested in the metaphysical implications of the disguise, using it as a means to investigate, and eventually resolve, the disparity between appearance and essence" (p. 63). My argument is that Shakespeare is equally interested in all these questions even in the earliest plays, and that there is no "resolution" to the disparity between appearance and essence in his comedies—there is, rather, a reveling in disparity and dislocation. In her essay on *Cymbeline,* Hayles makes the amazing claim that "what is missing in the early plays is any sustained exploration of the psychological possibilities of the disguise" (p. 232).

2. For a useful introduction to the topic, see the essay by Mircea Eliade, "Mephistopheles and the Androgyne or the Mystery of the Whole," *The Two and the One* (New York: Harper & Row, 1965); and Carolyn Heilbrun, *Toward a Recognition of Androgyny* (New York: Knopf, 1973), especially her survey of literary history, pp. 3-45.

3. Cf. Leo Salingar, *Shakespeare and the Traditions of Comedy* (Cambridge: Cambridge Univ. Press, 1974), p. 44.

4. T. G., "The Rich Cabinet," in John Dover Wilson, *Life in Shakespeare's England* (New York: Barnes & Noble, 1969; rpt. 1911), p. 174. The argument came, in part, from Deuteronomy 22:5: "A woman shall not wear anything that pertains to a man, nor shall a man put on a woman's garment; for whoever does these things is an abomination to the LORD your God."

5. Phillip Stubbes, *Anatomy of The Abuses in England,* ed. F. J. Furnivall (London: N. Trubner, 1877-9; rpt. 1965), p. 73. For a comprehensive study of this aspect of antitheatricalism, see the fine recent study by Jonas Barish, *The Antitheatrical Prejudice* (Berkeley: Univ. of California Press, 1981), especially pp. 80-131; Barish notes that in the characters of Falstaff, Hamlet, Edgar, and Cleopatra at least, "Shakespeare provides a positive version of the phenomenon of self-change, a glimpse into its transfiguring possibilities" (p. 130).

6. Thomas Greene, "The Flexibility of the Self in Renaissance Literature," *The Disciplines of Criticism,* ed. Peter Demetz, Thomas Greene, and Lowry Nelson, Jr. (New Haven: Yale Univ. Press, 1968), pp. 241-64.

7. A. Bartlett Giamatti, "Proteus Unbound: Some Versions of the

Sea God in the Renaissance," *The Disciplines of Criticism,* pp. 437-75.

8. In *The Tempest,* Prospero quotes Medea's speech in Book VII of the *Metamorphoses;* see my discussion in Chapter Seven.

9. Sir Philip Sidney, "An Apology for Poetrie," *Elizabethan Critical Essays,* ed. G. Gregory Smith (Oxford: Oxford Univ. Press, 1904), I, 200.

10. See John Russell Brown, *Shakespeare and His Comedies* (London: Methuen, 1962), pp. 45-82; C. L. Barber, *Shakespeare's Festive Comedy* (Princeton: Princeton Univ. Press, 1959), pp. 176-7; and Alexander Leggatt's fine discussion of Portia's role in the casket scene, *Shakespeare's Comedy of Love* (London: Methuen, 1974), pp. 128-37. The result of Bassanio's correct choice, Leggatt argues, is pure release: "One feels that she [Portia] is eager also to release the wealth of Belmont, so long hoarded up, into the world" (p. 136).

11. The parallels and similarities between Christians and Jews have become a staple of modern criticism of the play. For a recent version of this argument, which relates Shylock's role to that of the scapegoat, see René Girard, " 'To entrap the wisest': A Reading of *The Merchant of Venice,*" *Literature and Society,* ed. Edward W. Said (Baltimore: The Johns Hopkins Univ. Press, 1980), 100-19. Girard was anticipated by C. L. Barber (pp. 167-8, 179-83), among others.

12. In *The Harmonies of The Merchant of Venice* (New Haven: Yale Univ. Press, 1978), Lawrence Danson shows how Portia/Balthazar derives from the tradition of the *puer senex* (pp. 121-2). Danson argues that "Portia's lesson is intended for each of the principals at the trial—Shylock most directly, but also Antonio and Bassanio" (p. 122).

13. Sigurd Burckhardt, *Shakespearean Meanings* (Princeton: Princeton Univ. Press, 1968), Chapter VII: "The Gentle Bond." In *Comic Transformations in Shakespeare,* however, Ruth Nevo says that "the maskings and unmaskings and reconciliations of the rings episode become mere comedy-game flourishes upon the theme of letter and spirit" (p. 138).

14. Danson's final chapter offers one of the most persuasive, balanced readings of the final act, especially pp. 175-9 and 183-8.

15. Ruth Nevo offers a dissenting view: "Portia's disguise has not been a device whereby her own self-discovery was extended, a means

whereby she can be herself and not, or more than, herself at once and, we believe, for ever" (p. 138).

16. My discussion of Rosalind rests on the prior general interpretations of the play by C. L. Barber; John Russell Brown; Harold Jenkins, "As You Like It," *ShS* 8(1955), 40-51; Helen Gardner, "*As You Like It*," *More Talking of Shakespeare*, ed. John Garrett (London: Longmans, Green, 1959); David Young, *The Heart's Forest* (New Haven: Yale Univ. Press, 1972); and Alexander Leggatt.

17. The verb "translate," which is repeated as a comic threat by Touchstone against William ("translate thy life into death"—V.i.56), has been a key metamorphic term in several of the plays, especially *A Midsummer Night's Dream*.

18. Arguing against the received critical tradition, Peter B. Erickson, "Sexual Politics and the Social Structure in *As You Like It*," *MR* 23 (1982), concludes, however, that Rosalind's involvement has a serious negative side, since she must eventually "resume a traditional female role in order to engage in love" (p. 71); her disguise is not truly transforming but merely "a protective device" (p. 70). The play, he concludes, "is primarily a defensive action against female power rather than a celebration of it" (p. 82). I argue, to the contrary, that the stereotypes of femininity have been invoked by Rosalind in order to be dismissed, and that a deeper energy which essentially transcends ordinary sex roles—which I still term "feminine," admittedly—is revealed throughout the play, and the other comedies of sexual disguise.

19. For the iconographical associations of Hymen, see Chapter Two, n.14.

20. See appendix to Arden edition, ed. Agnes Latham (London: Methuen, 1975), pp. 133-5.

NOTES TO CHAPTER FIVE

1. William Hazlitt, *The Characters of Shakespeare's Plays;* quoted in the Signet edition, ed. Wolfgang Clemen (New York: New American Library, 1963), p. 136.

2. David Young, *Something of Great Constancy: The Art of "A Midsummer Night's Dream"* (New Haven: Yale Univ. Press, 1966), p. 157. Young's path-breaking book anticipates several of my own points. On the Ovidian sources of the play, see Young, pp. 164-5; Geoffrey Bullough, *Narrative and Dramatic Sources of Shakespeare*

(New York: Columbia Univ. Press, 1957-1975), I,367-76; Walter F. Staton, Jr., "Ovidian Elements in *A Midsummer Night's Dream*," *HLQ* 26(1962), 165-78; and the Arden edition, ed. Harold F. Brooks (London: Methuen, 1979), pp. lviii-lix. Shakespeare's apparent indebtedness to Apuleius' *The Golden Ass* is more problematic; see Bullough; Frank Kermode, "The Mature Comedies," *Early Shakespeare*, ed. John Russell Brown and Bernard Harris (New York: Schocken, 1966), pp. 218-9; Sister M. Generosa, "Apuleius and *A Midsummer Night's Dream*: Analogue or Source, Which?," *SP* 42(1945), 198-204; D. T. Starnes, "Shakespeare and Apuleius," *PMLA* 60(1945), 1021-50; and the Arden edition, pp. lix-lx. Both Ovidian and Apuleian incidents could have been found in Reginald Scot's *Discoverie of Witchcraft*.

3. Marjorie Garber, *Dream in Shakespeare* (New Haven: Yale Univ. Press, 1974), p. 70.

4. R. W. Dent, "Imagination in *A Midsummer Night's Dream*," *SQ* 15(1964), 115-29. See also the excellent study by Garrett Stewart, "Shakespearean Dreamplay," *ELR* 11(1981), 44-69, for a study of dream play and metalanguage in Bottom's vision; Stewart also has illuminating comments on the statue scene in *The Winter's Tale*. I have been partly anticipated in the argument that follows by David Bevington, " 'But We Are Spirits of Another Sort': The Dark Side of Love and Magic in *A Midsummer Night's Dream*," in *Medieval and Renaissance Studies*, ed. Siegfried Wenzel (Chapel Hill: Univ. of North Carolina Press, 1978), 80-92. As Bevington notes, "Repeatedly in this play, a presumption of man's licentiousness is evoked, only to be answered by the conduct of the lovers themselves. This representation of desire almost but not quite satisfied is to be sure a titillating one, but it looks forward as do the lovers themselves to legitimate consummation in marriage and procreation" (p. 87). My chapter, as will become evident, argues that the consummation cannot occur before the "representation of desire" has been deliberately summoned into existence and then exorcised.

5. Victor Turner, *The Forest of Symbols* (Ithaca: Cornell Univ. Press, 1967), pp. 105-6.

6. Garber, p. 77.

7. Young, p. 161. See also J. Dennis Huston's discussion of Bottom as the play's focal point of parody and the spirit of play: *Shakespeare's Comedies of Play* (New York: Columbia Univ. Press, 1981), pp. 94-121.

8. C. L. Barber offers a vastly more generalized view of the function of dramatic exorcism: "In promoting the mastery of passion by expression, dramatic art can provide a civilized equivalent for exorcism. The exorcism represented as magically accomplished at the conclusion of the comedy is accomplished, in another sense, by the whole dramatic action, as it keeps moving through release to clarification," *Shakespeare's Festive Comedy* (Princeton: Princeton Univ. Press, 1959), p. 139. Alexander Leggatt, *Shakespeare's Comedy of Love* (London: Methuen, 1974), p. 111, makes a similar point.

9. Jan Kott, *Shakespeare Our Contemporary* (New York: Norton, 1974), p. 228. The classical and Renaissance iconography of the ass does endow it with a legendary phallic potency. What Deborah Baker Wyrick terms the "licentious" tradition ("The Ass Motif in *The Comedy of Errors* and *A Midsummer Night's Dream*," *SQ* 33[1982], 432-48) has been fully documented in many places; cf. Beryl Rowland, *Animals with Human Faces* (Knoxville: Univ. of Tennessee Press, 1973), pp. 20-8. Wyrick's discussion of Bottom (pp. 443-8) relates his function and character in the play to the various traditions she discerns.

10. Garber, *Dream in Shakespeare*, pp. 78-80; Frank Kermode, "The Mature Comedies," p. 219.

11. René Girard, *Violence and the Sacred* (Baltimore: The Johns Hopkins Univ. Press, 1977), especially pp. 1-38. Girard's own essay on the play—"Myth and Ritual in Shakespeare: *A Midsummer Night's Dream*," *Textual Strategies*, ed. Josue Harari (Ithaca, N.Y.: Cornell Univ. Press, 1979)—focuses almost entirely on the four lovers, who bring upon themselves a frenzied crisis of "mimetic desire": "The more these characters deny the reciprocity among them, the more they bring it about, each denial being immediately reciprocated" (p. 202). Girard's argument that mimetic desire causes metamorphosis is narrower, or perhaps more precise, than my argument. For Girard, the play's animal images "are part of the process which leads from mimetic desire to myth. . . . Far from raising himself to the state of a superman, a god, as he seeks to do, the subject of mimetic desire sinks to the level of animality. The animal images are the price the self has to pay for its idolatrous worship of otherness" (p. 197). Formulations such as this sound little different from the standard Renaissance moralized commentary on Ovid, yet Girard drives his point to an un-allegorical literalness: "It can be said that mimetic desire *really works:* it really achieves the goal it has set for itself, which is the *translation* of the follower into his model, the meta-

morphosis of one into the other, the absolute identity of all" (p. 201). For Girard, "the conjunction of man, god, and beast takes place at the climax of the crisis and is the result of a process which began with the play itself. It is the ultimate metamorphosis, the supreme translation" (p. 207). Girard does not discuss the play-within-the-play.

12. Turner, p. 106.

13. *Christopher Marlowe: The Complete Poems and Translations,* ed. Stephen Orgel (Baltimore: Penguin, 1971), VI.274-81 (p. 89).

14. In *John Lyly* (Cambridge, Mass.: Harvard Univ. Press, 1962), pp. 318-30, G. K. Hunter offers an important discussion of *A Midsummer Night's Dream* in relation to Lyly's plays; see also the chapter on *Dream* in Leah Scragg's *The Metamorphosis of Gallathea* (Washington: Univ. Press of America, 1982), and the Arden discussion, pp. lxxxi-lxxxii.

15. See Kott for the most extreme statement of this position. See also the balanced discussion by Leggatt, pp. 103-6, and the useful Arden summary of critical opinion, pp. cvii-cx. For more on the fairies' background and Elizabethan attitudes to them, see the classic studies by Minor White Latham, *The Elizabethan Fairies* (New York: Columbia Univ. Press, 1930); Katharine M. Briggs, *The Anatomy of Puck* (London: Routledge & Kegan Paul, 1959); Keith Thomas, *Religion and the Decline of Magic* (Harmondsworth: Penguin, 1973), pp. 724-34; as well as the Arden summary, pp. lxxi-lxxvi.

16. Reginald Scot, *The Discoverie of Witchcraft* (London: Centaur Press, 1964), VII.ii (p. 123).

17. On the Elizabethan stage Robin Goodfellow was not always possessed of magical powers. In *Wily Beguiled* (Tudor Facsimile Texts, ed. John S. Farmer; rpt. New York: AMS Press, 1970), Robin is strictly a con man with no genuine powers of shape-shifting: "Ile put me on my great carnation nose / And wrap me in a rowsing Calveskin suite. . . . Ile play the divel, I warrant ye" (p. 33); his kinship is obviously with the Vice. In *Grim the Collier of Croydon* (Tudor Facsimile Texts, ed. John S. Farmer; rpt. New York: AMS Press, 1970), Robin is one of the devils, named Akercock; he soon appears as Robin Goodfellow, claiming powers similar to Puck's:

> When as I list in this transform'd disguise,
> I'le fright the Country people as they pass,
> And sometimes turn me to some other form,
> And so delude them with fantastick shows:

But woe betide the silly Dairy maids,
For I shall fleet their Cream-bowles night by night,
And slice the Bacon-flitches as they hang. (p. 52)

18. See David Young's discussion of the epilogue, pp. 124-5; Young's entire discussion of the play-within is essential reading.

19. Every essay on the play, it seems, discusses Theseus' speech: see, for example, Young, pp. 137-41; Barber, pp. 142-4; Garber, pp. 84-7; and the Arden summary, p. cxl. Girard, "Myth and Ritual in Shakespeare," pp. 208-12, seems unaware of these commentaries. Theseus' own status as part of an "antique fable" is investigated by M. E. Lamb in "*A Midsummer Night's Dream:* The Myth of Theseus and the Minotaur," *TSLL* 21(1979), 478-91; Lamb explores the Ovidian source suggested by her title, with Bottom a comic Minotaur. She concludes that these allusions to the monstrous suggest that love "can only be attained by the loss of self within the labyrinth of one's own irrationality" (p. 488). A complementary study by David Ormerod is "*A Midsummer Night's Dream:* The Monster in the Labyrinth," *ShakS* 11(1978), 39-52. Ormerod and Lamb cover much of the same ground from slightly different points of view.

NOTES TO CHAPTER SIX

1. Alvin B. Kernan, "The Henriad: Shakespeare's Major History Plays," *The Revels History of Drama in English, Volume III: 1576-1613*, ed. J. Leeds Barroll, Alexander Leggatt, Richard Hosley, and Alvin Kernan (London: Methuen, 1975), p. 299.

2. See A. R. Humphreys's note in the Arden edition of *Henry IV, Part II* (London: Methuen, 1966), pp. 91-2.

3. H. B. Charlton, *Shakespearian Comedy* (London: Methuen, 1938), p. 197.

4. Mark Van Doren, *Shakespeare* (New York: Henry Holt, 1939), pp. 139-140. Van Doren qualifies his statement, "after *The Comedy of Errors.*" For a more sympathetic and provocative study of the theory of farce and its relation to this play, see Barbara Freedman, "Falstaff's Punishment: Buffoonery as Defensive Posture in *The Merry Wives of Windsor,*" *ShakS* 14(1981), 163-74. Freedman's work here and on *The Comedy of Errors* (see entry at Chapter Three, note 6) ought permanently to dispel the older, depreciatory view of farce.

5. Charlton, p. 196.

6. William Green, "Introduction" to *The Merry Wives of Windsor* (New York: New American Library, 1965), p. xxix. Ruth Nevo, in *Comic Transformations in Shakespeare* (London: Methuen, 1980), argues to the contrary that "the *character* of Falstaff has not changed. The craft, the shrewdness, the brass, the zest are all there. The very accents and rhythms, the vivid similes, the puns, the preposterous hyperboles, the loving ingenuity with which he enlarges upon his monstrous girth . . ." (p. 155).

7. "'A Received Belief': Imagination in *The Merry Wives of Windsor*," *SP* 74(1977), 186-215.

8. J. A. Bryant, Jr., "Falstaff and the Renewal of Windsor," *PMLA* 89(1974), 296-301; Jeanne Addison Roberts, "'The Merry Wives of Windsor' as a Hallowe'en Play," *ShS* 25(1972), 107-12; Jeanne Addison Roberts, "Falstaff in Windsor Forest: Villain or Victim?," *SQ* 26(1975), 8-15. See also Professor Roberts' *Shakespeare's English Comedy* (Lincoln: Univ. of Nebraska Press, 1979), and the entries at note 11. In *Shakespeare's English Comedy,* Roberts argues that in both Falstaff's and Bottom's cases, animal metamorphosis "becomes an ironic metaphor for stasis . . . a penultimate stage in a series of illusionary changes which culminates in a restored reality wherein it becomes clear that there has been no change at all" (pp. 125-6). See also her essay cited earlier, "Animals as Agents of Revelation: The Horizontalizing of the Chain of Being in Shakespeare's Comedies," in *Shakespearean Comedy,* ed. Maurice Charney (New York: New York Literary Forum, 1980).

9. J. A. Bryant, p. 298. In *Anatomy of Criticism* (New York: Atheneum, 1969), Northrop Frye comments, "Falstaff must have felt that, after being thrown into the water, dressed up as a witch and beaten out of a house with curses, and finally supplied with a beast's head and singed with candles, he had done about all that could reasonably be asked of any fertility spirit" (p. 183).

10. In the middle of his paranoia, Ford recites the names imputed to him: "Wittol!—Cuckold! The devil himself hath not such a name" (II.ii.293-4). Ford's unintended pun on "witall" alludes also to the devil Falstaff, who had called Ford a "jealous wittolly knave" (II.ii.266), and who is the embodiment of all wit in the play.

11. Cf. the specific comments on this allusion by J. Dover Wilson in *The Fortunes of Falstaff* (London: Cambridge Univ. Press, 1944), and J.I.M. Stewart, *Character and Motive in Shakespeare* (London: Longmans, 1949). The entire argument is usefully summarized by

Philip Williams, "The Birth and Death of Falstaff Reconsidered," *SQ* 8(1957), 359-65.

12. John M. Steadman, "Falstaff as Actaeon: A Dramatic Emblem," *SQ* 14(1963), 230-44, traces the Renaissance iconography of the Actaeon myth in detail, showing how closely Shakespeare followed Renaissance versions of the myth rather than Ovid's. Steadman also links two other transformations—Falstaff's hiding in the buck-basket and his disguise as the witch of Brainford—with a variety of classical and Renaissance sources; the prototype of the woman-disguise, he says, is the story of Hercules and Omphale. Steadman believes all three scenes "involve deliberate parody of stock examples of *libido*" (p. 243). Cf. also Leonard Barkan's important study, "Diana and Actaeon: The Myth as Synthesis," *ELR* 10(1980), 317-59, which traces the iconography of this story through a vast array of historical permutations; as Barkan notes ironically, in the case of Falstaff, "Actaeon's sexual crime has become mere impotence" (p. 352). In *Animals with Human Faces: A Guide to Animal Symbolism* (Knoxville: Univ. of Tennessee Press, 1973), Beryl Rowland traces other historical and iconographical associations of the deer from the Middle Ages on.

NOTES TO CHAPTER SEVEN

1. Lytton Strachey, "Shakespeare's Final Period," *Books and Characters* (quoted in the Arden edition of *The Winter's Tale,* ed. J.H.P. Pafford [London: Methuen, 1966], p. xxxix; G. Wilson Knight, *The Crown of Life* (London: Methuen, 1947). See also the surveys of criticism on the romances by F. David Hoeniger, "Shakespeare's Romances since 1958: A Retrospect," *ShS* 29(1976), 1-11; Robert Merrill, "The Generic Approach in Recent Criticism of Shakespeare's Comedies and Romances: A Review-Essay," *TSLL* 20(1978), 474-87; and Wayne A. Rebhorn, "After Frye: A Review-Article on the Interpretation of Shakespearean Comedy and Romance," *TSLL* 21(1979), 553-82.

2. Marjorie Garber, *Dream in Shakespeare* (New Haven: Yale Univ. Press, 1974), p. 219.

3. K. M. Lea, *Italian Popular Comedy* (New York: Russell & Russell, 1962; rpt. 1934), II.629

4. *The Works of Thomas Campion,* ed. Walter R. Davis (Garden City, New York: Doubleday, 1967), p. 273.

5. Reuben A. Brower, "The Mirror of Analogy," *Shakespeare: The Tempest,* ed. D. J. Palmer (London: Macmillan, 1969), p. 174; rpt. from *The Fields of Light* (New York: Oxford Univ. Press, 1951). Cf. Garber: "metamorphosis in the romances achieves a serenity, a sense of peace, which seems compounded at once of wisdom and of resignation. The poet is confronting his own craft" (p. 141).

6. Northrop Frye discusses these issues at far greater length in *A Natural Perspective* (New York: Columbia Univ. Press, 1965), among other places.

7. *The Winter's Tale* (New Variorum Edition), ed. H. H. Furness (New York: Dover, 1964; rpt. 1898), p. 395. Charles Frey, in *Shakespeare's Vast Romance* (Columbia: Univ. of Missouri Press, 1980), quotes these passages in another context (p. 27).

8. *Variorum,* p. 392.

9. See, for example, Howard Felperin's exemplary discussion in *Shakespearean Romance* (Princeton: Princeton Univ. Press, 1972), pp. 241ff, and Marjorie Garber's briefer description of it, pp. 184-5.

10. See the far more cynical interpretation of the Pygmalion myth in George Sandys' commentary of 1632, in his translation, *Ovid's Metamorphosis* (Lincoln: Univ. of Nebraska Press, 1970), pp. 484-5.

11. From *Dido, Queen of Carthage,* II.i.4-5, *The Complete Plays of Christopher Marlowe,* ed. Irving Ribner (New York: Odyssey Press, 1963).

12. *Christopher Marlowe: The Complete Poems and Translations,* ed. Stephen Orgel (Baltimore: Penguin, 1971), p. 21.

13. See, for example, the bear scenes in *Mucedorus* (scenes ii and iii), and the Arden discussion, p. 69.

14. Geoffrey Bullough, *Narrative and Dramatic Sources of Shakespeare* (New York: Columbia Univ. Press, 1957-1975), VIII.141. Charles Frey, in *Shakespeare's Vast Romance,* notes only "the explosive mixture of horror and humor" in this scene (p. 141). Garber discusses the bear as a common symbol of immortality and resurrection (pp. 172-3). In his long psychoanalytic study, "*The Winter's Tale:* Loss and Transformation," *AI* 32(1975), 145-99, Murray M. Schwartz says of the bear: "Oral violence is not only externalized but depersonalized and dehumanized, so that its expression becomes a function of the 'natural' world, outside the civilization of the court, and outside human control" (pp. 158-9).

15. David Young, *The Heart's Forest* (New Haven: Yale Univ. Press, 1972), p. 132.

16. Felperin, pp. 240-2. In "Hermione's Wrinkles, or, Ovid Transformed: An Essay on *The Winter's Tale*," *CompD* 5(1971), 226-39, Martin Mueller notes that Hermione's wrinkles distinguish her from the youth and beauty of Pygmalion's statue, and suggests that the dominant myth of the play is that not of Pygmalion but rather of Alcestis.

17. Douglas Peterson, in *Time, Tide, and Tempest* (San Marino, Calif.: Huntington Library, 1973), argues however that we cannot be certain that the "statue" is truly Hermione until she speaks, but then also says "we remain uncertain even after Hermione has descended from the scaffold and has embraced Leontes" (p. 208).

18. Cf. Charles Frey: "All interest centers in the point of crossing over, the strange margin between timeless being and timeful becoming" (pp. 94-5).

19. Brower, p. 165; Young, p. 172; Alvin Kernan, in *The Revels History of Drama in English, Volume III: 1576-1613*, eds. J. Leeds Barroll, Alexander Leggatt, Richard Hosley, and Alvin Kernan (London: Methuen, 1975), p. 465.

20. Brower, p. 173.

21. Garber, p. 191.

22. Cf. Coppélia Kahn, *Man's Estate* (Berkeley: Univ. of California Press, 1981), pp. 222-5, for a recent, thoughtful discussion from this viewpoint.

23. See Frank Kermode's enlightening discussion in the Arden *Tempest* (New York: Random House, 1964), pp. xxvi-xxx and xxxiv-xliii.

24. Quoted in the Arden edition, p. xl.

25. Stephen Orgel, "New Uses of Adversity: Tragic Experience in *The Tempest*," *In Defense of Reading*, ed. Reuben Brower and Richard Poirier (New York: E.P. Dutton, 1962), p. 125.

26. Orgel, p. 127.

27. Frye, *A Natural Perspective*, pp. 158, 157.

28. Harry Berger, Jr., "Miraculous Harp: A Reading of Shakespeare's Tempest," *ShakS* 5(1969), p. 272.

29. Cf. Felperin's chapter on the play, pp. 246-83. One of the best recent essays on the masque, which surveys all the other works quoted here, is Ernest B. Gilman, " 'All eyes': Prospero's Inverted Masque," *RenQ* 33(1980), 214-30.

30. See Frank Kermode's discussion of the Nature-Nurture opposition in the Arden edition, pp. xxxiv-liv.

31. See Orgel, pp. 128-9, and Brower, pp. 167-8.

32. Brower, p. 168.

33. Robert G. Hunter notes that Prospero's forgiveness lacks "tenderness" because he knows that "to forgive unregenerate evil is safe only when . . . the good are in firm and undeceived control," *Shakespeare and the Comedy of Forgiveness* (New York: Columbia Univ. Press, 1965), p. 240. Quoting this passage, Harry Berger adds that "*control* here should be understood in a more restrictive sense than Hunter intends it; it is a control exerted nowhere but in the never-never land of magic and romance. This is why Prospero connects despair to his lack of "spirits to enforce, art to enchant," in the epilogue" (pp. 269-70).

34. Arden edition, p. lxviii. A thorough review of the evidence, which I find convincing, has recently been made by Young, *The Heart's Forest*, pp. 148-53; he concludes that Shakespeare "was deliberately resorting to the organization and manner of the pastoral tragicomedies of the *commedia dell'arte*" (p. 152). See also Jackson I. Cope, *The Theater and the Dream* (Baltimore: The Johns Hopkins Univ. Press, 1973), pp. 242-4; Bullough, VIII.259-61; and the Appendix.

35. Young, p. 156; see his discussion of magic in the play, pp. 159-70. Many other readers have noted this equation as well.

36. Shakespeare was apparently consulting two versions of Ovid, an original text and Golding's translation (Arden, pp. 148-9), when writing his own version. Cf. T. W. Baldwin's discussion, *William Shakspere's Small Latine & Lesse Greeke* (Urbana: Univ. of Illinois Press, 1944), II.443-52. Here is Golding's version:

Ye Ayres and windes: ye Elves of Hilles, of Brookes, of Woods alone,
Of standing Lakes, and of the Night approche ye everychone.
Through helpe of whom (the crooked bankes much wondring at the thing)
I have compelled streames to run cleane backward to their spring.
By charmes I make the calme Seas rough, and make the rough Seas plaine,
And cover all the Skie with Cloudes and chase them thence againe.

By charmes I raise and lay the windes, and burst the Vipers jaw.
And from the bówels of the Earth both stones and trees doe draw.
Whole woods and Forestes I remove: I make the Mountaines
shake,
And even the Earth it selfe to grone and fearfully to quake.
I call up dead men from their graves: and thee O lightsome
Moone
I darken oft, though beaten brasse abate thy perill soone.
Our Sorcerie dimmes the Morning faire, and darkes the Sun at
Noone.

(*Met,* VII.265-77)

37. Arden edition, p. 149. In "The Magic of Prospero," *ShS* 11(1958), however, C. J. Sisson sees in the quotation only a mistake: "It is difficult to reconcile ourselves . . . to his claim to have opened graves and to have resurrected the dead. But the fact is that Shakespeare has been unwary in his borrowing from Ovid, and has read too much of Medea into Prospero's speech. For this was one of Medea's especial powers. Here, indeed, and not for the first time, we may truly say that Shakespeare had too much education, not too little. The invocation, in fact, conflicts with his conception of Prospero as a white magician" (p. 76). Sisson's comment can no longer be accepted, I believe. In "Prospero, Agrippa, and Hocus Pocus," *ELR* 11(1981), 281-303, Barbara A. Mowat says that this speech makes Prospero seem "a kind of pagan enchanter" (p. 288), but his abjuring of powers suggests the more beneficent tradition of the wizard. She attempts to distinguish among the traditions of the "magus," "enchanter," "wizard," and, on a different level, the performing magician; she links Prospero with each of these traditions.

38. Berger, p. 281.

39. Reginald Scot, *The Discoverie of Witchcraft* (London: Centaur Press, 1964), V.v (p. 100), V.i (p. 94). See Bodin, *De Magorum Demonomania,* Lib.II, cap.ii; the reference to Agrippa is *De Occulta Philosophia,* Lib.I, cap.lxxii. Scot refers to or quotes from Ovid's Medea speech at least four times (I.iv; XII.vii; XII.xv; XII.xxi), and refers as well (VI.vi) to the passage on Medea in the *Ars Am.* II.99-106, and to her magical treatment of Aeson in *Met,* VII.261 (XII.xviii). Ovid's versions of Medea were evidently very well known.

40. *The Works of Thomas Middleton,* ed. A. H. Bullen (London: John C. Nimmo, 1885), V.ii.17-29 (V.442-3).

41. Sandys, p. 335.

42. David Young observes: "this last achievement might seem to be the one really 'unnatural' act of Prospero's magic; but it is surely meant to sound like a rehearsal of the Day of Judgment, an event that for Shakespeare's audience was to be the last chapter in the story of the natural world as they knew it" (pp. 183-4). Apuleius relates parallel powers in the witch Meroe: "Verily, she is a magician, and of divine might, which hath power to bring down the sky, to bear up the earth, to turn the waters into hills and the hills into running waters, to call up the terrestrial spirits into the air, and to pull the gods out of the heavens, to extinguish the planets, and to lighten the very darkness of hell"—*The Golden Ass*, trans. Adlington (New York: Collier, 1962), p. 76.

43. My colleague Stuart H. Johnson helped me clarify this point. In "This Rough Magic: Perspectives of Art and Morality in *The Tempest*," *SQ* 23(1972), Robert Egan makes a somewhat related point, in more extreme terms: what Prospero surrenders here is "that aspect of his art by which he presumed to rise to a Jove-like stature over other men, refusing to forgive them or accept their kinship as fellow beings until he had made them over in the image of his own faulty moral perspective. In drowning his book he does away not with the essence of his art but with that same volume that he has prized above his kingdom—above the society of his fellows: his blind absorption in the ideal to the exclusion of the real and the human" (p. 181).

NOTES TO APPENDIX

1. This is not the place to mount a history of Renaissance Italian drama. For a broad survey of the topic, which includes all essential bibliographical references, see Louise George Clubb, "Shakespeare's Comedy and Late Cinquocento Mixed Genres," and Ninian Mellamphy, "Pantaloons and Zanies: Shakespeare's 'Apprenticeship' to Italian Professional Comedy Troupes"; both essays are in *Shakespearean Comedy*, ed. Maurice Charney (New York: New York Literary Forum, 1980).

2. Torquato Tasso, *Aminta, A Pastoral Drama*, ed. and trans. Ernest Grillo (London: Dent, 1924), p. 89.

3. Giovanni Battista Guarino, *Il Pastor Fido*, trans. Fanshawe,

ed. Walter F. Staton, Jr. and William E. Simeone (Oxford: Clarendon Press, 1964), pp. 98-9.

4. Ludovico Ariosto, *The Comedies of Ariosto,* trans. and ed. Edmond M. Beame and Leonard G. Sbrocchi (Chicago: Univ. of Chicago Press, 1975), p. 129.

5. See K. M. Lea, *Italian Popular Comedy* (New York: Russell & Russell, 1962; rpt. 1934), I. 201-12 for a summary of the typical plots. All subsequent textual references are to this edition.

6. Henry F. Salerno, trans., *Scenarios of the Commedia dell'Arte: Flaminio Scala's Il Teatro delle favole rappresentative* (New York: New York Univ. Press, 1967), p. 379.

7. New York: Russell & Russell, 1969; rpt. 1928.

Index

287

Library of Congress Cataloging in Publication Data

Carroll, William C., 1945-
The metamorphoses of Shakespearean comedy

Bibliography: p.   Includes index.
1. Shakespeare, William, 1564-1616—Comedies.
2. Metamorphosis in literature.   I. Title.
PR2981.C37 1985   822.3'3   84-42877
ISBN 0-691-06633-7 (alk. paper)